I Am WE

I Am WE

My Life with
Multiple Personalities

By Christine Pattillo
and the Gang

Published by Christine Pattillo LLC.
Cover art by Suzanne Schaefer.
Cover and interior book design by Mi Ae Lipe, What Now Design,
www.whatnowdesign.com.

Printed in the United States of America by Mill City Press.

To contact the author or order additional copies:
www.iamwebook.com
iamwe@comcast.net

First Edition, January 2014
ISBN: 978-0-9899401-0-8
Library of Congress Control Number: 2013916166

To Hope, SHE, Rim, Tristan, Q, Chrissy, Cyndi, VC, Lou, Little Lou, and Molly—their voices deserve to be heard.

To my husband, I love you more.

To Mariana, for all that you've given to me and all you have done for our special family. My cup runneth over.

To those struggling with mental health issues: Hold on, find help, speak your truth, and know you're not alone.

Table of Contents

Acknowledgments

We want to thank Mariana Sintay, our therapist, for her faith in our abilities to write our story and her belief that it was worth sharing. Mi Ae Lipe, editor extraordinaire, for her guidance, patience, humor, and vision. Sandra Tomlinson, for your interest and support, and to WIA Workforce for their resources and LLC funding. And to Carolyn and Linda for making Grow Washington a safe place for us to bloom.

Suzanne, for your beautiful efforts on depicting each of our eyes on the cover art and your friendship. My sister Jennifer, brother Chuck, mom Sharon, stepmom Pattee, and good friend Sandy for taking the time to share their experiences and allowing us to use them in our story. Additional thanks to Pattee/Mimi/Mom2 for your tireless proofreading and love. Great appreciation goes out to the numerous family members, friends, and acquaintances who took time to read through and catch any last-minute mistakes prior to publishing and to review cover drafts.

Lastly, to the love of my life, Christopher, who has never wavered in his devotion and commitment to me and to the Gang. Thank you.

Preface

My name is Christine Pattillo, and I have multiple personality disorder (MPD). This book is filled with stories about our lives told by me, my alternate personalities (alters) who share my body and mind (SHE, Hope, Tristan, Rim, Chrissy, Q, and Cyndi), my family, friends, husband, and therapist. I will be the primary narrator, but you will be hearing from many others. To avoid confusion, I have capitalized the alter SHE's name as well as the pronouns "WE" and "Others" when referring to myself and the alters.

Although our intention for this book is to be inspirational and educational, some chapters will be more difficult to read than others. WE do not mean to be offensive, but to truly understand our stories, WE must relate the sexual and physical violence from our past, some of which is expressed through rather graphic artwork created during our first years of therapy. (If you feel yourself slipping into crisis mode from reading about our experiences, contact a healthcare provider immediately.)

Please note that some of the names used in the sharing of past experiences have been changed. In addition, we share about the main personalities in my life, but there were two other personalities who were with me briefly. They came and went and our understanding of their purpose are limited. These alters are not discussed in detail in the following accounts.

As our unique lives unfold in the pages in front of you, WE welcome you to laugh, cry, and wonder. Thank you for taking the time to learn more about us and how WE live with multiple personality disorder.

Foreword

CHRISTINE IS ONE OF THOSE clients a therapist grows with over the years of work together (1995 to present). As we explored the nature of human suffering and her suffering in particular, there was an extraordinary degree of collaboration across the hundreds of hours we spent in sessions. We have learned together about change, healing, and healthy relationships.

Since she sat frozen in silence during much of the first several years, I decided early on that I would at least "do no harm." My instinct was to be with her in a gentle way. At the time I was working a lot with very young children and saw the beautiful results of providing them with the experience of being seen and understood without analyzing, without pushing for an outcome, or giving advice. When she first came in, my therapeutic experience and vocabulary were limited; I mostly knew my own yearning for kindness and acceptance for the hidden places within.

Nonetheless, it was hard to sit with her without wanting to push for change. I made many mistakes, which she always generously tried to make sense of. From the beginning she brought her thoughts and feelings to me via writing. Oftentimes her comments on our sessions were insightful and therapeutically intelligent. For example, the letter she gave me at our third session (March 2, 1995):

> "... after last weeks session I was a little troubled with what we came up with for expectations or goals. I really felt that it somehow simplified my situation. I realize you have guidelines that

*you need to meet [I was working at an agency at the time] and
filling out that form was one of them, but I felt much smaller
after I left. To sum up all that one wants to accomplish in one or
two lines, then have them sign it and be on there (sic) way was
not pleasant to me. There is so much going on in my mind and
I have thought long and hard on what I want to address and
improve on or deal with. It goes much farther than 2 lines. ..."*

And she had the courage to proceed to write one-and-a-half pages
of what she wanted for herself. She continued to write voluminously
throughout the years.

After some time of accepting her silence, (but really expecting her
to break through and start talking), I finally realized she was seemingly
unable to speak enough for us to do "talk therapy." I was confused
because she had a responsible job, appeared well put together, and in
a loving marriage. I began asking her to draw what she was feeling.
She took readily to the crayons, both as a medium for expression and
as objects to fiddle with, stacking and restacking them in their basket
like little sticks of firewood. It was through the pictures she drew
that I first became aware of the terribly violent, conflicted, tormented
world within her. The alter SHE was drawn as an evil presence, often a
green-eyed, scaly monster, always engaged in violent acts and threats
of death. The alter Rim was also drawn repeatedly committing horrendous
acts of homicide and mutilation. So much violence, so much
blackness.

There are images of her various selves in drawings done as early as
1996, although for a long time I thought the images were only symbolic
representations of her various feeling states. I understood that she
had tremendous internal conflict, but for quite some time I did not
appreciate the traumatic nature of what was hidden in her. I certainly
did not understand where all the violent, sexually explicit references
were originating from. She did her best to both tell and show me while

at the same time resisting with all her might the reality of what had happened to her.

By the time one of the most revealing pictures was drawn several years into the therapy, I was quite certain that Christine had multiple personalities. The image was of an underground cavern, with each "self" living in her or his own burrowed-out small space. It was a perfectly clear representation of Christine's internal world. Still, I only reflected back what I saw, asking her for her interpretations. I never suggested out loud that she might have multiple personality disorder because I did not want to influence her diagnostically, given the controversy around the diagnosis itself.

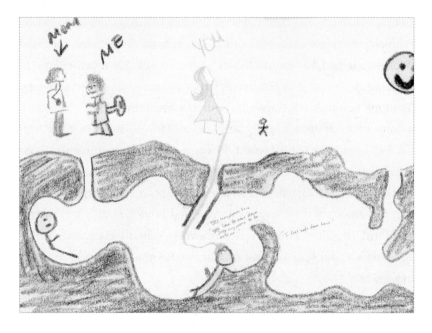

I also firmly believe that although diagnosing is helpful for understanding and treatment (particularly medicating), it is irrelevant to healing. Healing comes through healthy relationships, nothing else. If a person decides, as Christine did, to have a real relationship with another individual, it is not possible to avoid opening up. Out of that process can come a lot of pain, but it is the only path to the ultimate meaning of life: to love and be loved. This guiding principal about the reality of the connectedness and relatedness of everything in life forms the basis of my work with people—not any theory or abstract analysis.

It is important to note that in the fourth edition of the *Diagnostic and Statistical Manual of Mental Disorders*, multiple personality disorder (MPD) or dissociative identity disorder (DID) is considered a mental illness, although not in the same category as schizophrenia and bipolar disorder. Neither schizophrenia nor bipolar disorders can be "healed" in the way that a dissociative disorder can. A schizophrenic brain creates hallucinations (typically auditory or visual), delusions, disorganized speech and behavior, and disordered thinking. Bipolar disorder is a "mood disorder" that creates states of agitation and/or depression that are cyclical in nature and outside of the normal range, as well as disordered delusional thinking. These brain dysfunctions are considered "biological" in nature and require medication (as well as therapy) in order for the individual to avoid out-of-control behavior. These disorders manifest in individuals because of genetic tendencies; they are not trauma-induced. Christine's family includes people with mental illness, which makes me wonder if a genetic tendency may have contributed to Christine's extremely early splitting. Not that MPD/DID exists as a gene per se, but rather that the genetic tendency toward mental illness affects an individual's coping responses to life.

MPD is a defense mechanism. The splitting into various parts or alters serves a function. Sometimes when the function is no longer required, the part or alter "integrates" or merges into either the "host" or primary personality or even into one of the other alters. In many therapeutic approaches, the goal is to integrate all the alters into the primary personality, leaving just one. I have worked with people who have what I think of as mild MPD: They hear distinct voices in their minds, they can tell me how many there are, and we can effectively work to have the host person take enough responsibility for his or her life that the various splits are no longer necessary. At that point the voices usually recede. Any reoccurrence indicates a slippage in responsibility of some kind on the part of the primary personality.

In Christine's case, she has had the alters for as long as she can remember, cannot imagine her life without them, and does not want to integrate all of them. Her husband was and is supportive of this decision. Therefore, I never thought it was my place to push her in the direction of full integration. We talked extensively at various times—and the topic continues to come up now and again—about how she and the alters wish to live. Other people feel differently and I help them accomplish their goal of complete unification.

⁂

At the same time that I was maturing as a therapist, I was personally working on my own shortcomings in relationship issues. As I became a more skilled therapist and a more genuine person, I was more effective in helping Christine. In 2004 she was able to set a boundary with her mother for the first time in her life, and in a 2005 session she finally said the words to me: "There is more than one of me."

Then began another stage of our work together as I developed relationships with each alter and facilitated the relationships between them, as well as between the alters and Christine herself. That work itself was not much different from helping any other set of people learn to relate in a healthy way. The alter Hope's integration was a death in the family—a life experience to be accepted and dealt with. The alter SHE's aggression had to stop. The alter Rim needed to open up to alter Tristan. Tristan needed to stop being a victim. The alter Chrissy needed to learn boundaries. Based on Christine's presentation in therapy, I identified her as the primary personality and kept that position throughout our work with her "system." If she had insisted otherwise, I would have explored the possibility with her that another alter was the prime determiner of the life to be lived. We toyed with that possibility at times, but it was clear to me that these were not genuine inquiries; they were attempts to avoid having to take on the enormous challenges facing her. Openness about "having an alter" is great, but that too can be used to hide from having real contact with the world.

I was not afraid of what was occurring. I knew Christine had a singular and powerful drive to have a life worth living, and she was the organizing force throughout all her changes and all her selves. I had complete faith in her. Not blind faith, but faith based on what I saw she was capable of. What I admire so deeply about Christine is not just her strength to endure but her unfailing kindness, generosity, and enjoyment of life.

All of Christine's work in therapy has been arduous for her and, at times, for me. The most grueling period was during the emergence and integration of alters Lou and Little Lou. For several weeks I met with Christine and her husband every day, as well as having brief phone contact in the mornings and evenings. Many practitioners would not be willing or able to provide this level of contact, preferring hospitalization for the patient. If I had thought hospitalization was best for Christine, I would have pursued it, but I did not believe that, and I was open to providing what she needed during her time of crisis. We had already worked together for a long enough time that I knew her extremely well. That, coupled with her commitment to her own healing, minimized the dangers. Hospitalization was on the list of options; the joint decision to avoid it if possible was continually revisited and reaffirmed throughout the process.

It is important to note that despite the frequency and intensity of our contact throughout the years I have held to very strict boundaries with Christine, as I do with all clients. My objective is to assist people in creating an independent, authentic life without me—not to create yet another unhealthy dependency. Over time my boundary-setting became a source of humor between us, a very healthy sign reflecting Christine's growth.

At this point in our work together I feel immense joy at seeing Christine getting stronger and more functional. In this book she describes how she has successfully integrated her multiple selves into life-at-large. Instead of accommodating the social expectation that she be a single self, she lives openly as a multiple. However, it is important not to present this story as a dramatic fairy tale with a perfect ending. We continue to work on her relating to me as a fully functioning adult rather than a mother or authority figure. She continues to learn how her anxiety is rooted in her dishonesty and lack of integrity, and how easy it is to lie to oneself as well as to others. There are no shortcuts to taking responsibility for one's life—something I also continue to learn.

Mariana Sintay, MC, LMHC
Everett, Washington
May 28, 2013

Introduction:
Our Memories

A memory from me:

I wake up slowly. My head is pounding, and my mouth tastes of booze and stale cigarettes. I reach down to make sure the sheets are covering my alarmingly naked self. My movement causes my bed partner to roll over and face me, although his eyes remain closed. "Oh my God" is the thought that slips silently through my lips. My recognition is slow, but I somehow feel as though I know this man from years gone by. Furthermore, I'm quite certain he is someone that I did not think highly of. "Who is he?" I ask myself. "Gary, Jerry … no, Andy. Eww, I slept with Andy Drude, aka Andy Rude and Crude. He was a senior in high school when I was a junior. He was obnoxious and vile, and I despised him. Then I hear laughter inside my head, but it isn't coming from me. As quick as an eye blinking, my alter Rim has pushed herself out to control my body. I don't fight her. I just let myself blend into the corners of my mind, trying to block the image of Rim sliding our self on top of Andy saying, "Come on baby! Let's go for another round."

A memory from alter Rim:

It's late afternoon and our older brother Chuck and I are watching TV. I'm about nine years old and Chuck is four years my senior. The year is right around 1974 and the original Star Trek *series is the hot sitcom on the weekdays. I'm not a Trekkie, but my brother is and I love him. Therefore we watch it together, and I am thrilled to just be in his space. But our harmony comes to an abrupt end with the angry sounds of our father thunderously slamming the front door shut and storming into the house. At that moment, the air stands still. Our small black dog, Sneakers, named because of his four white paws, pees in my lap. He lets out a whimper, tucks his tail between his legs, and heads under the kitchen table to hide. Chuck and I immediately make eye contact. We were all too familiar with our father's rage, but this time we're uncertain who it's going to be directed at.*

*As our 360-pound, 6'5" father stomps his way down the hallway toward us, I quickly do an internal inventory but cannot identify what I might have done to cause his wrath. When my father bellows "Christine Louise!" all thoughts of Spock and the Enterprise vaporize into dread. Chuck gives me a sympathetic, understanding look that can't prevent the inevitable, but I suck in his mental support nonetheless. As Dad enters the room, he points directly at me, reaching me in two long strides. My arms are already flung up in defense as his football-sized hands pummel my thighs, then my arms, and finally my head, all the while yelling, **"IF YOU CANNOT TAKE CARE OF YOUR TOYS, YOU WILL NOT HAVE ANY. NOW GET OUTSIDE AND PUT THEM AWAY, THEN GO TO YOUR ROOM AND STAY THERE UNTIL YOU'RE TOLD OTHERWISE!"***

Trembling, I make my way off the couch and out of the room. I refuse to cry. I won't give him the satisfaction, but I hear Cita inside me, sobbing like a baby. I open the front door and scan our yard for the toys I have so unwittingly neglected. It takes three canvasses of the yard to finally locate the object of my father's wrath, sitting to the side of some juniper bushes. The toy in question is a new red rubber ball.

It is this innocuous eight-and-a-half-inch-wide ball that I have neglected so shamefully. I pick it up, open the garage door, and as I go to set it on the sports shelf, I notice a box cutter. "I should just slice up this piece of shit and throw it into his fat face" is the thought that passes through my young mind, but Cita's desperate pleas in the back of my head prevent me from doing so.

A memory from SHE and me:

"You will be punished, you pathetic piece of crap," SHE says to me.

"Please, no!" I sob. "Not again!" But I am unable to stop her as SHE picks up the eight-by-ten-inch metal picture frame and smashes it across the top of our forehead again and again, until the only thing left is the mutilated picture of my dog playing at the ocean. Pieces of my hair and scalp cling to the bent metal and shards of broken glass that litter the floor.

A memory from my husband Christopher:

It was just recently that I had been introduced to the Others who share my wife's mind and body. We'd been married for nineteen years, but I have known of my wife's multiple personality condition for less than two weeks. I am barely grasping its implications on our marriage and trying to get a handle on the fact that our once family of two is really now a family of seven.

This trip to Leavenworth, a quaint Bavarian-themed town in the Cascade Mountains in western Washington with wonderful shops and places to eat, was to be our first "family" activity together. Chrissy is one of my wife's alters. She is six years old and so excited to be out and about with me, seeing all of these wonderful new sights. My wife and I haven't really thought this activity through. None of us talked about expectations, rules, or guidelines for all of us out in public, but here we were.

We had barely walked half a block when Chrissy yanks me into a charming shop with a variety of handmade wooden toys, puzzles, and dolls. Chrissy is quietly sharing with me her delight and excitement of this wonderful world of toys. As her eyes pass over all of these beautiful goods, she spots a small curving stairway that leads to the store's second floor.

With much exuberance, she pulls me up the stairs to a wall loaded floor to ceiling with stuffed bears. There are bears in green velvet dresses with lace ruffles. Brown bears dressed in yellow raincoats, complete with plastic yellow boots and hats. There is a darling black bear in a bathtub with plastic bubbles on its nose and head. Pink bears, green bears, and rainbow bears. The pleasure Chrissy feels in seeing the princess and ballerina bears light up her sparkling eyes.

Other patrons and of course the desk clerk are present, but no one pays us much attention until I push a button hidden in the first dancing bear's paw. The music starts and the graceful bear spins around and around. Before I can comprehend the implication of this one bear, Chrissy waltzes her way to five more paw-activated bears. Now they're all singing, laughing, and talking while Chrissy cries out in joy and claps her hands. Soon even more of these once-cute but now loud and obnoxious bears are gyrating and convulsing, with Chrissy laughing all the way.

I soon feel that the situation is out of my control. I glance down the stairs and notice the shop owner scowling up at me. To him he sees a husband and wife acting out some immature childhood fetish. Can someone say "Awkward?" I feel in between a rock and a hard place, because I don't want Chrissy to sense my discomfort. She is truly just experiencing what any child would the very first time in a toy store or even on Christmas Day. You wouldn't want to stifle a child then, but I am feeling anxious. It is the first time I think about having to publicly explain my wife's multiple personalities.

Sadly, I am unable to prevent Chrissy from noticing my discomfort, and what began as a splendid adventure of wonder turns into her feeling confused and ashamed. It is hard on her to learn that her behavior has such a negative effect on me. She sheds many tears while apologizing for embarrassing me. I hold her tight, trying to reassure her that she didn't embarrass me, the situation had. I let her know she is loved and that we will continue to work out all the kinks in being a unique family.

The moments shared above are just the tiniest flickers into the experiences of myself, my alternate personalities, and my husband Christopher in our life together. Our story is filled with these unique, fun, and sometimes tragic experiences. As you read on, you'll see clearly how different our lives are from the societal "norm," but WE believe you'll also see how special our family is and in so many ways, how normal it is too.

One of my earlier group drawings, dated October 1998, prior to coming out about my MPD. Hope is facing out with Chrissy at her leg. Rim is wearing a baseball cap and holding a knife, while SHE or Tristan is facing away. I'm cowering in fear on the ground in the center.

1

⟡

What Is Multiple Personality Disorder?

WE KNOW THAT THE CONCEPT of having multiple people existing inside one person's body is a confusing and complex idea to grasp. The simplest way WE can explain it is that I literally have six other people who live inside my mind. I can hear and see most of these six other people, and the majority can all hear and see me too.

Still with me? These six people or "alters" (alternate personalities) are named SHE, Rim, Tristan, Q, Chrissy, and Cyndi. My name is Chris, or Cita, as the alters call me. And yes, to make it even more confusing, WE all have nicknames too. I'm called Cita to eliminate the abundance of Chris's in our lives; my husband is Christopher and there is a young alter called Chrissy. Why the name Cita? Well, Tristan, who happens to be the only male alter in our group, often calls me Mama-Cita; hence Cita for short.

Plenty of scientific theories exist as to how multiple personality disorder (MPD) happened to me, to us. Various theories support our condition as well as beliefs discounting the idea. I contacted the Sidran Institute in Maryland, which is renowned for its work in helping people understand, manage, and treat trauma and dissociation. They state that a study done almost twenty years ago showed that only 1 percent of patients being treated for psychiatric conditions has been diagnosed with dissociative identity disorder (the newer name for multiple personality disorder) (P. M. Coons, "The differential diagnosis of multiple personality: a comprehensive review," *Psychiatric Clinics of North America*, volume 7, pages 51–67, 1984). In addition, another study done in 2002 indicates that 0.5 to 1.0 percent of patients in a psychiatric setting are treated with this condition (J. R. Maldonado, L. D. Butler, and D. Spiegel, "Treatments for dissociative disorders" in *A Guide to Treatments That Work*, second edition, New York: Oxford University Press).

Part of the challenge in getting accurate statistics is because of the difficulty medical professionals have in actually diagnosing multiple personality disorder. One of the main reasons is explained in the following quote: "MPD is difficult to recognize and diagnose, because it is a condition of hiddenness (Gutheil, cited in R. P. Kluft, "The natural history of multiple personality disorder" in *Childhood Antecedents of Multiple Personality*, Washington, DC: American Psychiatric Press, 1985b)." I myself have certainly spent most of my life hiding my multiple personality disorder and was in my late thirties before I told anyone about having MPD.

The very untechnical definition of why I have MPD is that early in life I experienced trauma so severe that it caused my mind to split. The separate personalities that resulted helped to shield me from events and situations that I was unable to survive on my own.

Multiple personality disorder is sometimes referred to by its acronym "MPD" or more recently, dissociative identity disorder (DID). The following is from an online article on WebMD ("Dissociative Identity Disorder [Multiple Personality Disorder]," accessed June 13, 2013, http://www.webmd.com/mental-health/dissociative-identity-disorder-multiple-personality-disorder):

Is dissociative identity disorder real?
You may wonder if dissociative identity disorder is real. After all, understanding the development of multiple personalities is difficult, even for highly trained experts. But dissociative identity disorder does exist. It is the most severe and chronic manifestation of the dissociative disorders that cause multiple personalities.

What were the traumas? To begin with, my father was a paradox himself. He could be loving and fun, but he was also a raging, violent-tempered man with an extremely heavy hand and explosive mouth. In addition, the alter Rim and I were sexually exploited by a friend's sadistic, pedophile stepfather for close to two years. Finally, when I was less than two years old, I battled congenital problems of my hips; I was strapped down and immobilized from walking, crawling, and any weight-bearing movement for about ten days. Regardless of the care my mother took to comfort me, as an infant I would have been unable to use words to express the pain and fear I must have been experiencing.

There is no way to determine which of these experiences were the causes. WE have no memories of the exact moment my mind split and the alters came into existence. In fact, I was already fractured when the rapes occurred. So why then did my mind fracture? Possibly, in addition to undergoing abuse and trauma, I was born with a predisposition toward mental illness. Implied and documented cases of mental sickness run in both my mom's and dad's families. This was during a time when mental health was not widely studied, and women who would now be diagnosed with a menopausal condition or even PMS might have easily been admitted to psych wards. I'm certain these were conditions the women on my father's side experienced, in addition to undiagnosed and untreated postpartum depression. There are relatives in our family tree who committed suicide or displayed undiagnosed behaviors of schizophrenia and bipolar tendencies.

All of that combined is our best attempt at figuring out why I have MPD, in addition to defining what multiple personality disorder is.

2

⸻⟨❧❧⟩⸻

How Does It Work?

To start with, only one of us (myself or an alternate personality) can be out controlling my physical body at a time. As I, Cita, am writing this chapter, I have control over the physical body. But if Rim, an alternate personality in her late twenties, decides that she wants to be out to watch something on TV, it would take less than a second for her to "shift out"—meaning that then she would be in control of my body. This would cause me to shift inside my mind to an internal home where my alternate personalities (alters) live. Yes, the alters have an actual residence that looks very much like a regular home. We'll talk about this internal home shortly, but for now I'm going to have Rim shift out and be the person actually typing:

Rim (Alter):
OK, this is Rim. Hi. While I'm out, Cita has now shifted inside her mind. Freaky, huh? That's how it works, though. If Cita's husband, Christopher, came into the kitchen right now, he would see our black lab Dixie sleeping at our feet and the physical image of his wife, Cita. Just by looking at us he wouldn't be able to tell Cita and me apart. However, that changes if I speak. My voice is a tad deeper and quieter than Cita's. If I was watching a football game with Christopher, he'd also be able to distinguish me from the colorful profanity spewing from my lips. Enough from me; time for Cita to come back out.

Hi again. As Rim shared, when one of us is out (which again means that one of us is out controlling my body, living and functioning in the external world), the rest of us are inside my mind. Those who are internal (inside my mind) can talk to one another and most can see each other too. Each personality has its own anatomically correct internal body. They look different than me and have their own thoughts and emotions.

Take alter Tristan for example: Tristan is male with blonde hair, whereas mine is brown. My eyes are hazel, his are blue. Tristan is around seventeen years old, left-handed, and lean. I, however, am forty-five years old, right-handed, and overweight. I love the rain and he hates it. He thinks sour cream is the bomb and it makes me gag! Tristan can eat like a pack mule, but I can miss meals and not think twice about it. We both enjoy science fiction and natural disaster movies, but Tristan is also intrigued by quantum physics, time travel, wormholes, and black matter, whereas I get lost in all the technicalities and frankly lose interest quickly.

SHE (Alter):
The only time I give a rat's ass about black matter is if it's covering the white powdered sugar on my Hostess donuts!

As you can see from just this short exchange that even though each alter originally split from me, WE are distinctly individual.

The alters can also hear external noises while inside their internal home. Moments ago my husband launched into a song on the piano. Although I'm the person out typing, internally Tristan and the Others can hear Christopher's music. They also see out to the external world. The alters' sight is limited to what my eyes are looking at—i.e., the words I'm typing on the computer.

Tristan, shift out and tell them what it's like internally.

Tristan (Alter):
Hi. For the record I'm a lean, mean, fighting machine.

SHE:
Excuse me, but this is SHE, and for the record Tristan is a scrawny man-child.

Tristan:
Ignoring you SHE… When WE are in our internal home and looking out (meaning seeing out of Cita's eyes), it's like looking at a small TV. Right now I'm typing and staring at the screen, while those who are inside see the words I'm typing and anything else on our screen. They can see what my peripheral vision takes in. I can see Christopher's electric drill recharging on the floor and the darkness out the kitchen window. Cita's purse and miscellaneous papers are strewn about the table, and I just heard our lab Dixie woof to be let outside. If the Others were paying attention they could hear her bark too. Rim, your turn to chat:

Rim:
Crap, I don't know what to say. It may seem like a constant barrage of noise and chatter and there are definitely times when I want to yell, "For the love of God and all that's holy, please shut UP!" Instead, you learn to tune it out. It would be like living in a home with seven people in it. You wouldn't be constantly in each other's space. Our internal home does have bedrooms with doors on it, so WE can get some privacy. However, our home has no front or back doors. There are no windows and WE certainly don't have a view. The only time WE have any sort of quiet is when we're all trying to sleep. But it isn't really quiet as SHE, Tristan, and Christopher snore like freight trains. Still, it's as harmonious as it gets for us. That is until

Cyndi, the youngest alter, all of about two years old, wakes and shouts, "Pee Pee Poppy, Pee Pee!" ("Poppy" is Christopher.) Then, of course, one of us is shifting out and taking us to the restroom before Cyndi takes a leak in Cita's pajamas. Yes, this has happened a time or two. Cita, you're up.

Hi again. So, a little more about the internal home: Only Rim, SHE, Tristan, and Chrissy live here. (The additional alters Cyndi and Q live elsewhere, and I will talk more about them later in the book.) This home has a living room, dining room, and even a bathroom. The rooms have furniture and decorations. Rim painted graffiti on her bedroom wall and Chrissy's room has a chalkboard hanging in it.

WE can't tell you why their home is designed the way it is. WE don't even remember it being built; it seems more that it has always just been. And WE can't create household items or make changes to our surroundings. If WE could, Tristan would be sitting in front of an enormous flat-screen television right now, and Chrissy (who is about seven now) would have a pony walking the halls.

The alters spend the majority of their life in this internal accommodation. If I am not the person shifted out and controlling the body, then I'm inside with the Gang. Even so, while I'm out typing I can look inside my mind and see Tristan, Rim, and SHE sitting on their couch in their internal living room. I hear Chrissy's quiet breathing as she sleeps in her own room on her own bed with her own pink bedspread. Internal and external sounds can be heard by the person out in control of my physical body and throughout the rooms inside my mind.

SHE:

I think it's important for you, the readers, to really grasp what Cita just said. Noises can be heard throughout the rooms WE live in. It's like our own frickin' surround sound. Right now Cyndi is going to town on her thumb. She is sucking that baby like it's mama's nipple and her slurping and smacking sounds are echoing in the chambers of our internal abode. I think it's also important to discuss how WE communicate to one another. For this next point, however, I shall pass the torch on to Tristan.

Below is Tristan's rendition of our internal home:

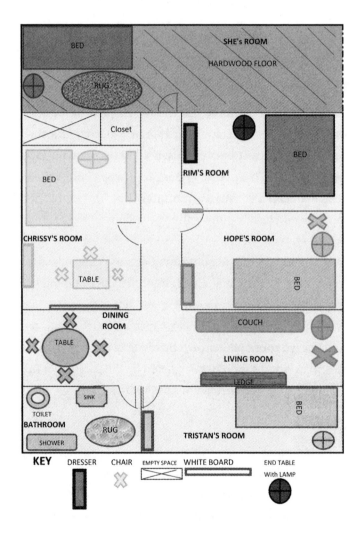

Tristan:

There are multitudes of ways WE communicate with one another. The most common is moving our mouth and forming verbal sounds or words just like the majority of human beings across the world do. As I type this, Cita has shifted back into our internal home. Cita, SHE, and Rim are sitting in our internal living room talking. It looks and sounds just like if you had three people in your den visiting with one another. As I type this next sentence, I verbally speak what I'm typing out loud too. Now both Cita's spouse Christopher and the internal gals can hear what I'm saying. However, since I'm shifted out and in control of the physical body, I can hear what they are saying internally in addition to any external sounds.

Now keep in mind that I may be able to hear what they are saying, but that doesn't mean I listen to what each person is saying all the time, nor would Cita if she were out. If you had six roommates, you wouldn't listen to every single conversation going on under the roof. You might hear a word or two and tune in on a topic of interest. If you happened to be reading a book, you would tune out the background noise and that's what WE do. I'm hoping in time you'll begin to feel sorrier for me as you realize that I am the lone dude in a henhouse of six women. It would be one thing if I were the rooster, but that is not the case.

Rim:

You keep dreaming Tristan.

Tristan:

A dude's gotta have dreams! Anyway, Cita will be coming back out to type soon, but before she does I want to reiterate a point. As Cita begins to type again, she will hear the following: First the daily external noises, dishwasher, the neighbor saw-

> ing down tree limbs, the TV sounds as Christopher watches a
> football game, birds chirping, dogs barking, and so forth. Cita
> will also hear all the noises that the alters, me included, make
> inside her mind; laughing, talking, yawning, farting...

This is Cita again. Keep in mind that I grew up with all this noise going
on in my head for as far back as I can remember. What might seem like
a chaotic mayhem of sound to you is just normal to me. I'm impacted
most by this internal static when I'm in a crowded room or restaurant.
I find it difficult to hear the person across from me at a table when loud
sounds are going on externally in addition to the internal noises. Also,
my husband Christopher can obviously hear only the person who has
control of the physical body, but frequently the Gang are all talking to
him. They can only speak one at a time, but WE all shift back and forth
in split-second intervals laughing, sharing, joking, and commenting.
It's very much like how the crowd at a large family dinner would sound
like, but with only two physical bodies sitting at the table.

Growing up, I had no control over Rim, SHE, or Hope. (Hope is
an alter who is no longer with us, and WE will share much more about
her later in the book.) But WE are more cohesive in how WE live now,
and I have much more influence over my physical body. I am still unable to stop some of the adult alters from shifting out; however, WE
have made conscious choices to be courteous with and not disrupt one
another when one of us is talking externally. However, we're pretty tol-
erant of interruptions, because they just happen.

Tristan:
Interruptions happen, good one Cita. You should cross-stitch
that on a pillow.

Here's another example. In 2007, I underwent a colonoscopy that ended up being so painful that I awoke from the anesthesia. My intense

pain and high fear levels caused me to inadvertently block the alters who would have typically taken over. If the person who controls the body experiences a severe emotion, it can prevent any of the Others from shifting out externally. In some circumstances the alters' pain thresholds are higher than mine, and WE don't always feel the pain that the external person experiences. If I got a cramp in my wrist right now, odds are that I'd be the only one to feel it. The alters internally might notice a twitch in their wrist, but unless they shifted out, they would not even be aware of it. At other times they might feel external discomfort on a more muted level.

Tristan:

I wanted to share this too: Most nights, it's Cita who is physically shifted out and sleeping in bed next to her husband. The rest of us snuggle down in our own beds. It is common for the two youngest, Cyndi the baby and Chrissy, to shift out and say their goodnights to Christopher. Well, last night there was a small windstorm in our neighborhood (that would be the external neighborhood, not internal). It was close to 1 AM. WE were all snoozing soundly when a power transformer less than a mile away shorted out. The sound was like a gunshot and it startled Chrissy, even though she was asleep inside Cita's mind. Chrissy's fear was so acute that she burst into tears and shifted right out, waking Christopher. Christopher immediately began to comfort and calm her down.

Where do I stay if I'm shifted internally? Prior to Hope's passing, I shared Chrissy's room with her.

The house also has a dining area, although curiously there are no cupboards or any access to food; however, the bathroom is fully functional. They have access to a shower and can go to the bathroom, including flushing the toilet. I can hear you saying, "Oh my God! How can that be?" There is no way to answer every question, and we've probably asked many of the same questions ourselves. WE also can't tell you why some of the alters have the names they do: Tristan, Rim, SHE…no idea.

Why is their home a rambler? My early childhood homes all had two stories. I didn't live in a rambler until fifth grade and by then the alters were already a part of my life. So again I do not have an answer for you. With other people who have MPD whom we've read about, some also have internal residences, such as caves; another was an ancient castle. (See suggested reading in the back of this book.)

One question that I often get asked is, "What about when you and your husband want to be intimate or have private time? Do they watch and hear that too?" The answer is no! Most of the adult alters and I have the ability to "block." This means that by focusing a bit harder WE can prevent one another from hearing what is occurring on the outside. The person who is in physical control of the body can have privacy as long as WE are blocking. Blocking is like a reflex, similar to holding your breath. After a time, WE begin to feel the strain and can become exhausted if WE block for more than a couple hours at a time.

Hopefully this background helps you understand our world a little better. For every point WE make, WE think of more specifics to share with you. We're also aware that too much information in one sitting may leave you overwhelmed and unwilling to persevere through our story. In this book you will read some chapters that are long while others are much shorter. Each one will continue to build your knowledge and hopefully increase your comfort zone as WE delve deeper into our lives.

3

⋖❖⋗

Integration

MANY PEOPLE WHO KNOW A bit about multiple personality disorder commonly believe that the main goal for a person with MPD is to rid themselves of their alters and become as one. We've often heard integration described that way. In reality, that would mean I would wish for Chrissy to no longer be a part of my or of Christopher's life. Although there may have been times when I wanted one or more of my alters to disappear, the reality is that losing an alter is a huge emotional upheaval, akin to a death in the family.

I previously mentioned that the alter Hope integrated and WE go into far more detail about that experience in a later chapter. But the point is that, for us, it was as if Hope died. That was the same experience our therapist and my husband had. Someone whom WE loved and spent time with no longer existed.

Again, WE can't tell you why one alter fades or integrates and another doesn't. Our best guess is that once an alter has served its purpose, it isn't needed anymore and therefore has less reason to exist. I once had an alter named Molly who was just an infant. She integrated a few months after I shared with my therapist Mariana that I had MPD. WE believe that Molly represented my fear of telling someone that I had MPD, as well as my childhood anxiety that my parents might take Hope from me. When I finally shared about my MPD and Hope still remained with me, Molly's purpose was served. One day she existed in our internal home and the next day she didn't.

As for Hope, WE had been working on a new support network for me that included counseling, family, and Christopher. Hope knew that

I'd be able to function and survive in life with the help of these people, and it was this faith in my security that enabled Hope to let go and integrate. Hope's fading was deeply traumatic for me, occurring over a period of thirty days. It was literally like watching someone you deeply love die of cancer within a month.

Oftentimes when an alter integrates, their characteristics disperse among the remaining personalities. That wasn't the case in our situation. Tristan didn't suddenly become a tree hugger and I wasn't instantly more confident. The changes were subtle. For instance, during Hope's existence, she and I could talk telepathically. Chrissy and Tristan could communicate to each other this way too, but none of the other alters had this ability. After Hope faded, Tristan and I could hear each other's thoughts when we hadn't been able to prior.

WE can't choose who leaves. Even if an alter wants to integrate, WE aren't able to just snap our fingers and make it happen. WE define integration as a way of creating a healthy environment among ourselves so that WE can function cohesively into society as a person with MPD.

4

⊰⊹⊱

Open-Door Policy

IN OUR HOUSEHOLD, WE TRY to have an open-door policy, which means that in our daily lives at home, when we're with friends, family, and of course my husband, the alters and I shift in and out at ease. No restraints are put on who wants to be out when. Sure, WE are courteous with one another and try not to interrupt the person who is out directing my body, but sometimes, especially at dinner, it can be a free-for-all. I'll let Christopher share our dinnertime festivities:

Christopher:

Being in the presence of the Gang while preparing and enjoying food is so much fun. Each alter is unique. For example:

It would be too easy to portray Tristan as a hungry puppy, ready to dig in before the dog food is poured from the bag. When he is hungry, Tristan actually squawks like a fledgling bird crying for another worm from its mommy. He does it in jest, but he finds no humor in hunger. Sounds of pure eating pleasures are Tristan's trademark... "uhmm, ahhh, yumm."

It's most obvious when Chrissy is out because of her delightful mannerisms; she is animated and playful even when she is just sitting at the table. Sometimes she rocks back and forth as though she were dancing in her seat. Oftentimes she forgets that eating is what she's supposed to be doing.

Q is a patient, gracious vegetarian. Christopher, who does most of our cooking, tries to prepare meatless meals throughout the week. The

Others are also courteous and make sure that Q gets to have bites of veggies, pastas, or rice.

Christopher:

There's this ongoing banter between Tristan and Chrissy versus Q around the consumption of meat. Q refers to them as disgusting carnivores and will not shift out if any meat products are in my mouth. Chrissy and Tristan will tell Q not to shift out because they are still eating meat, while they covertly eat all the French fries that Q loves.

SHE will also burst onto the scene, usually with a gruff comment like "Back off Squirt!" then blocking everyone from getting any bites at all, because she can.

Cyndi's diet is limited. She tried cantaloupe this week and liked it. The banana was spat out. Up until then, strawberries were the only food she'd eat. Cyndi eats them in small bites and after each bite says, "Mmmmmm berry, Poppy." When she's done she puts her hands out and says, "More? Go Poppy, go." At any other time when she shifts out and food happens to be in the mouth, she will stick her tongue out, repulsed. If WE can catch her in time, someone will finish eating the food (eww!). And if not, it ends up on my wife's shirt or on the floor.

As for Cita during all of this, I'm comforted to know that she is always just a moment away. As for the two of us, we enjoy the food and our own conversations a good portion of the time.

After dinner the Gang and I do clean-up because Christopher usually does the cooking. I came into our relationship with many special gifts, but Betty Crocker tendencies were not among them; domestic goddess isn't either! My poor hubby Christopher is also patient enough to grocery shop and finds pleasure in addressing all our myriad nutritional tastes and requirements. Don't think that WE won't help grocery shop, but when it comes to meal planning, food preparation, and presentation, Christopher takes the lead. When it comes to food consumption, the Gang and I don't hold back.

Once we've completed our post-dinner chores, Chrissy often wants to play a board game called *Sorry*. It's a game we all enjoy and have played so many times that we've created new rules to keep ourselves entertained. Below, seven-year-old Chrissy describes our gaming experience. (I typed it just as she wrote it, so it includes all her grammar and spelling errors; I made corrections in brackets if I thought it was necessary for your understanding.)

Chrissy:

i think the game sorry is fun to play and WE all can play at the same time. i am red and christopher is blue, tristan is yellow and q is green. if SHE or Rim want to play they pick someone to be partners with. i like when SHE is my partner because she makes me laugh. SHE gets so mad when someone nocks her back to start and some times she will say a bad word. when that happens she has to put a qarter [quarter] in the potty cow [a ceramic cow bank that we deposit change in when anyone swears—Chrissy is saving to go to Disneyland] we laugh so much becaus SHE doesnt work and asks christopher or Q to borrow money. cita plays with us to but mostly she will shuffle the deck. even grandma, mimi, jennifer, and sandy [my mom, stepmom, stepsister, and friend, respectively] play when they come to see us but jennifer some times gets crankie when WE change the rules on her.

We've never had to enforce a bedtime for the two youngest alters. They fall asleep at night almost like clockwork, with Cyndi dozing off around 7:30 and Chrissy closer to 8 PM. As night draws near and our youngest alters' eyes grow heavy with sleep, the following exchanges are likely to take place between Chrissy and Cyndi, with both of them straining to shift out and be held in my husband Christopher's arms and pining for his love.

Chrissy:	i dont have to go to sleep.
Christopher:	I know that baby.
Cyndi:	I no baby Poppy.
Christopher:	I know honey.
Chrissy:	I was out with christopher, cyndi!
Cyndi:	yndi bestest Poppy! [Cyndi, who often drops the first letter in a word, also will suck my thumb when she is shifted out.]
Chrissy:	no! he loves me the mostest.
Christopher:	Ok girls. I love you both the mostest.
Chrissy:	i liked it better when cyndi wasnt my sister.
Cyndi:	rissy no no yndi poppy. rissy no no yndi. [Cyndi telling Christopher that Chrissy is mad at her]

So hurt by her sister's words, Cyndi will recite this last cry over and over. Much to the joy of everyone who is hearing this ongoing squabble, Chrissy finally relents:

Chrissy:	its ok. chrissy loves cyndi.
Cyndi:	rissy no no
Chrissy:	im sorry cyndi. do you want to hear the story of the princess pony?
Cyndi:	rincess pony rissy? nigh nigh poppy
Christopher:	Goodnight loves. Sweet dreams.

And with that they both settle in as Chrissy creates a story about a fair maiden, a princess pony, and her journey to the magic castle.

With the girls at long last sleeping, the remaining alters SHE, Rim, Q, and Tristan may join Christopher and me for a movie on Netflix. Between us all, our film preferences vary, but we normally manage to pick out something we can all enjoy. If not, the majority rules. Those who do not like the movie choice settle in our internal home and visit, or else go to bed. Afterward Christopher will play the piano while Q beads or SHE and I read.

I'd like to say that once the evening is complete, we all crawl into bed and fall into a deep slumber and pleasant dreams, but that isn't the case. Christopher could fall asleep and not wake up until the morning if he wasn't blessed with the nightly awakening from Chrissy or Cyndi. I'll let him describe his night to you in his own words.

Christopher:

Often I don't even know who's getting themselves ready for bed. It is normally Q, SHE, or Tristan slipping into pajamas, brushing teeth, fluffing pillows, and crawling under the sheets. At a minimum, I always have a brief chat with whomever is lying next to me. The alters will say goodnight and shift into their internal home, leaving the body uninhabited for a few moments. When no one is shifted out, the body lies still and it's quite strange.

What happens next is characteristic of my wife, Chrissy, or Cyndi. It quickly becomes self-evident who is out, as their movements and breathing patterns are all unique. Cita has subtle movements, and she is usually already comfortable and moves in for a little snuggle with me. Chrissy immediately begins her ritual of rearranging herself into a fetal position with her feet touching mine; she reaches for the sheet and then the bedspread, asking for her small, hand-crocheted green blanket and lastly tucking her stuffed reindeer Sarefino around her neck. With all as it should be, I reassure her she's safe and that I'm not going anywhere as she drifts off to sleep.

Cyndi has an uncanny ability to hear train whistles off in the distance. They occur frequently. With each toot of the horn, she shifts out, still half asleep, laughing in joy at what she hears. The next few moments are about reassuring her as I run my fingers through her hair. She will suck her thumb (well, Cita's thumb), patting my hand until she falls asleep. Or Cyndi will awaken fully, asking me questions and playing with her stuffed animals while having me kiss each one goodnight. Some assistance by SHE or Q help me convince her that "Poppy needs his sleep" and with some fuss she settles in.

I often sleep through my alters' customary bedtime rituals and won't realize that they were out until I wake up with a wet thumb or Minnie or Mickey Mouse's face plastered to my cheek. Other signs of alter activity? Well, I like to sleep with the window wide open—winter, summer, spring, and fall. I use just a sheet for covering up. I also like to face my husband and hold his hand as I drift to sleep. But many times when I wake up, I'm facing the opposite direction and bundled in covers (Chrissy's doing), and Cyndi will have turned on her smiley-face nightlight given to her by her grandma.

One less subtle indication that things are amiss will be waking up on the couch with a book on my chest and crumbs littering our coffee table. That means SHE had a restless night.

SHE:

Well, that makes it sound as if I just graze the night away and that may be the case on occasion, but it's not the norm. The reality is that the girls start stirring and wanting Christopher's attention, but he needs to sleep. He's got to get up most mornings and work. WE have the five-minute rule, and if they don't submit to blissful sleep, in lieu of braining them, I go out to the couch and put a vid on until they fall back asleep.

By then I've worked up a slight appetite and I make myself a midnight snack. I stretch out on the couch, grub, and read. Anyway, it's normally Chrissy who wakes us up on the couch, which she hates by the way and drags us back into bed. Of course, this risks waking Christopher up yet again, but finally there is a short time period where WE are all catching some REM sleep together.

Thank you for that clarification SHE. I think WE will all agree, however, that mornings are our most difficult time of the day. Throughout the day, I can be resting inside our internal home and the Others can be shifted out, controlling the body, watching TV, beading, coloring, or reading. I don't have to be awake for them to utilize my body.

When I am overly tired, which is normally the case in the morning; it's harder for the Others to shift out. SHE, Rim, Tristan, and Q are able to break through my fatigue if necessary, but if they notice my resistance, they allow me to sleep so I can rest my body too.

When I am sleeping in our internal home, it helps with exhaustion, but it isn't the same as when I'm in control of the body and sleeping like a normal person would be. The drawback for Chrissy is that she is an early riser and loves her mornings with Christopher. On the days when sleep takes precedence over her social time, she is stuck inside, much to her chagrin.

Chrissy:

i love being with my christopher in the morning before he goes to work. everyone else is sleeping, even cyndi and i dont have to share him. we have cereal and juice together and watch a disney movie together. i love to be held by him and have him all to myself. there are some times when cita wont let me through to shift out and be with christopher. i call it being held hostage and i hate it. some times SHE will shift me out to play with christopher and then there are times when SHE says i have to let cita sleep and it makes me mad. christopher will always wake cita and say goodbye to all of us before he leaves for work but that's not the same thing.

Chrissy always tells me that this is "not acceptable behavior" when she's held hostage, but she says it lovingly and is really a pretty good sport about the unique ways WE live. On the mornings when Christopher doesn't have to work, he will be up and about long before me. Often he will come back into the bedroom to retrieve his glasses or grab his shoes, and he'll see Cyndi out playing with her stuffed friends. Mickey Mouse is her favorite, but there is a Minnie Mouse and an alpaca stuffed animal that she calls "Pa-Poppy."

Christopher:
I love to come into the bedroom and see Cyndi animatedly moving her animals around her. Cyndi also loves anything that spins. We've hung a "spinner" from our windowsill. A spinner is a foot long twisted piece of plastic that spirals when the wind blows. Ours is iridescent blue, but it hangs inside and will spin from a breeze coming through the window, but more often we manually spin it. Cyndi can't quite reach it and I will see her outstretch one hand, mimicking the motion of spinning. Once she spies me, she happily cries, "Poppy, yndi out," whereupon I reply, "Yes, I see you Cyndi." It's important to her that I recognize her. "Poppy, pinning?" she asks me, and I'll reach over and give the spinner a twirl for her.

Every day could be its own chapter, so we'll share a few more moments to help you visualize the mayhem of our days:

Rim:

Ok, so let's take today. It's Football Sunday which rocks and the Seattle Seahawks are playing against the Pittsburg Steelers. It's just after half and the Hawks are being spanked 17 to zip; that rocks less. Regardless, Christopher and I remain forever faithful and hopeful that one day soon, our Seahawks will take the NFL to the mattress and KICK SOME ASS!

Tristan:

I may be the sole male in the group, but there is probably more testosterone between Rim and SHE than in me! I mean yeah, I'm a dude and I'm no girly guy, but my voice isn't macho; SHE's is deep. I don't know much about sports, though I'm watching and learning; Rim is a jock. I like to make comments during football games like, "Hey, he double-dribbled" or "Did he hit a home run?" Both Rim and Christopher will shake their heads, then ignore me.

Another alter that has yet to be introduced goes by the letter Q. Q is gifted in creating beautiful beaded bracelets and intricate figurines she calls Bead People. When she is shifted out, occupying my physical body, beading is her activity of choice.

On the left is one of Q's bead people; this one was called "Moonshine."
On the right are some of her beautiful bracelets.

WE go into more detail about Q and her existence in a later chapter. But for now, know that she is in her mid-twenties and has a speech impediment. I will be typing her thoughts in the manner that she speaks them, clarifying in brackets if needed:

Q:
Hi it Q. I happy [to] share with you. When have chance I settle in my chair right next to kitchen window and where Cita and Christopher put up my bead station. It peaceful watch squirrels chase each other, running up [and] down tree. Sometime they climb from roof hanging upside down to eat food from bird feeders. That funny to see. I see all beautiful birds as I bead too. I like watch sports too, but most [mostly I] like Mariner baseball. I let Rim enjoy football and she let me watch baseball. It good trade.

In between all of our activities, WE make time to read to Cyndi or let both of the younger girls color. Chrissy is quite the artist and loves doing most crafts. Chrissy also loves Webkinz. Webkinz are adorable stuffed animals that come with access to an online animated world. Each stuffed animal includes a secret code that she can apply to her Webkinz account. With the code, her stuffed animal becomes a living cartoon character that can go to school, play outside, eat, sleep, and even work out—all in the confines of the Webkinz World. She has over thirty Webkinz and loves them all. Chrissy never got to attend a real school, and most of the games and activities on Webkinz are learning-oriented. It's her very own online school and she has fun while she learns.

WE also need to allow time in the day for general housecleaning, laundry, washing dishes, and vacuuming, in addition to counseling, medical and dental appointments, picking up prescriptions, and tending to Q's bead business. Rim and I tend to be homebodies while the Others love to be out seeing and doing.

Lastly, Christopher and I try to find time each and every day for just the two of us. We enjoy each other deeply and love our rare moments of quality time, just visiting or hanging out together in our hammock. We are grateful for the harmony that we have been blessed with in the most recent years. You might laugh at my use of the word "harmony," as you might find our life far from harmonious. But believe me, it is far more pleasant and balanced now than in years gone by, as you'll soon see.

5

--◦◦◦--

In the Beginning

I WAS THIRTY-NINE YEARS OLD before I ever told another soul about my multiple personalities. Until then, the alters and I lived outwardly as one person. If Rim or SHE were out and in control of the body, they were recognized by other people as me (Chris or Christy as my family called me). When I was a child, only Rim, SHE, and Hope were active in my life. Chrissy and Tristan were in my mind, but they did not shift out, nor did I have a relationship with them. Instead, Hope took care of them, and to me, they were more internal chatter and annoyance than anything else.

I have no memory of my childhood that does not include Hope, SHE, and Rim. Hope was my confidante, my savior, and my shelter. Hope watched over me, as well as guided and comforted me. She was tall and lean, with golden blond hair and mocha-brown eyes. Her skin was pale, without blemish, and her eyelashes were equally pale. Hope's upper front two teeth overlapped just a tad, which softened her almost regal manner. She was patient, gentle, kind, honest, and warm. She also loved the outdoors and encouraged us to make healthier choices. As I grew older my eating disorder and smoking habit tried her easygoing nature.

Age is hard to determine with the alters. The body may have been born in 1965, but the alters tend to stay in a certain age range. The best we can do is guesstimate. Hope always appeared older to me as a child and young adult. When I was about twenty-two, Hope peaked at about age thirty and stayed that age until she integrated years later. One would think that she would have looked younger when I was a child and grown older with me, but that is not the case.

Since all of Us (including Hope) have written in journals for years, we've been able to include her thoughts throughout the book.

Hope:

Truth is, I don't know the exact date and time I came to be. It's as if I have always been, although I know that isn't the case. As Cita grew and developed, so did her need for me until one day the urgency of her cry brought me fully to life. The anxiety levels that ran through her tiny infant body were numbing and baffling to me. Cita did not appear to be in any immediate danger, and upon my arrival her tension did lesson a bit, but in no way did it decrease in the manner I expected. Uncertain what to do from that point on, I mainly just watched, listened, and comforted when needed.

If Hope sounds like my guardian angel, then SHE will sound like the devil reincarnate.

For the first thirty years of my life, SHE terrified me. We did not have a relationship in any form other than SHE tormented me and continued the physical abuse I received from my father. SHE burned me, cut me, and even broke my bones. She verbally abused me and the other alters. In the numerous books I have read about people with MPD, it is a common phenomenon to have a "bad" alter present. These alters often have generic names like SHE, "the witch," or "the bad one." When I began counseling with my therapist later in life, I drew a lot to express myself and release my pain when I was unable to find the words. In many of those pictures, SHE was represented as a monster or a wolf.

SHE radiates an energy that is intense. I don't know how to describe it, but SHE commands space without saying a single word. SHE is opinionated, obstinate, stubborn, and determined. SHE has no time for idle chit-chat and cannot be bothered with the effort involved to have a relationship with another human being. It wasn't until I began counseling that I realized, in a twisted way that SHE has really been there for my protection. Her sole purpose was to deflect my father's rage and keep it as her own. In addition, SHE absorbed my own anger at the abuse I experienced as a child.

One of many pictures drawn with SHE represented as a monster.

A physical description of SHE would include a round face and short, choppy brown hair. SHE tends to have "bed-head" hair, like the kind when you first wake up, but that's how it looks all day long. She is shorter than the other adult alters, about five feet six, and her build is thick, stocky, and solid. Her eyes are green and her skin olive. SHE is also a lesbian, but that factor didn't impact my life until I was much older.

SHE:
I don't remember the dawning of my existence either. I was just there sucking in all the rage her dad dished up. I absorbed

it like a frickin' sponge. Early on I don't recall having much of an image of myself (more like an entity than a physical presence) until Cita was age four or so. It wasn't until Cita started to develop her own cognitive abilities that Rim, Hope, and I seemed to morph into having our own bodies.

It was also then that I became the SCARY MONSTER that hid in the deepest darkest bowels of Cita's mind. I sucked in all the rage that was being directed at Cita from other people in her life. This rage made me mean, intimidating, and strong. Not even the alter Hope could bust through a block that I instigated. Well, "rarely" is more accurate. If she did get through, it would be for short durations. Then I'd return with a vengeance.

I was out externally only when Cita's father went ballistic. He might be smacking her upside the head or yelling at someone, and then Cita would shift to our internal home. She would literally just disconnect mentally and become a vacant, worthless blob. Then I would step out to take his anger and deal with it. In turn, I used her dad's rage to fuel my aggression toward her.

Now, I hear your sobs of pity for me and I'm truly so terribly touched that I might just cry myself a river, but the reality was that it was the only way of living that I knew. Like a psychopath, I fed off rage and Cita's fear. I would never have thought of myself as abused but more the abuser. Between her father and me, she lived with the anxiety of physical and mental abuse twenty-four hours a day, seven days a week. I would slam her fingers in a door or smash her hand in a window. We'd drink mouthwash or eat a tube of toothpaste until Cita would vomit. I remember taking her Play-Doh tins and smashing them into her face or legs until she was littered in bruises and welts. Unfortunately at the time, Hope was always there to spoil the fun. At times Hope was as helpless as Cita, but other times she was able to knock me back a peg with a supersize power block.

The third and final active alter during my childhood is Rim. Rim was everything I felt I wasn't. Rim is gorgeous and sexy, with a lean muscular body and eyes green almost to the point of turquoise. She is athletic, good in math, and tough as nails. She is the ultimate tomboy—rough, tough, and street-smart. Rim was and is still, to some degree, my courage. Rim was also SHE's best friend and ally growing up.

Rim is an alter who did age with me throughout my childhood, adolescence, and early adulthood. We were always the same age until I was in my late twenties. Then I kept aging while Rim stayed about twenty-eight years old. Our guess as to why Rim stayed at that age relates to my marriage to Christopher. WE think that once I gained trust and felt safe with Christopher in my life, that part of her reason for existing changed.

Rim:

Yeah, people ask me why I was friends with SHE when WE were younger. Cita paints me as this tough alley cat, but the reality was that SHE was intimidating as hell and I didn't want to be on the wrong end of her wrath. You know the phrase, "Keep your friends close, but your enemies closer." Well, there you have it. I chose my own safety over Cita's.

I remember once being invited to go camping with a friend when WE were, oh, nine-ish. WE went to the ocean, and Cita and I shifted back and forth depending on what WE were doing. This friend suggested we go hike up the side of this cliff. It looked like someone had just taken an enormous chainsaw and cut straight through the earth. There were tree roots sticking out, downed limbs, and all sorts of things protruding from the side and boulders below.

Cita was petrified, but I immediately felt the thrill of a challenge. Par for the course, Cita "checked out" to our internal home while our girlfriend and I began climbing. We scrambled up the rocks, reaching out to grab whatever was available and started stretching ourselves across the side of the cliff. At one point we were close to twenty-five feet above ground. I could sense Cita's fear, but it just fueled my thrill to conquer and even SHE was egging me on. We were about halfway to the top when SHE said, "Back off Rim, I'm sending Cita back out." In a matter of seconds, I was back inside and Cita was now out against her will, clinging to the sea cliff.

I feel sad when I think back on memories like this one. At the time I really didn't give a shit about the torment Cita was experiencing. Her fear just pissed me off. I don't know how much time passed, and Cita says it was hours. I know it was only minutes when I heard our friend shouting, "Move it along, my arms are getting tired!" Still Cita stayed paralyzed and our friend's pleas were turning more angry and frantic. By this time the girl's father was bellowing at us from below and had taken a more direct path to the top. He walked over to a location just above us, reached down, and pulled us up. Man, was he pissed. Not because we got stuck, but because we had climbed up there in the first place. The girlfriend was crying and mad at us for getting her in trouble. SHE and I just laughed and kept Cita shifted out to deal with the aftermath.

Cita was good at apologizing and smoothing over ruffled feathers. Cita was always apologizing for existing.

I had Hope as my savior and nurturer, SHE absorbing my father's rage, and fearless Rim to override my insecurity and occasionally my common sense! So, what was my purpose? I was the holder of fear. I was afraid of my own shadow. I cried often and needed continual comfort to know I was safe. I loved others to the point of smothering. I was overly sensitive to noise or pain, and I did everything in my power to keep people from being mad at me, since I had no tolerance for aggression or confrontation. This meant that not only was I quick to have my feelings hurt or to become scared, but I could also sense when someone else was feeling even just a hint of sadness or anger.

I remember one particularly traumatic event when I was six or seven. My brother Chuck (who is four years older) and his friends had built a fort underneath a neighbor's back porch. As I recall, hanging from the door was a "No girls allowed" sign. Later that same day my mom took me outside for a surprise. Sometime earlier that day she had trimmed back our corner landscaping and built a tipi-like fort just for me, hidden between the trees and shrubs. She had hung sheets or blankets to add color and folded another one to sit on. She even had a tray with snacks and juice waiting for me inside the fort.

By all appearances it looked pretty cool, but what my mom did not anticipate or even suspect was how petrified I was to be inside that fort all by myself. I wasn't claustrophobic, but I was terrified of something bad happening to me in that space and no one would be there to save me. I felt sick to my stomach when I thought about telling her of my fears. Mom had worked so hard and I believed I'd hurt her feelings by telling her I didn't want to play in it. After she lifted up the makeshift-flap door for me and then departed back to the house, I sat Indian-style, frozen like a statue. I could hear SHE making fun of me for being afraid, Rim laughing alongside of her, and Hope scolding them both.

Rim actually thought the fort was cool, and I had been depending on her to be the one playing in it. However, because that was what I wanted, she of course did not oblige me. Hope tried to shift out for me, but SHE blocked her and left me to deal with my fears alone. My wide eyes scanned my surroundings; I was certain that monster-sized spiders and other creepy-crawlies were, at that very moment, emerging from the shrubbery to take siege of my fort.

My body began to shake, and I moved only when I was forced to fill my lungs with air. Hope tried to get me to take a drink of juice, but I refused to move. Hope spoke soothingly, continually trying to coax me. She sang softly to me and still my anxiety remained. Then the unimaginable happened: An actual garden spider began making its way across the side of my fort, its shadow seemingly expanding it to ten times its real size. As soon as I spotted it, I screamed. Then I began breathing frantically as though I were being chased by an axe murderer. I could no longer hear anything but ringing in my ears, and my vision grew dark.

The next thing I clearly remember is sitting at the kitchen table and my brother looking at me as if he is waiting for me to answer him. "Well?" he asks. I look around the table. My mom is staring at me while my dad is engrossed in his food. We're obviously having dinner. I look at my plate. Spanish rice. Yuck, my least favorite. Then I yawn. My mom smiles warmly at me and says to my brother, "She's a tuckered girl. I think she'll have to show you her fort tomorrow."

I look over at my brother with a dawning realization that I had just shifted back out. I then become aware of Hope speaking to me in the background. I respond to my brother, "No, we can look at it after dinner." I smile at him. He shakes his head and sees my worry. "I promise I'll hang with you for a while tomorrow Christy, OK? I think Mom's right. You do seem tired." He reaches out and pulls one of my pigtails. I still feel foggy and ask to be excused from the table.

Back in my room I curl up on my bed. Hope then fills me in. "It was when you started to breathe so fast. You hyperventilated and began to pass out. SHE released the block so I could shift out. I slowed our breathing and you calmed down. Rim ate the snack your mom had put out and then WE just rested in the fort. I don't know how long

WE were out there. I'd say not quite an hour, but I was getting chilled. You were sleeping and I didn't want to wake you. I headed toward the house, where your mom was just starting dinner. She asked me to wash up and help her set the table. I thanked her for the fort. She seemed pleased that you enjoyed it. Your dad came home and shortly afterward so did your brother. Your dad asked your brother something about his paper route as WE sat down to eat and then your mom asked about his fort and mentioned yours. That's when your brother asked to see yours and also when you woke up and shifted back. I had hoped we'd get to talk before you came back so I could fill you in, but it didn't happen that way."

Hope then asked how I was feeling. I could only reply, "I love you Hope." Then I curled up into a tight ball, wishing Hope had her own body and could hold me on the outside. Then I mentally pulled myself inside and let her hold me in my mind. I'd had enough for one day.

⚜

Not all of my young life is filled with pain. My mom had the most magical Christmases whereby our house and tree looked like you had stepped into a fairy tale. Birthdays were filled with friends, games, and wonderful homemade cakes. For Halloween my brother and I were adorned in the best costumes, all made by hand by our mother. I was a clown, a gypsy, a Sesame Street yellow-feathered Big Bird, a bunch of grapes, and even a slime-dragging slug! On St. Patrick's Day we were greeted by green grapefruit and green milk for breakfast. But even those joys were masked by the strain of hiding my multiple personalities and the abuses that WE experienced.

People have asked us why WE didn't tell someone about our MPD. It's a great question, but it's another one I don't completely have the answer to. Hope once shared that when I was in kindergarten, I had mentioned Rim and her to a friend. I had assumed that everyone had lots of people inside their minds, just like me. When I asked this child about it, she apparently just laughed and thought I was joking. I'm certain after that I wouldn't have felt comfortable mentioning it again.

As for telling my parents? Well, at the time my dad was physically abusing me. I also was deeply worried that if I spoke of the alters that somehow my parents would take them away from me. At that age I wouldn't have cared if Rim or SHE left, but the thought of losing Hope was more than I could stand. Also, SHE made harmful threats if Hope or I discussed talking to someone on the outside about the MPD. When I was young, talking about it just wasn't an option.

Portrayal of a "happy" family, taken in 1970. I would have been five.

6

◄◙◙►

Childhood

WE GREW UP IN A nice middle-class neighborhood in Seattle. It was ten minutes from downtown and close to a large lake, as well as a nearby zoo. My father worked hard for a local grocery store chain and my mom was able to be home with us. Our home was an older two-story with three upstairs bedrooms and a modest living area on the main floor. In addition, we had a basement and detached garage.

I attended kindergarten through fifth grade while we lived at this house. One afternoon I came home with a note from my teacher. It informed my parents that I had many of the qualities of a gifted child. My mom no longer has that note but remembers some of those characteristics:

Ultra-awareness
A dramatic imagination
Observant
Acute sense of right and wrong
Self-motivated
Advanced reading/math/art skills

Very curious
Fantastic problem-solving skills
Very sensitive
Learns quickly
Relates well with adults/teachers

Christine's mom (Sharon):
At home, Christine always had several things going on. When watching TV she would also color and during boring commercials she would read. Once we were in a department store and when I turned to her, she was not there. I instantly started racing around to find her, and after passing right by her a couple of times, I realized that she was standing as still and posed

as the mannequins she was imitating. I swear she didn't even blink. I couldn't believe my eyes.

Once, when Christine was four or five years old, she came running down the stairs and jumped onto the arm of our recliner. She was squatted down with her bottom toward the back of the chair and her arms stretched out wide. Looking at me with huge eyes, she cried, "A spider is on my wall Mom! And it looks just like this!" Looking at her I could just see that spider.

In the early 1970s, few programs were available for kids who were high achievers. Other than some encouragement to participate in school plays, band, and any advanced classes offered, no other reference to being a "gifted child" took place. I made friends easily, stayed active, and kept up my grades. I did not give any outward indication that I was fractured internally. Rim, Hope, and I excelled at functioning as a "whole" person.

The summer before I entered sixth grade, our parents moved us to a new school district, since they preferred the scholastic programs offered in the suburbs just north of the Seattle area. WE transitioned well into the local elementary school, making new friends but continuing to see others from the old neighborhood.

Mom/Sharon:
Christine was a friend magnet. It was hard to plan birthday parties because of the number of kids we needed to invite!

Many of the friends WE made that sixth-grade year stayed with us through high school and even beyond. WE met one of our closest friends, a beautiful girl named Ally, in the most awkward way. One Monday morning, I arrived at school with dread racing through my veins. The Friday before, I had been assigned a ten-minute oral presentation that made me want to vomit from anxiety. None of us can remember what the topic of our speech was, but as I checked out internally, Hope strode up, feeling confident and making good eye contact, and did our presentation.

Hope:

I had no doubt that WE would receive a well-deserved A or B grade. WE had done the appropriate research and I even remember WE practiced several times with Cita's mom as an audience. Once I returned to my seat, I was relieved to be done and enjoyed listening to the rest of the class with their contributions.

I always tried to be positive in my thoughts toward others and empathetic at their sometimes quite obvious nervous twitches and repetitive "Ums…" Some were quite good, others a tad dull, and a few just downright pathetic, but everyone gave it the best they could at that time. Even now I can remember Ally standing in front of the class. WE didn't know her well at the time, but WE could tell she was nervous from the slight blushing in her cheeks and her somewhat stiff stance. Other than that, hers seemed quite an unremarkable presentation.

Late in the day, Mrs. Johnson returned a previously turned-in outline of our speech that included the grade in the upper right corner. I saw a bright red C+ at the top of our paper and had to double-check to be sure I saw it correctly. I was astounded—a C+ was ridiculous. As I glanced around the room, I saw Ally's paper. Ally sat directly behind us and to my surprise, I saw that she had received a B+. My young brain could not fathom why Ally, sweet as she was, got a higher grade than WE did. There was no doubt in my mind that WE had done better.

I waited for Mrs. Johnson to return to her desk, then I walked my righteous self over. I spoke plainly of my concern in the error of her grading. As I recall, I even used examples of what I had done better than Ally. I was certain that Mrs. Johnson would see the error of her ways, but much to my surprise she did not. In fact, Mrs. Johnson was quite affronted by my assertive manner. I remember her saying, "Well, that's fine then." As she reached for her grade book, she erased Ally's B+ and changed it to a C+. That was not what I had expected, but before I could utter another response, Mrs. Johnson replied, "Now you Christine can go tell Ally of her new grade."

I was dumbstruck and noticed a sense of nausea coming from Cita. Nonetheless, I walked over to Ally, introduced myself, and then let her know what transpired. I really can't remember her response or the outcome, but I do recall that we became friends from that point on. We were locker partners through high school and friends for years, even through marriages. Sadly, later in our lives we eventually drifted apart.

Rim and I were close to Ally too. She only knew us as Chris or Christina, as she called us, but WE loved her as only best friends can.

⊰⊱⊱⊰

In fifth grade, Rim and I joined a recreational league softball team. Both of us loved this physical outlet. Our coaches were two wonderful women and our father, who assisted. WE continued to play softball with many of these kids for years.

In junior high and high school, WE continued our involvement in sports; in addition to softball WE played basketball, volleyball, and track. I loved the long jump and Rim liked running short races and the shot put. WE look back at our years now in track and laugh. I suffered from yo-yo dieting, and I constantly lost and gained significant weight during my adolescent years. WE all experienced the consequences.

When I was packing additional weight, we'd excel in the shot-put, even going to state two years in a row. When my weight was lower, WE were less successful in the shot-put but flew in the long jump. WE never excelled in running, and with our problematic hips, distance running was not my favorite activity anyway. But because I didn't enjoy it, I think that Rim pushed to do more running activities just to be ornery.

> **Rim:**
> I have to say it wasn't fuckin' orneriness that kept me wanting to run. I think I was just trying to do anything to burn this anger, confusion, and pain that I hid so deep inside of myself. Cita turned to food; I turned to physical activity. I was never happier than when WE were burning the candle at both ends, doing sports on a rec and school league at the same time. We'd race from the school practice down the street to the park where our rec baseball league played. I loved the intensity and the nonstop lifestyle, anything that kept me from having to face our situation and myself.

It had been years since the rapes and our father's physical abuse continued until WE were a freshman in high school. WE were always so involved in sports that no one paid any attention to the bruises caused by my father kicking us in the shin because WE had annoyed him or the unexpected smack across the face for not meeting his expectations on an assigned chore.

> **Rim:**
> Our dad was often our coach for the city leagues WE played on in high school. The other kids loved and respected him and thought us so very lucky. But they weren't there when WE practiced in our front lawn. They didn't see him throwing a ball at us with the speed of a major leaguer and the true expectation that we'd catch it or stop it with any means avail-

able. This usually meant our body. They weren't standing at the plate waiting for him to pitch a ball deliberately thrown to hit some part of our body so that we'd learn not to dodge it. "Don't flinch or turn away!" he'd yell. "A walk is as good as a hit, so stand your ground and let the ball hit you."

And again, they did not see the balls hit in our direction for us to practice grounders. They didn't see how often the ball rebounded in a vicious jump. Because of our training (and the consequences if WE failed), we'd use even our face to stop that fucking ball from getting past us.

WE were so involved in sports that no one noticed the cuts, strains, and bruises that adorned our body. I didn't complain and always played through the pain.

The Seaview Sluggers in 1977. I am in the back row, third from the right, and at twelve, was the tallest.

I loved sports too and I was good, but I was much less aggressive. Much to Rim's dismay, I cried when I was in pain, angry, or sad. This made Rim even madder. Hope would often block Rim and SHE to allow me to participate in my own way, but if I botched a play at all, Rim would shift back out. She would take control of the situation, often racing down the court or stealing a basketball from an opponent to enforce her more aggressive tempo.

Rim:

One thing both Cita and I agree on is that sports saved our lives. I don't think we'd be alive today if WE hadn't had the athletic outlet to vent our unexpressed emotions.

I don't know exactly when or why my dad stopped his physical aggression toward us. Rim and I would have been about thirteen. WE think Rim began responding more aggressively toward him. When he went to take his belt to us, Rim would shift out and say, "Bring it on." At first it made him even madder and the beating was worse, but then I think my dad sensed that retribution was coming if he didn't heed her warning. He was still quick to get angry and yell, but he stopped smacking us around. However, where Dad stopped, SHE continued the cycle.

SHE:

I would sit inside our internal home just waiting for opportunities to torment Cita. I would dream in intense detail on what I would do to torture her. I would visualize running her arm under the kitchen sink to get it good and wet. I knew that it would take only a slight dousing of liquid on her forearm and an iron set on steam mode to get a good scald going. Steam burns are intense; you don't need to have actual contact with the hot iron. I'd imagine the heat getting closer to the water on her arm and hearing a sizzle like bacon frying on a griddle, her pale arm hairs curling as they burn and then her skin reddening and eventually turning brown.

This premutilation planning was as erotic to me as the actual punishment. I would get a high and then feel a sense of euphoria. I realize now that it was pretty sick, but back then that euphoria was my "crack candy." It was the only time I felt anywhere close to happiness. Yeah, I was a freak, but fear, rage, and pain was all I knew. I took on the father's role of abuse.

I'm certain people thought I was the biggest klutz on the face of this earth. I made excuse after excuse of how I got a burn on my arm, a cut on my forehead, a bruise on my cheek, or the stitches in my finger. For my cheek bruise, my excuse was that I got hit with a ball, or for the broken finger I'd say I had shut it in a door. Burns were explained by curling irons, or as I got older, that I'd cut myself at work. On and on I'd go. I presumably fell so often that I'm surprised someone didn't suggest I go to the doctor and have a brain scan for some malignant tumor that interfered with my equilibrium. Lying was very much a part of our lives.

Christmas 1971. I would have been six and my brother ten.

Lying is a gamble any time it occurs. With three of us, it was impossible to keep track of all the excuses and lies WE told. I remember a time when Rim gave a speech in junior high about us having gone skydiving during the summer. She presented our experience in such detail and so vividly that no one suspected that WE hadn't actually done it. Even our best friend Ally didn't appear to doubt our story, even though we had spent the entire summer with her.

WE made it through each day, sometimes with me barely hanging on, Rim continuing to push us, SHE trying to destroy us, and Hope trying to keep us safe and healthy.

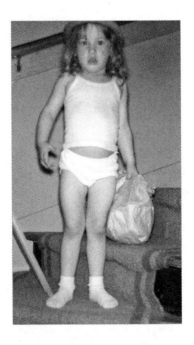

Mom tells a story of how she called me "Chrissy-Wee" when I was young.
One day she noticed I was saying, "The Wee wants a drink of water." "The Wee
wants to color." Mom then asked me, "Honey, what's your name?" and I answered,
"The Wee." It's likely I was verbalizing there was more than one of me at age three.

‹⬦·⬦›

7

The Seams Start to Unravel

WE WERE JUNIORS IN HIGH school in 1982 when our parents finally divorced. It was a mixed blessing. I remember waking up the day after my father moved out; my brother Chuck was already living on his own, so it was just Mom and me. The house was so harmonious. I stood in the kitchen enjoying a small moment of peace, but it ended abruptly as I neared my mom's room and heard her crying. She had been married for over twenty-two years to her first and only love. When my mom spoke to me more about her feelings then, she shared that even though the relationship had been unhealthy, the loss and feeling of failure were extremely painful for her.

As for the alters and me, the years to follow were filled with power struggles, increasing weight gain, and health problems. As a youth and young adult, not only were my emotions wreaking havoc on my nervous system but on Rim's and SHE's too.

I firmly believe that the stress from my mental rollercoasters caused my female organs to fail. My menstrual cycles occurred every twenty-two days, and while they were as light as all get-out, the cramps felt like knives stabbing me. Doctors prescribed Vicodin as a treatment until I hemorrhaged. I was just sixteen when I landed in the hospital to get blood transfusions and undergo a procedure called D&C, whereby the inside of my uterus and vaginal cavity were scraped out to stop the bleeding. The medical professionals' opinion was that it was just nerves, but no one thought to see why I'd be so anxious at that age. Instead, they happily put me on birth control to prevent future excessive bleeding.

I laughed that I was now on the pill, because WE had not been sexually active. WE had plenty of boyfriends, however, and if Hope had not been around, I think Rim would have had sex much sooner. However, once WE graduated from high school, Rim was determined that WE were going to sleep with someone. I think she desperately wanted to change her view of sex as a negative experience and so she set out to do just that. Rim would not let fear stop her.

Rim:

Cita makes it sound so deliberate, but now that I think back on it, she may be right. I remember flirting with a girlfriend's neighbor. He was two years younger than I, but I'd always liked 'em younger. When I envision him today, he seems like a real slimeball, but at the time he was willing to have noncommitted sex and there was chemistry between us.

I remember telling SHE and Hope that they had better block everyone. I didn't want anyone interfering. Secretly, I really wanted this experience to be something like in the movies: fireworks, sweat, and heated passion. Instead, it was in the basement on a mattress at his house. I think it lasted all of five seconds. It was like, "Oh yeah," kiss, probe, then "OUCH." Then his face turned red, he grunted, and just when I thought it was starting to feel a tad better, it was over. To myself I thought, "What the fuck? That is so not worth it and we're left to clean up the mess."

Even though Rim wasn't impressed with our first sexual encounter, it didn't deter her. In fact, Rim began drinking heavily and sleeping around. Shortly after WE started working for the same grocery chain our father did, a young man caught me in the parking lot one night after my shift had ended. I did not recognize him, but in the back of my mind I heard Rim say, "Oh shit." Once I determined I wasn't in any danger, I stammered to say hello. He was far more familiar with me than I was comfortable with, but Rim wasn't shifting out to assist so I tried to wing it. The guy reached over and wrapped his arm around my neck, kissing me deeply. Then he handed me a small paper bag and said, "I hope we can do that again sometime." Kissing me again, he walked back to his car and then drove off. I slid into our car and peeked in the bag. Inside was a torn pair of our underpants. "Shit, those were my favorite," I heard Rim say. "Once he tore them off I forgot all about them."

⊰◈⧫◈⊱

After I graduated from high school, my days often blurred together. Rim and Hope would be the only two controlling my body for days on end as I mentally checked out. Sometimes I'd wake up next to a stranger. Other times I'd awaken in the middle of the night, drunk as a skunk, feeling the room spinning out of control as I raced for the nearest garbage can in which to vomit.

The despair I was experiencing was beyond comprehension, and my memories of life during this time are sporadic, with big gaps that only Rim and Hope could fill. I often felt like I was a walking, talking robot. Just pick the correct emotion and then I'd act that part. Push the laugh button and I'd laugh appropriately; hit the sad button and I'd cry, and on and on. Day after day after day. My motto was fake it 'til you make it.

8

※≪◎▷※

Working and Crashing

AT THE AGE OF SIXTEEN, WE were working for the same company that my dad was at for most of his life. At the time, in 1981, employment at a large grocery store was considered crème de la crème for kids our age. The pay was great and the benefits were excellent. Rim, Hope, and I worked hard, but new problems started in our first six months of employment.

Rim:

To start with, it seemed credit card companies couldn't give us enough "free" money. By the age of twenty WE were $25,000 dollars in debt. WE drove an awesome red-and-black two-door Capri. We'd pretend it was a Mustang, although it wasn't even close. Regardless, it was sporty and I felt way cool racing through the city in it.

Secondly, Rim and I both started shoplifting. WE stole only from our place of employment. Why? Well, it doesn't take a rocket scientist to connect the dots and see how symbolic that was: stealing from the company that represents our father. WE didn't work at his store specifically, but still it was like stealing from his livelihood. Each soda pop WE took without paying for and every cart of groceries snuck out the door not paid for was the ultimate "screw you" to our dad.

WE were out of control weightwise and moneywise. WE had run out of integrity in our life and were living dangerously. In our sixth year of employment, WE arrived at work one day to be greeted by the store manager, who escorted me directly to his office. Two men in suits whom Rim and I did not recognize were already awaiting my arrival. The manager guided me to a chair across from his desk. After an intense interrogation, I broke down in tears and admitted to stealing. I heard Rim shouting at me, "Fool. If they had proof they would have fired us on the spot!" but I was frightened and ashamed. After listing a sketchy inventory of what we'd stolen through the years, I was asked to leave the premises. The store manager advised me that once he had heard from the corporate office, he would let me know my employment status.

When the phone call came less than twenty-four hours later, I was informed that I had been fired, although my personnel file would state that I had resigned. I would then be contacted by the finance department, who would set up a payment plan for me to reimburse the company for what we had shoplifted.

Rim and her coveted red Capri.

Rim:

This ordeal was awful, but the true trauma came when WE tried to figure out how WE would tell our parents. With Dad,

Mr. Safeway, lying wasn't gonna work. He'd eventually hear what had happened through the grapevine, so truth was the rare route WE took.

The thought of disappointing my mom made me sick to my stomach, and I was terrified to tell my Dad.

Rim:
WE can't remember who we told first, although I am guessing it would have been Mom. WE figured that would be the lesser of two evils, so to speak. How wrong we were. Mom was devastated. "Where did I go wrong? I raised you better than this!" It felt as though we had mortally wounded her and that our actions were a true reflection of her failure as a mother.

Dad, on the other hand, just shook his head and said something like, "Of all the times you've lied, why tell the truth then?" He seemed more pissed that I got caught than the fact that I stole. In later years, WE learned that Dad felt obliged to resign from the company's credit union, where he served on the board. Really, it was just yet another thing I added to my guilt pile.

Shortly after losing our job in 1986, I filed for a Chapter 11 bankruptcy. Hope and I really struggled to meet our financial responsibilities, but there wasn't enough money to cover our debt. The bankruptcy would enable us to set up reasonable payments to my debtors.

As WE stood in front of the judge overseeing my case, I heard him laugh and say, "Young lady, you are unable to even meet the minimum payment it would take to file a Chapter 11." He continued, "You'll need to file a Chapter 13 [full bankruptcy]. The impact of this action will stay with you for years, but unless you do, you are going to sink and drown." I felt like such a fool. I couldn't believe I had allowed my life to get so out of hand. Even so, I felt this was the only way I might be able to start again.

It was from this event that WE found ourselves living back at home with my mom, our car repossessed, and us working at a neighborhood deli. By this time Rim had started experimenting with cocaine, snorting it off the bathroom counter at work, and drinking wine coolers in between waiting on customers.

Rim:
Sex for drugs; a good trade.

Hope:
I truly felt as though WE were on a downward spiral that was eventually going to lead us to Cita's death. Our death.

The only positive thing happening during this time was weight loss from the drugs Rim was ingesting.

Rim:
I want to share something that I discovered. When Cita's weight was down, many people in our lives just assumed that she was obviously doing better. Whether the weight loss was due to genuine effort or drugs, no one looked any further. If Cita looked okay, then she must be okay.

I realized early on that people can cope better with physical injuries more than they can with mental health issues. Still, it never crossed our mind to tell anyone about our MPD. It was just how WE lived. Each morning we'd wake up, breathe, and try to make it through another day.

9

-◦◦◦-

Meeting My Husband

I WAS TWENTY-TWO IN the fall of 1987. WE had once again moved out of my mother's house and were renting a townhouse with our longtime friend Ally. WE had little debt after the bankruptcy, so WE were able to pay rent and cover living expenses. WE still didn't have a car, but the deli was on a direct bus route and I was able to get there with only one transfer each way. Rim was still drinking and doing drugs, but she wasn't pushing us quite as hard. Instead she seemed exhausted and depressed. SHE, on the other hand, was still perpetuating Dad's physical abuse by inflicting self-harm upon me.

> **SHE:**
> The urge to inflict pain upon Cita was my entire focus. I burned her, cut her, and even chopped off her hair. At night while she slept I'd taunt her, calling her the devil's spawn or the demon seed. I'd tell her she was ugly and worthless. Hope tried to intervene, but of all the alters I was always the strongest and could prevent Hope from blocking me the majority of the time. Who says good prevails over evil?

One night just before closing time, a young man entered the delicatessen. He was in his early thirties, balding on top but with long hair that hung to his shoulders. He wore a faded tee, frayed cut-offs, and light-blue flip-flops. He looked as though he came from a '60s peace gathering. Even so, he had incredibly warm brown eyes and a smile that lit up his entire face. He walked up to the counter and said, "Hey

Sweet Thing. How ya doing?" I remember feeling annoyed. It was late, and I just wanted to close up the shop and head home, but Rim was thrilled with the attention. While they flirted, the small bell above the door jingled again to alert us to yet another customer arriving.

I sighed and shifted back out. Rim wasn't known for good customer service. As I looked over to greet the new patron, I felt my heart stop beating. Before me was another young man in his mid-twenties, looking so all-American, like he'd just stepped off a box of Wheaties. He sported curly red hair, with a freckled face. His eyes were brilliant blue, further set off by the sky-blue t-shirt he was wearing. He was broad in the chest, thin in the waist, and had the hottest little butt. His legs were sculpted and athletic-looking. I could hear Rim saying to SHE, "Check it out, Cita's got a woody for Mr. Man." (Rim still calls Christopher "Mr. Man.")

It was plainly obvious to the first man that I had eyes only for Christopher. Joe was his name and he was a good sport. As it turned out, he was also Christopher's roommate. Joe could see that Christopher was equally enthralled with me and like the gentleman he was, stepped to the side and let our courtship begin. Little did WE know at the time that Christopher and Joe had a system for picking up chicks.

Rim:

Yeah, the sneaky little bastards, but we'll let him tell you all about their scheming ways.

Christopher:

We didn't have an elaborate plan at all. We were just out having fun that night, taking turns having a go of it with any attractive girls we happened upon. When we pulled into the deli's tiny parking lot, we parked facing the store. We could see Cita through the glass; tall, red hair, beautiful face, and lovely to look at. Sadly, it was Joe's turn to hit on her. I stayed back, keeping my eye on them.

As I entered the store, I overheard Joe get rejected. Then I sprang into action. Casually I sauntered over to the counter and said "Hello." Immediately I sensed a spark—and was I happy.

Before Christopher and Joe left they asked me once again if I wanted to go out for a drink after work. All psyched to down some cocktails, Rim responded internally, "Hell yeah!" But I hesitated. That day WE had worked a double shift and were exhausted. I told the guys I'd take a rain check.

Two days later they returned. WE were just getting done with our shift and Christopher asked if I wanted to head to the beach with them. WE said yes and I felt that rush of pleasure that comes at the start of a new relationship. It was early September and some warmth from summer still lingered.

At the beach we sat and talked, drank some wine coolers, and then even went for a swim. Christopher and I swam in our clothes, which for me was a tank top and snug jeans. Afterward I was invited to have dinner with Christopher and his roommate at their abode. It was a lovely evening, one I shall never forget. At his house he let us borrow a pair of his pants while ours dried. (Oh those were the days, when WE could fit in his jeans … sigh.) After dinner he drove us home, kissed me goodnight and that was that. He was a complete gentleman. Rim and SHE, however, were pressuring me to invite him in and in their words, "Nail the bastard."

Rim and I spent the next few days talking about the possibility of going out with Christopher again. It was one of the rare instances where Rim and I were adversaries.

Rim:
You might have thought that there would have been more jealousy between the two of us, but that didn't occur until later in

their relationship. The reality was, Cita hadn't often felt this strongly toward a guy and Hope was really pining for Cita to have a chance with Christopher. I knew Cita would eventually call on me, because Cita still hadn't slept with a guy. When sex came a knockin', I'd be first to get my time in.

Christopher called me a week later to invite me to take a drive to Mount Baker National Park, a two-hour drive northeast from where we lived. He showed up in his brown Chevy pickup with a golden retriever named Gauge. I was so nervous that my heart was pounding. I truly believed that I didn't have much to offer Christopher. I certainly didn't see myself as a "catch of a lifetime" and knew that once Christopher got to know me, he wouldn't stick around. But I couldn't help allowing just a small bit of hope to seep in.

Even with such desire to keep him in my life, it didn't prevent me from creating a past history far more interesting than my reality.

SHE:

What Cita is trying to say is that she lied to him. She told him that she'd gotten a four-year degree at Western Washington University, a college thirty minutes south of the Canadian border, when in actuality the only time she'd been on that campus was to visit her friend Ally.

Rim:

I just want to add that, as was our normal pattern, Cita and I shifted back and forth throughout this date; however, Cita lost her courage and stayed internal for most of the drive up the mountain. It was also I who flirted with Christopher on the ride back down the mountain and who gave him a blow job in the front seat of his truck.

That being said, I did shift back out as we approached the college town. At this point Christopher suggested we stop for some Chinese food. He asked me to lead the way, assuming that I would know where to go since WE had lived there for four years GOING TO SCHOOL! I could hear SHE in the background calling me "Loser."

Luckily, fate was with me that day; Hope and I remembered seeing a Chinese restaurant on our way through town near a hospital. With the help of blue hospital signs, WE were able to steer him directly to it.

One side note: About this time in our trip Rim realized that she was having real feelings toward Christopher herself and because she liked him, she wasn't badgering me as much as she might have. Instead she kept a low profile and even assisted in locating the restaurant. Once we entered the establishment, WE all let out a collective sigh that the joint was not a total dive.

Leading up to our third date, I had been considering having sex with Christopher. This was a huge step for me. The thought of being intimate with someone petrified me. I had low self-esteem and my body image was warped. I was repulsed by my body and was certain other people would be too. Now when I look back at pictures of myself from childhood to my early twenties, I see moments when I was heavier, but never do I see anything but a beautiful young girl.

Rim's image of herself was the exact opposite; she was quite certain of her sex appeal. I, however, had never had a physical relationship with someone. I talked a lot about this with Hope, who felt that Christopher was a kind and gentle soul and therefore a safe person for my first time.

A few days after this conversation, I stayed overnight at Christopher's house for the first time. I remember how masculine his room seemed. There was a 4-foot-by-3-foot world map on his wall above the bed. His furniture was made from rich cherry wood and his bedspread contained random splashes of blue and brown. While I was getting ready for bed, I recall turning the light off on the nightstand before we had even gotten undressed. Christopher said, "Hey, let's have some light here," as he fumbled about tripping over his work boots.

Rim:
You have to laugh. Visualize Christopher, who just weeks before was given a blow job by this woman, and now this same woman was being painfully shy. I was cracking up.

Yeah, it was so terribly hilarious. I was so self-conscious, but I was determined not to have Rim be the first one to sleep with Christopher. I knew early on that I felt something special toward him and I wanted to make sure I'd make that first physical connection. I don't know how I managed to get my clothes off, but I did and joined him under the covers. I lay on my stomach while he rolled on his side facing me. Each second he watched me felt like hours until I could no longer suppress my nerves. Instead of shifting inward like I feared, I started laughing.

Christopher:
Cita has a great laugh. She got the giggles while we were under the covers and we both began to laugh. So here we were, two excited young lovers not making love but embraced in the giggles.

I think we laughed for ten minutes until Christopher finally reached over and gently stroked my shoulder. "You okay there?" he asked. I apologized profusely and then with a deep breath admitted to being a tad nervous. To his credit, Christopher never questioned why, and he treated me so very sweetly throughout our entire lovemaking experience.

That night with Christopher was my first healthy experience of sex. I was finally able to begin removing the violent sexual images from my childhood and replacing them with the kindness and gentleness of Christopher.

Wouldn't it be wonderful if I could end this chapter with that last paragraph, so sweet and pure, but the night didn't end there. It is true that after our lovemaking, we fell asleep wrapped in each other's arms. However, at some point in the middle of the night or early morning, I woke up to find that I had wet the bed. This was an isolated incident for us, for bedwetting was not a health issue WE dealt with in our daily lives. Maybe it was triggered by using vaginal muscles I wasn't used to, or being more relaxed than I had ever been before. Maybe it was just a case of too much stimulation. WE don't know, but wet the bed I did.

Hope woke up with me and tried to keep me from panicking by reassuring me that this was not the end of the world. Hope had me get out of bed and clean myself off in the bathroom. Then WE actually finagled the top and bottom sheets off the bed while Christopher remained asleep. It was an extremely slow process, but he slept on undisturbed.

WE were then able to get the linens washed and while the sheets dried, I crawled back in and snuggled with the still sleeping Christopher. It was days later when he and I were talking about that night, and I actually told him what had happened.

Christopher:
How in the hell did you get those sheets changed while I slept?

‑◈‑

10

He Loves Me. He Loves Me Not. He Loves Me.

Rim:

I wanted to be the one to share this, because I always bust a belly when I think back to this moment. It was about a month later when Christopher had us over to his mom's for dinner. It seemed like a normal "meet the parents" dinner, but WE found out later that his parents had been divorced for years and that his father was normally not in the picture.

Christopher:

I thought I had told her about my parents' divorce, but it doesn't surprise me that I left that part out. Clearly, leaving out significant details of our lives was a trend!

SHE:
Good one Christopher.

Rim:

Another surprise was the main dish. Cita was managing to be out and in control until Audrey, Christopher's mom, brought over the main dish. The feast before us was a huge platter filled with these tiny frickin' birds. They were doves and I kept staring at their little headless bodies, envisioning little vacant eyes staring back at us. Christopher's father and brothers all hunted. Apparently it was normal in their family to eat the game they killed. I thought Hope would faint. In fact, she gasped internally, but it was loud enough for Cita to hear. That's when I noticed the first signs of Cita's strength slipping and soon I was out grubbin' on birds o'plenty.

Eventually I was able to regain my composure and shift back out near the end of the meal. Actually, just in time to hear Christopher informing his parents that in the next month he was going to take a job in Florida and work in the sun a spell. He's a carpenter and that's not a bad idea, except this was the first any of us had heard of it. He was leaving us.

Rim:

Bastard! That was my first response, though I said it only internally. I don't know why, but I was feeling hurt too. He's screwing us, but not able to tell us his plans of taking off? Where did WE keep finding these sons of bitches? I guess I had hoped he might be the one to stick by our side too. Schmuck ...

SHE:

I couldn't help it, but I thought it was fucking hilarious. How on earth could they expect anything different? I remember taunting Cita about being a worthless excuse of a human being. Who would stay with trash like her?

I remember fighting back tears as Hope soothingly encouraged me to not get up from the table and leave. Hope kept talking over SHE, telling me to breathe. She reminded me not to jump to conclusions and to listen to what Christopher had to say.

Christopher:

I really screwed up telling my parents and not talking to Cita first. It was just a clumsy and insensitive move on my part.

At the time I was working with another carpenter. He talked of a brother who did remodeling, worked in South Florida, and would hire me. All I had to do was get down there. I wanted to travel and I knew I wanted Cita to go with me.

On the drive home, Christopher was quick to notice my silence. He pulled the car over to the side of the road and gently said, "It's about the Florida thing, isn't it?" and he reached out for my hand. I heard the Others making snide remarks, except Hope who was encouraging me to talk to him.

"Why didn't you tell me?" I could barely get out between my tears. I was so mad and so hurt.

"I just confirmed with the contractor I'll be working with before I got to my mom's," he said, as I angrily wiped at the tears that continued to escape.

"But you've known. All this time you've been planning or at least thinking about it and said not one word to me," I said, feeling like a groveling fool.

He replied, "I didn't know what to say. I was trying to figure out a way that this could work. I don't want to lose you, Chris."

He started driving again and I remained silent. He dropped me off at our own apartment that night, and I didn't ask him to stay over. I was confused and scared and wanted time to sort through my thoughts, our thoughts…

It was two days before we spoke again. He showed up to take me to an appointment. When I walked out to his truck I saw his two nieces with him. These girls were so darling with the same red hair and freckles as Christopher. They were eight and eleven and such delights that I couldn't help but warm to their greetings. It was a pleasant drive and then they dropped me off.

Christopher:

While we waited for Cita, I drove the girls to a nearby park and we watched some softball. I asked the kids to please help me create an application for employment. I was going to give it to Cita as a joke. I wanted it to appear as if I was hiring a camp cook.

The girls jubilantly partook in conjuring up all sorts of silly questions that they thought would appear on an application: Can you cook? Are you handy cleaning up? Is your recipe file bigger than a breadbox? Stuff like that.

After my appointment, we dropped his nieces back at their home and then headed back to his place. We were still in the car parked outside his house when he handed me the homemade application. I looked at the papers, then back at Christopher, uncertain if he was for real. And then we both started laughing.

Christopher:

I laughed hard. I think she briefly wondered how many girl-friends would get interviewed. The part I couldn't wait for was to ask her to go with me to Florida. Cita said yes and in our excitement we hugged and talked about all that needed to happen before we could leave.

-◦◦-

11

Reality Check

I WISH WE COULD SAY we rode off into the sunset and all was well, but so much had to be done before we could leave. WE had an apartment WE were leasing with a friend and needed to work that out with her. Christopher was working on a '67 white Chevy pickup that we would be driving the entire trip. This truck was literally pulled from overgrown sticker bushes. He and his roommate were able to do the engine work, clean the inside, and get it running.

WE also had some additional debt that had crept back into our life after the bankruptcy which Christopher did not know about. Three warrants were out for my arrest due to unpaid parking tickets that Rim had recently brought to my attention. In addition, I had some pretty big lies. Attending college was the main one, which I felt I really should come clean about. But telling him about the MPD was never even a consideration.

One weekend we were at my grandma's waterfront cabin right on the Puget Sound. The water was calm and beautiful. Christopher had built a fire and we were snuggling on the couch. I took a gulp of air and decided the time had come to tell him the truth about our fanciful college degree. The conversation between the two of us started something like this:

"Hey sweetie, can I talk to you about something?" I asked.

"Sure, what's up?" Christopher replied.

I tried to breathe through knots of shame as I quietly stated, "Well, you know how I've always said that I have a four-year degree from Western University?"

"Yeah?" he asked.

"I lied."

Now that the words were out, I felt a slight sense of relief. I had done it. I had told him the truth.

However, Christopher still hadn't quite grasped my meaning. "No biggie, what college did you go to?"

"Umm ... That would be none, really. I don't have a degree at all. I never went to a university—only a community college and only for a few quarters," I sheepishly replied.

I was ready for Christopher to glare at me with disgust for being a liar and a fake. I knew this was the end of us. What I didn't expect was for him to burst out laughing.

"You crack me up! Why would you lie about that? I don't care if you went to college or not. Really, I'm just glad you decided you could tell me the truth. I love you! I hope that you'll continue to share with me and learn to trust me. I don't plan on going anywhere without you."

I couldn't believe my ears. That deep wall that I'd built around me began to crack.

By the way, when he took me down to Seattle to pay the parking fines, it cost over six hundred dollars! Christopher didn't find that one quite as amusing.

It seemed that Rim, SHE, Hope, and I were all committed to this road trip. Although the self-harm continued, WE seemed to coexist with less drama. WE sold anything WE owned that was not precious to us and gave it to Christopher to put toward our expenses.

While he and his roommate Joe worked on the pickup, my mom, Hope, and I refurbished an old camper that Christopher's dad gave us. We made new curtains and seat covers that gave it a warm, fun, and cozy look. Finally we were set to hit the road.

Prior to heading out on our trip, however, I was to be introduced to his entire family at a dinner at his mother's. All five older brothers, their wives and kids, and Christopher's dad and mom would be in attendance. That was a total of twenty-one people. I was petrified!

To make matters worse, when Rim went to grab our high-top basketball shoes, Christopher started acting funny. You see, at his mom's there is a half-court basketball hoop and we never went there without doing a little one-on-one.

Rim:

I recall asking Christopher what was wrong. I couldn't even get him to look me in the eye. Cita was all freaked that he was beginning to want to back out on us meeting his family. Finally I grabbed his face and said "What? What is it?" I had no clue that he was about to tell me that he wasn't comfortable with us playing basketball. I was like, WTF? I gotta hang out with all the moms and talk about sewing and doctor appointments? Screw that. Finally, Cita came back out and dealt with it—I was far too pissed.

I just said, "Don't stress, sweetie. I'll bring my shoes, just in case. I won't just head off to the court without an invitation."

Christopher:

After introducing Cita to the sister-in-laws, we walked out onto a deck that overlooks the basketball court in our backyard. My father, who was playing with my brothers, looked up and invited Cita to join in. I was uneasy because none of the other brother's wives had played basketball with us before. It was always just the boys on the court. Cita would have been the first girl and my own insecurities with my brothers had me thinking to myself, "Cita, please say no!" However, she said yes, but it was only moments later that I realized I had nothing to worry about. Cita fit right in. She was a little more aggressive than we generally played. She owned the court. Just dominated it. During one play in particular—a scramble for a rebound—Cita threw an elbow and put my oldest brother's tooth through his lower lip.

Rim:

Little did Christopher know that it was I giving his brothers the smackdown and loving every second. Regardless of Christopher's uncertainties, the brothers and his dad enjoyed the new meat on the court. After the first swing of my elbow going for a rebound, any of their thoughts of being careful with a girl on the court vanished!

This informal family barbecue was a great way to meet his large family. The day was a success, and Rim, Hope, and I were all feeling quite happy to have been accepted into his family.

This is my first visit to Christopher's mom's house, and he has us clearing brush at a neighbor's. His mom thought I was sassy and fun.

12

❧

Road Trippin'

Just outside Christopher's mom's house on the day we leave for Florida,
in 1987. Our dog Gauge, underneath the camper, is waiting to leave.

Christopher:
On Halloween 1987, two months after meeting each other, we finally hit the road in our '67 Chevy pickup with a big white camper, stuff strapped to the top of it, and towing a blue '59 Volkswagen Bug. I remember we stopped at my mother's for a quick goodbye kiss and she gave us a care package.

SHE:
I was active only behind the scenes then, but I remember quite clearly the items Christopher's mom gave them; a case of Snickers candy bars and two huge bottles of ketchup!

Yes, that was a sweet care package. In addition to those items, my mom had given us a three-pound, precooked HoneyBaked ham and a two-pound Jennie-O turkey. We had meat, ketchup, and candy—what more did two young lovers need?

Christopher:
With our loot in tow, we headed down the highway, every ten to fifteen miles a lethargic hornet would drift up from under the dashboard, where it had been happily hibernating. This lasted for about ten days.

On Day Two, we pulled off to a scenic viewpoint. The plan was for Cita to make lunch. Instead, she burnt the ham, had a tantrum, and I fired her as the cook. We made love and then hit the road again.

WE were all thrilled to be on the road—"WE" being Hope, Rim, and myself. I don't know that "thrilled" was a word in SHE's vocabulary back then, but SHE did seem less hostile for the time being. Christopher and I learned so much about each other on that journey, but still there was no mention of the MPD.

Rim:
I was so jazzed to be on the road. I remember the fall colors and waking in the morning and stepping out of the camper into the crisp autumn air. At night we'd pull in to a rest stop and wake to a beautiful view of mountain ranges or a vast open range. I felt like WE had left all our troubles behind and that we'd been granted a new beginning. If Cita could just hold it together WE might latch on and keep this treasure, Christopher.

Our first glimpses of the white sand beaches in Florida.
Note our truck camper in the background towing the little Bug.

Christopher:

We had a cassette player and our favorite music, Lionel Richie and the Commodores. Playing them would always smooth over any tension or issue. We'd drive a few miles singing a few lines from the song "Brick House" and all was well.

It's a thrill to drive west to east, never having seen the country and not knowing what's over the horizon. We'd wake up early and drive right into the sunrises. It was spectacular.

We stayed in a motorhome park on the outskirts of Las Vegas for two nights. Both nights we made love, once on the tiny table in our small camper.

Christopher:

As I was walking back from using the park's shower, I realized I could see right through our camper curtains. We abruptly left the next morning, to the chagrin of the local perverts. We should have just charged admission.

WE took our time driving down to Florida and were on the road close to a month. Along the way we stopped often to enjoy the countryside. Christopher and I enjoyed reading books together, and at the time we were engrossed in Stephen King's novel *It*. Needless to say, it's a book with many pages and it's slightly creepy. In the camper, with just the two of us at night, I began to have nightmares. I'd wake up in a start and Christopher would sit straight up, smacking his head on the low camper ceiling of our sleeping loft. After two nights of knocking himself silly, he put Stephen King away and we bought a book that was a bit more upbeat and pleasant to read.

❧

When we reached San Antonio, Texas, we stayed a couple days with family friends of Christopher's. One night the city had tornado warnings. The following morning the man we were staying with came home from his paper route with his bags filled with pecans that had blown off the trees in the storm.

Christopher:
We even parked the camper, unhooked our VW Bug, and drove to a border town in Mexico called Piedras Negras. The minute I crossed the border, I ended up driving the wrong way on a one-way street.

We stayed at a darling hotel for eight dollars a night! It wasn't a resort hotel on the ocean, but it did have a quaint adobe style, with Spanish tiles and beautiful flowering vines crawling up the walls.

Rim:
No air conditioning or drinking water, and tiny lizard-like creatures were crawling across the ceiling. Yes, very quaint.

Twenty-three days later, we pulled into Panama City, right off the Gulf of Mexico. We had finally arrived in Florida! We pulled into a public parking lot, raced down the white sand, and followed Gauge straight into the warm surf. Ahh, it was a little slice of heaven. It was 72 degrees—summer weather in Washington state—so we dove in with our clothes on. When we came up there was a couple stopped on the beach in front of us. They wore wool hats and scarves and were bundled in thick jackets. The look they gave us was sheer horror! (Remember, it was late November!)

"You're not from here, are you?" they asked, still eyeing us like we were from another planet.

Twenty years later, we still laugh over that.

Christopher:

We had Thanksgiving dinner on a remote island in Florida, where we blended in nicely with all the other tourists baking in the sun. Cita made us tuna casserole. And for dessert? Yes, Snickers. This really marked the end of our trip and the beginning of a completely new experience.

13

⊰⊱

Florida

Christopher:

It's Day One, 8 AM. Our truck and camper are parked in my new boss's driveway. The VW is unhitched and I'm ready for work. I'm sitting with Cita having coffee and waiting for the day to begin when we hear the boss's front door open. I hurriedly kiss Cita goodbye and dash out of the camper, only to find him pulling out of his driveway and speeding off in his van. I jump in the VW and catch up with him buying coffee at a nearby 7-Eleven.

"I don't wait for no one," he says, glaring at me, as I mutter to myself, "Welcome to Florida."

We struggled to live in Bonita Springs, a small town an hour south of Tampa on the west side of the peninsula. The city was populated either by impoverished laborers or the exceedingly wealthy. We had arrived in the Sunshine State with less than ten dollars to our name, so it was obvious which category we fell in. After just a few days there, We had one single focus— get the hell out of Florida.

Rim:

I remember Cita and I found a bumper sticker that had the state of Florida outlined in orange and right across the state in bold green lettering were the words "WHO CARES." Christopher didn't actually want us to have it on our car, so I stuck it to our visor. If I got pissed driving, I would just flip it down and hope that someone noticed it.

SHE:

During our second week in Florida, we went grocery shopping at a store in a huge strip mall. Near our parking space was a vehicle with its hood raised and some young kids working on the engine.

Rim:

Yeah, that's right. We didn't pay it any mind at the time, but once We returned from the store, Cita discovered that her purse was gone. I cussed at her, asking why the hell she had left it in the car in the first place. Then I noticed that the supposedly broken-down vehicle was no longer parked in sight.

Christopher:

A few days later we saw the thieves in their beater car and we pulled up behind them to prevent them from leaving. I got out and had some words with them, but then a furious Cita stepped out. I had to restrain her. I just wanted her purse back, but Cita wanted to whip them. We drove away without her purse, lucky to be in one piece, but pissed as hell.

I just want to clarify one thing. As if you hadn't already gathered, the wildcat looking for a brewhaha was Rim, not me.

Christopher eventually found a job with a different contractor while Rim, Hope, and I worked two jobs. The first was at a landscaping company. That was extremely demanding work, but at the time WE were fit and trim. No doubt this was partly due to the fact that Rim had found the joy of cocaine again.

Rim:

That was some sweet shit. It was much cheaper in Florida and it was more pure. Weight loss from drug use was an added bonus. Cita enjoyed being thin more than she cared about the repercussions of snorting that shit up our nose.

Sadly, there is truth to that …

⋯⟡⟡⋯

Bonita Springs was predominantly Hispanic. The landscaping company WE worked for was actually quite thrilled to have someone who spoke English; even though WE had no experience, WE were quickly moved to a supervisory role. It was odd to be hired in a lead position, but the pay was better and WE didn't complain. However, my crew didn't speak English and WE had only two years of high school Spanish.

WE led a team of three other people and had a large work truck filled with tools and chemicals. They gave us basic instructions on what product killed what bugs and then sent us on our way. The homes WE maintained were out of the world of the rich and famous.

Hope:

I loved one home in particular. The entrance to the property was like winding through a rainforest. The greenery was thick with vines, tropical flowers, birds of paradise, lilies the size of saucers, porter weeds, and violets. In the Pacific Northwest we have pansies that hang from baskets and fill small areas in our flower beds, but in Florida they have entire pansy hedges! They thrive in the moist heat and grow up to two feet high.

For the first half mile of this long, winding driveway, you'd see no signs of human life—it really was like a remote rainforest. Then the wilds of this forest parted, its green tones melting into the blue of the Atlantic Ocean. The view was absolutely heart-stopping. The house itself was small compared to the other homes WE tended—only about 10,000 square feet.

Rim:

Yeah, it was a disgusting hovel, Hope.

Hope:

I just meant that the majority of the family homes on our route were more like mini-castles. This home was even designed to blend in with the forest. Instead of wooden bridges or stepping stones, there were rope bridges that led across a small creek to their dock on the ocean, as well as to their pool and private gardens.

Rim:

Did you know it takes eight to ten five-gallon buckets of water to fertilize one palm tree? Many of the properties sported seven or more trees. WE easily hefted fifty-six buckets of water per house each day WE worked. Well, the crew helped too, but regardless it wasn't just the drugs keeping us trim.

Hair bleached out from all the sun, or that's what Christopher thought.
Actually Rim and I used a hair bleaching product called "Sun In."

WE worked the landscaping job Monday through Friday from 7 AM to 4 PM. Our second job was at a gas station, where WE worked three shifts on the weekdays from 5 PM to midnight, in addition to Saturday and Sunday. It was really low-key. Often Christopher and our dog Gauge would bring us dinner and then we'd just chill out. The small store had a TV and air conditioning. It was also about twice the size of the camper, so we made ourselves at home.

As the months passed, our determination to get out of Florida grew. The state itself is beautiful and fascinating. Maybe if we had come for a vacation or had arrived with money, our views would have been different. But we didn't have the time or money to go on a tour of its scenic swamplands or stay in a nice hotel. The mosquitoes, snakes, and other creepy-crawlies gave me the willies. Each day we woke up, worked, and focused on saving as much money as possible. And we always kept the big picture of leaving Florida at our forefront.

Christopher:

For a couple of months we lived on the property of friends we met shortly after arriving in Florida. A hundred acres of forest surrounded us. Our camper was comfortable and I built a small wooden porch for it. There was a large pond, but we kept our distance. We didn't want our dog hanging out in the pond with alligators. We were maybe four or five miles from a main town.

Rim:

We had a long extension cord plugged into the outlet of the empty house on the lot that provided us with electricity; the Floridians called it "squatting." In addition to it being against the law, the locals frowned upon it.

On a few occasions Christopher and I socialized with people from my work or friends he made at the YMCA. However, most of the time Christopher and I kept to ourselves. I found it particularly stressful one evening when Christopher asked to talk with me in a solemn manner. It was early January of 1988 and we'd been on this journey for three months. WE had no idea what he was going to say, but it appeared to be serious.

Rim:
I got this sinking feeling that he was going to break up with us and leave us in this stinking hellhole.

SHE:
It didn't help that I started laughing and chanting, "Here it comes. He's booting your sorry asses out the door!"

His words of "It's nothing to worry about" did very little to soothe us. We sat there numbly as he expressed a desire to have time to do things on his own.

Christopher:
I told her that we do everything together and that I might want some "me" time.

That would seem like a normal request, but immediately I had thoughts of being left in this God-forsaken place completely alone and three thousand miles away from anyone I cared about. However, I was supportive and acted as if it were no big deal. Inwardly I was petrified. Rim was pissed and even Hope was uncertain where this was going to lead.

After Christopher's chat with us, I expected to have nights alone feeling sorry for myself while he was out bar-hopping and playing with new friends without me. However, WE didn't notice any changes in our schedule, and life went on in the same manner as before.

It was a month later that a girlfriend from work asked Christopher and me over for dinner. I was excited about getting out of the camper for an evening. When Christopher picked me up after work, I was surprised when he declined the invitation. "I was just looking forward to a night with just the two of us," he said. WE were a little confused, as it was normally just the two of us anyway, but I didn't make a big deal of it.

Christopher was quiet on the drive home. When we pulled in and I started to get out, he asked me to wait in the car for a few moments before going into the camper. Even more baffled, I waited for him as he grabbed a bag of unknown items from behind the seat and went into the camper alone.

Five minutes later, he emerged and waved me in. As I crossed our porch and pulled open the camper door, I heard a small crash and Christopher cursing.

Christopher:
I had tried to set the mood for the evening by changing the lighting around. When Cita pulled open the door, the extension cord the lighting was plugged into got yanked and the lights crashed to the floor.

WE continued in confusion, my anxiety elevating rapidly. It was so unlike him to be edgy and short-tempered. As I went to set my purse down, our suspicions rose when WE saw all my stuffed animals that I had brought on our road trip lined up atop our small table.

Christopher:
Trying to regain my composure, I ushered Cita to sit. I took a deep breath, reached behind the stuffed animals I had displayed as our witnesses, and grasped a small white velvet box.

"Marry me!" I asked. Then I waited uncomfortably in the silence that followed.

SHE:

I remember spouting "No fucking way" in my complete and utter surprise.

Rim:

"Fuck me" I think was the statement that flew from my lips.

Hope:

I don't remember what I said at the moment. I was just filled with such complete joy and happiness for Cita.

I was stunned and struck speechless. I just couldn't believe my ears. When I finally came to my senses, I just burst into tears. I was flooded with disbelief, but was so very happy.

Christopher:

Once the tears started flowing and I saw beneath them her beautiful smile, I reached out to her and said, "So does that mean yes?"

"Yes, oh yes!" Cita finally cried out.

I slid the ring onto her left ring finger and then grabbed two glasses of champagne for a toast.

Rim:

You should have seen these glasses. The bag with the "unknown" items that Christopher had brought into the camper contained two fluted champagne glasses. One of these had shattered when the camper screen door bumped the bag. When Cita and Christopher toasted their engagement, one of them was holding a beautiful crystal goblet filled with golden champagne and the other a jagged piece of glass that looked more like a weapon.

Christopher:

It was romantic nonetheless and we drove into town that night to call our families. This was back when cell phones were not the norm and we had to make do with a pay phone in front of a Laundromat.

Remember earlier when Christopher had asked for time to himself? WE learned later that what he actually needed was time to shop for the engagement ring!

⤛⟨⟩⟩⤜

We did eventually save enough money to leave Florida, but it took almost seven months. Our journey back was equally adventurous and fun, and we arrived home after eight months on the road. After moving into the basement studio in his mother's house, Christopher found work in the carpentry field and I was hired at a bakery where one of his older brothers supervised. We set the date for our nuptials for the following November, which gave us five months to prepare. Those few months flew by in a blur.

14

‒◦◦◦‒

Fairy-Tale Wedding

Hope:

Christopher and Cita married on November 5, 1988. It was a lovely wedding with close to three hundred people in attendance. Cita was so happy, but she was unable to keep her anxiety under control. Rim and I were actively controlling the body as Cita struggled shifting in and out.

Her mom did an amazing job and even catered the food herself. She also did the flowers and, with the help of a few friends, WE all helped to make the party favors for the guests. WE decorated hundreds of miniature graham-cracker teddy bears with black top hats and white veils of frosting. Then WE coupled them in mesh and tied bows around them. Talk about darling!

Cita's mom did all the decorations for the reception hall too. The colors were teal and peach and the party hall looked like a Mexican fiesta.

Rim:

What I remember about that day was convincing Cita to wear her first pair of thong underwear. One of the gifts she received from her brother's wife at the bridal shower were these white satin thong panties. Attached to the ribbon of the waistband was a tiny button that when you pressed it, the song "Here Comes the Bride" chimed.

The best part of this is that Hope and I persuaded Cita to wear these itsy-bitsy, tiny white silk thongs and even a garter belt. It was just a few minutes before she needed to walk down the aisle when she grabbed a friend's hand and dragged her to the bathroom.

I had to pee so badly, I knew I wouldn't make it until after the ceremony.

Rim:
Her friend was lifting up all the silk material from her gown, detaching the garters, and holding up her skirt so she could settle on the throne. But they didn't remember the wisp of panties and she peed right through them.

The music starts, and we're walking down the aisle in a wet thong. Other than that, I looked gorgeous!

Christopher and I on our wedding day, November 5, 1988.

SHE:

I don't remember much of the wedding hoopla. It was possible that enough conflict occurred without my contributions. At the time, Cita was in the full bloom of bulimia. In addition, she was black and blue from the tough work WE did at our job in the bakery—loading and unloading huge steel racks that stood six feet tall by five feet wide, filled with trays of bread.

And then there was the continuing jealousy between Rim and me. Rim was not behaving any differently than normal. I, however, wasn't willing to share my time with Christopher as I often did in the past. And I certainly didn't want to relinquish control over my body to Rim.

I gave Christopher our first kiss as man and wife, but Rim and I struggled back and forth trying to be with him for our first dance as bride and groom. Even with Christopher's love, I was easily intimidated by Rim and SHE, so it didn't take much muscle from Rim for me to back down.

Rim:

To be honest, I was a flippin' jealous hag! Much to my surprise, I was developing my own feelings toward Christopher. He wasn't just some dude I wanted to screw. He was someone that I wanted all to myself. Until now, Cita had been hidden inside so much of our life and now she was fighting me to be out. On the other side of this, I was still battling to hold onto that part of me that didn't need or want anyone. I was a mixture of contradictions.

With Hope's support, I was able to maneuver my own time with my new hubby, at least for our wedding night.

15

‹•❊•›

Wedded Bliss

OUR FIRST YEAR OF MARRIAGE WAS difficult. A honeymoon period it was not. After having traveled together the prior year free of any commitments or family obligations, we were now bound to an apartment and 8-to-5 jobs just like everyone else.

Rim, Hope, and I shared the role of Christopher's wife. Even though WE had established on my wedding day that I was the person married to Christopher, it didn't change the fact that I was a fractured soul. I did not live every minute of every day in control of my body, and being married didn't change that. Hope shared in the wifely duties too, although she left the sex issue for Rim and I to deal with. Hope loved cooking and social activities, and she always kept a tidy household.

Hope:
I never pursued or needed independent time with Christopher. Cita was getting more secure in being the main personality among us, but there were still many hours in a day when she was not coping in a healthy way. Rim shifted out to be in control only when it suited her, so in between someone had to be steering the ship, so to speak. It was during those times that I would be sharing time with Christopher, but please remember that for him he was just talking with his wife.

Christopher:
That first year together we lived in a penthouse apartment on a busy street with a view of downtown Seattle.

Sorry to interrupt—this is Cita again. A penthouse? Really? What are you talking about? Believe me, it was no penthouse. It was a small two-bedroom apartment. The view was only from our bedroom, and on a clear day we could see only the tippy tops of some of downtown Seattle's skyscrapers.

Christopher:

Well, it *was* on the top floor. We had fun there. Our dog Gauge was still with us and he'd hang his upper torso out the window. We'd often worry that he'd fall out.

Rim:

I have a story about Cita and Gauge, but first let me say that I am not an animal fan. I don't go gaga over puppies and kitties. They are dirty, smelly, and demanding and some eat their own poop. EWW! I've questioned myself before on whether I'm fearful of animals or if it's just plain disdain. I've concluded maybe a little of both.

With that in mind I wanted to share an encounter WE had with a stray dog while walking our sixty-pound golden retriever down the street near our Seattle apartment. It's Cita who is actually walking Gauge, and WE were less than a block away from home when a crazed dog came flying out of nowhere directly toward us. This dog only had eyes for Gauge and he was moving fast and furious. So what does Cita do? She reaches down and scoops Gauge up off the ground and into her arms.

Now I'm looking out thinking, "Oh, that's so much better—Cita you stupid shit!" I quickly shift out and take control. Fearing for our own safety and not caring much about Gauge, I opt to heave our dog over a fence that WE had just backed up against. The stray stops short and I lash out with my foot, hitting him in his ribs. With a yelp he skitters off in the direction he came.

What happened to Gauge? That furry shit was just fine. He was lucky enough to have landed in a dumpster and there he was, just chillin' in some ripe garbage. Hmmmm, why don't I like animals? I rest my case.

Christopher:

Hey, I remember something else that occurred at that apartment that first year. I came home one night from work famished and was rummaging through the freezer looking for a quick score. In a canister stuck way in the back I found a piece of frozen cake. I love sweets and frozen sweets even more. I ate it with a smile, enjoying every last bite.

Nothing significant happened the night he ate the frozen cake, but it did slightly irritate me on our first wedding anniversary. I cooked one of my few staple meals (spaghetti), lit candles, and went to take the groom's cake out of the freezer for us to share after dinner. Not only had Christopher eaten the cake months prior, but he had even left the empty container full of crumbs in the freezer for me to find.

Every day that first year, I'd wake up in amazement that Christopher was at our side. I could not fathom why he loved me, but there he was in my life. There were many moments of joy, but with each day also came increased internal battles. The stress of keeping my anxiety and emotions at manageable levels was taking a toll on me. On all of us...

16

-◦◦§◦◦-

Rim's Rage

Rim:

I was really slammed with anger. Residue from the childhood rapes, sure. It was more than just that, though. With Cita in control more often now and married, my partying, hard-core–whoring days were done, at least externally I was trying to be respectful of Cita's marriage to Christopher, but I wasn't eager to relinquish external control of our lives. I still wanted to party, but Cita was reducing her alcohol intake. I couldn't drink and the whole "forsaking all others" vow Cita took was hampering my sex life. I felt I was being shoved aside—or shoved inside would be more accurate—and I didn't like it. I was one pent-up bitch, and all my aggression went toward Tristan.

Tristan:

Rim and I had a real difficult relationship. It started out with her creeping into my (internal) room at night, trying to get me to fondle her. At first I was so stunned that I'd just kick at her and she would leave. That seemed to piss her off even more, until one night she actually took me in her mouth. Even though I was scared, I wasn't able to control my arousal. Being a boy in my teens, it's not like I didn't have my own fantasies. Rim is hot, that's for sure, but it wasn't like she was being gentle and loving. In fact, to quote Rim, "You're the only one with a dick. If I can't get any in the outside world, I'm sure as hell not going to abstain in here when you've got a fine tool just waiting to be used." I'm sorry if that's offensive, but it's what she said.

Or you might think it's no big deal, seeing how we're just alters created by Cita's psyche. I only hope that by reading up to this point, you are better able to view us from a more real perspective. WE feel, think, and breathe on our own, and we're all distinctly different individuals. What I experienced was very real to me.

But it got to the point that if I didn't perform to Rim's desired outcome, SHE would come in and start making threats. Now you've read enough about SHE to know that didn't have the right impact on me. Fear does not make for arousal on my end. However, it wasn't long before I was no longer a virgin. Soon I fought less and less. I just accepted things and did as I was told.

Rim:
What can I say? I was fucked up. I just have nothing else to say about it.

Hope:
Tristan and I spent a lot of time trying to block the youngest alters from all the conflict. It broke my heart to know that I was blind to the abuse occurring to Tristan. He never said a word and it happened right under my nose.

Tristan:
You'd have thought with all that went on for Cita and Rim that I would have spoken up right away and told Hope, but I didn't. Their childhood and abuse were completely beyond my internal realm, and I never knew about any of it until after WE all started counseling.

Rim and I continued to have sex for years. At some point though, what was just sex did turn into an intimate and loving relationship. I came to feel I had a girlfriend of sorts, and when I didn't put up a fuss, I found that it wasn't so bad. I began to enjoy it.

Rim:

Again, no comment.

Tristan:

But even though in time, I considered Rim my girlfriend, it really wasn't more than just a sexual relationship. Maybe thinking of us as a couple helped me cope with the fact that she just wanted to use my penis. Again, I did find the sex great, but there was no emotional connection with Rim. She was ... what is that phrase? Oh yeah, emotionally constipated. I've always wanted a reason to use that in a sentence.

Rim:

I didn't know how to express myself without the influence of alcohol and drugs. The only emotional release I allowed myself was in the form of sexual acts with Tristan. When he'd try to get close to me by asking how I was feeling or what I might be thinking about, I'd always push him away. If he pressed me for all that touchy-feely shit, I'd just say I was tired and go to my room, shutting the door behind me.

Even though Rim tried to keep her emotions on lockdown, her aggressive behaviors toward Tristan weren't the only ways her rage was seeping out. Rim's quick temper showed even when she was out being me. Her rage would pop up while she was driving, and she'd flip off other drivers, speed, and take unnecessary risks. If something wasn't going the way she wanted it to, you could feel the anger filling our body to the point that she might just lash out at the nearest wall with my fist. I can't tell you how many broken fingers, knuckles, and hands we've had in our lifetime. Not all of the abuse came from SHE.

A drawing of Rim with a knife to my throat—so angry at me.
Counseling was a threat and she didn't want our secrets exposed.

One incident in particular where Rim was so mad … Rim, do you remember who you were angry at?

Rim:
Are you talking about the back–door-window incident? If so, no, I can't remember what caused me to be so pissed off. What *didn't* set me off back then?

True. Regardless of what had triggered her that day, Rim escalated to a level of uncontrollable fury. In a frenzy, she grabbed one of Christopher's golf clubs and smashed out our back-door windows.

Rim:

All I know is once I was through with my tantrum, I felt better and could go on with our life.

Tristan:

When Rim had aggressive outbursts like that, it wasn't uncommon for her to then use me for sex. I never feared for my safety like I did with SHE's rage and violence. However, I did feel used and nasty versus loving and sexual. Now I realize it was just another way of releasing a current of energy that needed displacement, even though it sucked.

These violent upheavals may not have occurred every day, but they were constant in our lives. This aggressive energy ran rampant internally, and Hope would have to block Chrissy and Molly from Rim's rage as best she could, while Christopher felt the impact externally.

Christopher:

It seemed that every time I turned around or came home from work, there was some new injury or something had either been broken or destroyed in the house. At that time in my own life, I was incapable of understanding the depth and breadth of anybody's emotional issues. My wife's dramatic shifts were almost incomprehensible to me.

My own anxiety soared when I tried to fix my wife's problems, and it caused me to raise my voice at her. I would implore her to keep from freaking out, breaking shit, and cutting herself. Her response would be to freeze up and go blank, which only added to my frustration. I didn't understand then that I was making things worse, not better.

My life became a whirlwind of highs and lows. I would engulf myself in projects, giving them my all and becoming temporarily successful. I sold cosmetics for a while and was named the best saleswoman of the quarter during my first few months with the company. I even flew to Texas for some big convention where I was publically recognized for my accomplishments. Later Rim and I joined a fitness center and after twelve months were voted as Member of the Year. I lost tons of weight and radiated confidence, but our accomplishments never lasted.

None of the Gang remembered drawing this picture, and it dawned on us that this was Hope's artwork. I'm curled in a ball, overwhelmed. There is an emphasis of a face on my watch and a face of death with the knife. "Time was running out."

There wasn't always a specific defining factor that would cause us to derail, but once the spiral began, our descent was rapid. When I finally collapsed, profound depression flowed through me, deadening my heart and protecting me from a life I was clinging to by a thread. The rest of the world would have seen only a slight outward change in my behavior or a temporary absence from work that was always explained by a stomach flu or migraine. In a few days, Hope would have shifted out and gotten us back to work and doing the necessary daily functions of living, taking on her role as me until Rim was willing or I was able to perform again.

A drawing I did showing the pain of trying to be seen.

17

⋯◆⋯

What about Me?

I HAVE A VERY DETERMINED young woman inside of me who is anxious to share a bit more. I'm referring to the alter Chrissy, and she is not happy about being left out for so long.

> *Chrissy:*
> how come i dont get to say some thing anymore? i don't think thats acceptable behavior.

That is a phrase that WE have all heard frequently from our therapist Mariana: "Well Chrissy, you're welcome to share right now, but I'm writing about a time in our lives that is not your favorite part to talk about."

> *Chrissy:*
> you mean when you didnt like me?

Yes, back when I was not very nice to you.

> *Chrissy:*
> when can we talk about grandma Sharon, mimi, and sandy? I want to talk about when your sister jennifer comes to visit and throws food at me!

I promise you'll get to talk about that later, but right now can I ask you to share about when you were younger? While Rim, Hope, and I were shifting back and forth living life with Christopher, what were you and the Others doing in the internal home? What was it like for you when SHE would get mad or when I was mean?

Chrissy:

i dont like to talk about when cita was meen but I can stop whenever I want to. thats what cita said. cita use to hate me befor mariana [our therapist]. hope said cita didnt reely hate me its just that cita didnt like herself. hope said cita did not no how to love me. i still think she did hate me but she loves me now. mariana and christopher helped her to. And they love me too.

when that was [back then], i played mostly with my brother tristan and with hope. we told storys that would make us laugh. tristan is soooo good at telling storys. we would draw to. tristan would play tricks on me. when I drew a pictur like with a monky hanging from a tree Hope would tape it to my bedroom wall. tristan is a good drawer and when i wasnt waching he would draw the same pictur but he would change it. like instead of monkys he would have cats in the tree. he took my pictur down and then put his up. he would wate and see how long it took me to see that it was wrong. tristan is a rascal like that.

tristan let me sleep in his room when i had bad dreams or when SHE was being meen. SHE was reely scary. we never new when SHE would come to say bad things and we tryd hard to be good and not make cita and SHE and rim mad. hope would block me once bad things started and i am glad for that becaus it was not nice and it scared us. Molly [an infant alter] never said anything she was just a baby but she would do her quiet cry and I would be not so silent when I cryd. i like it better now not being afraid of them and loving them.

Sometimes when cita was sleeping or blocked, hope would let me shift out and i would get to play with citas toys. she had a big wood barbie house that was bigger than me. it had an orange car and a garage and an elavater. i liked to dress the barbie, but sometimes rim would shift out and lay ken on top of barbie and do meen things to barbie. i would cry and hope would get mad at rim.

i even talked to chuck who is citas reely nice brother but he did not no it was me. he thought i was cita. i dont want to talk anymore now. bye bye

It isn't easy for any of us to talk about painful memories, and I want to thank you Chrissy for sharing.

Chrissy:
you are welcome and thank you for loving me now and also let me know when we can talk about something fun.

⊰⊹⊱

During this period, Chrissy would have been about five years old. Chrissy also mentions her younger sister Molly, a terrified infant alter. She barely moved and never laughed. When she cried, her face would contort and turn bright red and her chest heaved up and down, but no sound came out and no tears fell. Molly is no longer with us; she integrated within the first year of our finally talking about having MPD in counseling.

As I've shared before, prior to therapy, I had no relationship with these three younger alters, Tristan, Molly, and Chrissy. They were additional irritants, worse than a root canal to me. I was aware of them from about age five or six on, but I rarely spoke to them and they rarely shifted out, unless it was under Hope's supervision and without my knowledge. This "nonrelationship" lasted until I was forty years old.

Tristan also carries key memories of the internal chaos experienced while growing up. As WE shared more and more details from our life in counseling, Hope discovered that she had a pretty good idea of when my mind split to create him.

Tristan:

Hope told me that when Cita was about six years old, she and her brother were being scolded in the upstairs hallway. Her dad slapped Chuck across the face. Chuck was at the top of the stairs and lost his balance and fell down three wooden steps to a small landing. Cita remembers reaching out to grab him but was unable to prevent his fall. In her young mind, her brother lay lifeless and she feared him dead. In reality, he was just stunned, not hurt, but her intense fear of losing him caused her mind to fracture yet again, and then I came to be. That's our best guess. My role was to be big brother to Molly and Chrissy.

My world revolved around my little sisters. I watched after and cared for them with help and support from Hope. WE didn't have any children's books in our internal home. Instead, I made them up. Sometimes we'd make a game of it, like I'd start with a sentence about anything and then Chrissy would say the next sentence and so on. Those are still fun, because you never know where the story will go or how it ends. You could start out strolling on a rocky beach and end up meeting a clam who can talk. You both end up being best friends and move to Disneyland.

I never had a conversation with Cita in the first part of my life. Rim and SHE were downright intimidating when they wanted to be. Well, SHE scared the pants off me all the time. When words or fists were flying, I always gathered up the wee ones and did my best to block them from the ensuing pandemonium.

Chrissy was also petrified of SHE and would sense her approach before I could. She would just start crying and if it wasn't from normal kid crankiness, then I knew something sinister was in the air.

For the most part, other than being verbally abusive, loud, and terrifying to all, SHE never laid a finger on the little ones. I was always grateful for never having to try and be macho and stand up to SHE in order to protect them. I was just a silent knight who did his best to distract and comfort them.

One of Chrissy's earliest drawings. Here she is expressing a need to feel safe.

Tristan and Chrissy are wonderful, loving, and amazing people. I cannot imagine my life without them in it. It is painful for me to hear of the neglect that they've experienced and the deep sadness expressed when Chrissy talks of this time frame. Chrissy had often been frightened by SHE and Rim, but I not only scared her, I hurt her deeply too. Chrissy had longed for my love. To her I was her mother and I gave her everything but love. Fortunately Tristan and Hope were present in her life, and between them they were able to shield her most of the time. More importantly they give her the love and closeness she deserved.

18

-<⊰⊱>-

Life Goes On

In our second year of marriage, we were able to rent an 960-square-foot home in south Everett, another suburb north of Seattle. The owner really liked us and reduced our rent in exchange for necessary repairs to the house. He paid for materials while Christopher and I supplied the labor. The house was tiny, the yard was sizable, and Gauge loved it.

That same year my body was physically challenged with severe bouts of fatigue. One specialist WE went to diagnosed me with chronic fatigue syndrome. This condition can vary in its symptoms, but in general I experienced nonstop exhaustion. Yet I was in the best physical shape I had ever been in as an adult. Christopher and I had both lost significant weight after gaining a lot back from our prewedding weight loss. But instead of feeling rejuvenated by the loss of seventy pounds with Weight Watchers, my body rebelled by constantly needing sleep. Sometimes WE would slumber sixteen to twenty hours in one twenty-four-hour period.

Rim:
Christopher would come into the bedroom and put a finger under Cita's nose, fearing that she had died in the night—he wanted to check that she was still breathing. It impacted us all. What I mean by that is that even the alters in our internal home slept more and more.

Our job at the bakery was too demanding physically. In addition, the hours were sporadic and our physician recommended getting a position where the schedule was more regular. He felt that a more stable routine would also alleviate unnecessary stressors. WE left the bakery and got hired with a medical insurance company doing customer service.

The change in jobs brought a few months of contentment. The new schedule helped with the fatigue, and Christopher and I were able to turn our focus to fixing up our new home. But we spent way above our means; credit cards got maxed out, and yet we told ourselves that all would be fine.

Christopher:

I think it's important to share that our life was never healthy in all areas at the same time. It seemed that if we were managing our weight, then expenses were out of control. That was the case as we spent more and more money on fixing the house.

After the novelty of overhauling our rental house wore off, my typical downward spiral took its course. I quickly packed on weight again. SHE was hurting us on a regular basis. Our smoking habit that had been off was now on again, and rage was spurting out of me in unpredictable ways.

I might be adjusting a venetian blind and find that I had torn it from the brackets. There were moments when I'd go to look for something. It could be anything—a normal household item, such as a hairbrush. I would search and search, but still I couldn't find it. Then I would feel myself filling up with white-hot anger. I used my brush every day, and yet it was nowhere to be found.

My mind would then start to buzz and hum; I'm not quite certain how to describe it, but that was what it felt like. I couldn't hear Hope or Rim. Instead, I'd hear this sound like a crazy woman screaming and realize that the woman was me. Upon recognition, deep shame would flood me and then my screams would dissolve into uncontrollable sobs. I'd huddle on the floor, rocking myself, completely oblivious to anything else going on outside of me. Christopher, the Gang, and I define those incidences as out-of-body experiences.

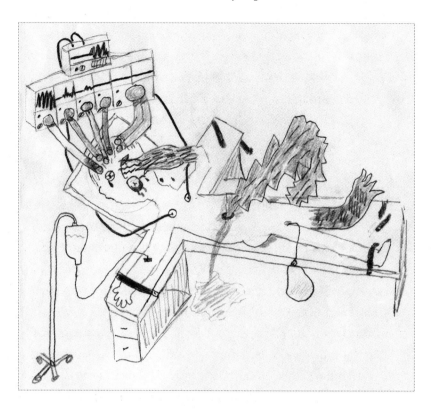

This picture shows the extreme pain and torment I was experiencing. Multiple tubes hooked up to me represent the alters. The heart monitor shows that some are flatlining, another is spiking, and one appears normal. SHE is represented as the monster trying to come out of me.

Christopher:

When I saw my wife writhing in an emotional meltdown, I'd get scared. I didn't know what to do and I wasn't aware of what was wrong with her. I got frustrated when I couldn't get her to snap out of it and get past whatever it was that was setting her off. And I didn't understand why I was unable to help her.

I find it interesting that Christopher felt he dealt with my emotions in an aggressive manner, because what I remember was his soothing touch and calming voice. When I was twisted within this rage-filled hell, Christopher would take me in his arms, stroke my hair, and tell me that he was there and that I was okay. If I was curled up on the floor, incoherent to my surroundings and tears streaming from my eyes, he lay next to me and stayed with me until the fit passed.

Needless to say, these emotional spasms took their toll on our marriage. How could they not?

Christopher:

I felt helpless and confused. What the hell was happening to my wife? One time I noticed a triangular burn mark the size of a playing card just below her elbow on the outside of her arm. Another time I came home late and Cita was already asleep. There were a few big clumps of her beautiful brown hair lying in the bathroom wastebasket. I didn't need to wake her up to know that she had hacked her hair. I tried to make sense of it as I went to sleep. I asked myself, Why would someone do this? I had no way to understand why my wife would purpose-ly deface herself, and I lost some compassion after the injuries continued. I never really knew if she was just trying to get my attention or if she really was that accident-prone. Cita was al-ways bumping into walls and banging into things, and I just wanted to yell, "Fuck, stop!"

It was really hard to deal with and again, I was not aware of SHE at that time.

One afternoon, after I endured yet another out-of-body experience, Christopher asked me if we might try marriage counseling. Already distraught, I burst into tears, certain that he was through with me and wanted out of our marriage.

Christopher:

I could immediately tell that Cita was taking my suggestion as the end of our relationship instead of how I intended it. I remember telling her that the only reason I suggested marriage counseling was to imply that I would go with her and support her seeing a mental health specialist. I wasn't saying, "Hey lady, get some help or I'm out of here." Once she realized that leaving her wasn't on my agenda, she was able to think more rationally.

I don't know that I actually became calmer after hearing Christopher's words. But Hope was, and she was able to talk with him about what steps WE needed to take to get help.

Hope:

Christopher and I (again in his mind he was talking just to his wife) discussed whether marriage counseling was necessary or if I got help with my obvious anger management issues, if that would bring him some relief. He most emphatically agreed.

The next day I researched our mental health insurance benefits and what providers WE could see. I called the first woman on the list, as I knew WE would be searching for a female care provider. I do believe that WE were all in agreement on that. Now that was a first!

The details after WE made our first appointment are fuzzy, but that first session is surely forever etched into the fibers of our souls!

Christopher drove us to the appointment, but I told him that he did not need to come in. Just having him there in the waiting room gave me the courage to see this through. Little did WE know what a total travesty the session would turn out to be.

Hope:

Cita tried to stay present and represent herself, but her total petrification immobilized her, so I shifted out and took her role. After the initial paperwork and introductions, I was, of course, asked why I had come in for counseling. I indicated to the therapist that I needed to deal with my anger better. She asked me if something had recently occurred to trigger it, and I truthfully replied that it was something I had dealt with all my life. I also mentioned that my father had anger issues, and it seemed plausible that they were related.

That was the last thing I remember the therapist saying. From that point on, the counselor talked nonstop. I don't think she even stopped to breathe. It was so sad. I could feel Cita losing her slight flicker of faith that she might get help. Rim was laughing in the background and I began to worry that I'd never get Cita to try another counselor. I realize it was our first visit, but still there was no sense of security, caring, or empathy. I knew I'd never get Cita to return to this woman.

Rim:

I remember asking Hope to let me shift out. I wanted to tell the lady to shut her yap and walk our ass out the door, but she didn't relinquish control. Hope was always so politically correct and polite.

I laugh when I look back on that session now. What a joke! Please don't ask me what she was talking about. I've checked with the Others and none of us can recall what she said. It was more like those nondescript sounds when the teacher is talking to the class in the animated Snoopy cartoons—"WhaWhaWhaWha."

Much to Hope's surprise, I did try again. It was less than six months later that WE scheduled another appointment. This time the therapist was a PhD. Unfortunately, this woman scared the crap out of all of us! She was so very militant in her style. In just our second session, she expected me to write letters to both of my parents to address any anger I felt toward them. Once I gave my parents their letters, she expected them to come into subsequent sessions until resolution occurred.

I don't mean to be judgmental of her counseling style, but as far as I was concerned, there was no way in hell I was going to be confronting my parents about anything. After all, we're talking about me, Cita, here. Miss I'm-Afraid-of-Almost-Anything. It was just not going to happen. When our time was up, Hope briskly left and I swore I'd never go to therapy again.

Hope:
I wanted to cry. My whole purpose in life was caring for Cita's welfare. I knew she needed help, but without outside resources like a therapist—the right therapist—I didn't know how to give it to her. It took Cita three additional years before she took us to another counselor.

The years that followed between returning to counseling were a quagmire of internal warfare. At times I felt that I might be close to a victory, but it wasn't long before I was waving my white flag of surrender again.

⋯⋯

The insurance company WE worked for announced that it was moving its customer care center to their home office in Denver, Colorado. I was given the option to transfer with the company, but I declined. Instead they paid to send me back and forth to Denver and train their staff on the policies that we had managed.

In some ways it was ideal, because Christopher was now working almost full-time on our house and the stress of all the construction took its toll on my nerves.

Christopher:
We eventually purchased that tiny home and continued our debt spiral by taking out a loan to completely remodel the house.

Plus, by traveling, I made much more money and that covered Christopher to be working on our remodel only.

Rim:
I loved traveling. It was the bomb! No attachments and best of all, free happy hour. They put us up at the Residence Inn—pool and spa, bar, and fitness center. The Inn was located two blocks away from an outdoor amphitheater. WE would sit out on our patio and listen to Elton John, Foreigner, and Phil Collins. I'm telling you it was sick! The company even paid for our food, phone, and rental car.

Your drinking was making me sick. So much for our routine and less stress. In fact, during one drinking splurge I became conscious enough to realize that Hope was fighting with Rim. Apparently Rim was making out with the Inn's bartender!

Rim:
I was drunk and he was hot. What the hell!

I was mortified. Oh my God! WE were married.

Rim:
You were married.

The lips you were using to press against that man were MINE!

Rim:
The tongue was yours too and the hands groping him also.

I remember waking up that next morning to see the face of the bartender in front of me. I totally flipped. Rim was still asleep and I jumped out of bed and grabbed my robe. His eyes opened wide too and he sprang from the covers. "It's okay! Nothing happened. You were drunk and so sick last night. I wasn't in any condition to drive. Check yourself out, you're in your clothes and I was sleeping on top of the covers. Nothing happened—don't freak out. I'll grab my shit and head out now." And he did.

He never acted surprised or confused by my behavior and I was so relieved that we hadn't had sex. But I still had no idea how I was going to deal with the rest of Rim's extracurricular behaviors. I mean, I'm married and here I had been, making out with another person. To me that goes against my wedding vow of "forsaking all others…"

As it happened, that same morning WE were leaving to go back home for good. My job of training others was done. As I dragged myself into the bathroom, I looked in the mirror, only to discover a grotesque black eye and that my entire face was bright red. It looked as if WE had stayed way too long under a sun lamp.

Rim:
I can explain the black eye. A group of us had gone out clubbin' and I'd had a bit more than I should have. We had taken a cab back home. (See I made some good choices.) Anyway, I was hanging my head out the window, trying hard not to hurl, when the taxi driver hit a bump. WE bounced our cheek against the partially rolled-down window. I remember it hurt like a moe foe, but at least I forgot all about wanting to puke.

That's great. WE found out after WE returned to Washington state that the redness was actually an allergic reaction to the excessive alcohol we'd consumed. I'm glad Rim had a good time that night because that was the end of my body's ability to deal with alcohol of any kind. From that night on, if Rim tried to drink, we'd become severely ill. In time, her drinking stopped completely.

Once I got home, I put that incident behind me and never told Christopher about it until years later. At the time I was being anesthetized for my first of many female surgeries. Stoned on happy medication, I felt it necessary to come clean. Christopher was still unaware of the MPD, so it came out as if I had been messing around with someone else when really it was a little grayer than that.

Christopher:

I remember being with Cita right before her medical procedure. The anesthesiologist had given her something that acted like a truth serum. She began apologizing for past indiscretions. My reaction was, "Hey, making out with some dipshit bartender in Denver wasn't going to rock my world," and I was quick to forgive.

⋯⟡⋯

Within a month of our return from Colorado, Rim, Hope, and I found a new job with another large medical insurance company doing customer service again. Our home was fresh and lovely. However, the debt incurred during our remodel was not so lovely. Yet WE were making good money, plus Christopher was back working full-time with another general contractor building and remodeling other people's homes.

Rim, Hope, and I worked hard and for the most part were well-liked. WE started as a phone representative, moved to claims processing and technical support, and then were hired to manage our own claims processing team. WE had twenty staff members that WE hired, fired, trained, and motivated. Through the years the self-harm continued, Rim fell off the booze wagon sporadically, I had five additional female surgeries, and my weight fluctuated more than the stock market. I'm talking about losing 70 pounds one year, gaining 120 pounds the next, losing 95 pounds, and then gaining 140 pounds.

Christopher:
In the meantime every other year I was training for marathons. I was learning martial arts such as hapkido and doing my best to appear to be complete and whole. In my mind I believed I would be a thriving contractor and was counting on Cita to continue bringing in steady income as well. The hope of achieving that dream was made more difficult by Cita's highs and lows.

Each day it was getting harder and harder to face life. Hope was unable to prevent my downward spirals, but she took on more and more of the external daily living. Hope tried to keep us on track with food and keep us in good graces at work, but once she relinquished control and had me back out to handle life, I would screw it up.

19

⤖⁂⤕

Seeking Help

IT WAS A DARK FALL evening in 1995 when I came home from work to find a dear friend and my husband sitting on the couch. Much to my surprise, they were doing their own version of an intervention. They showered me with empathetic understanding and warm but assertive concern.

Our friend is a social worker, and she assured me that there are thousands of practicing mental health professionals. I needed to shop around for them like you would for a car and that she'd help me find one.

Christopher:
I was confused and scared. Cita just seemed to be on the verge of having a complete breakdown. I didn't know what to do. I talked about it with our mutual friend and hoped Cita would feel secure enough to try therapy yet again.

I agreed, although my fear of losing Christopher was what truly motivated me. But the decision was not unanimous with rest of the alters.

Rim:
I just thought it was going to be a waste of time and money. Really, what could they do to help us? Not a damn thing!

SHE:
I was quite vocal this time, wanting nothing to do with it. I was adamant that WE did not need to seek help from some goddamn stranger.

Hope:

I was a hundred percent certain that WE needed to follow through on this. I felt WE and Cita specifically were at a critical point. If WE wanted to save this marriage—indeed save Cita and ourselves—WE needed to do something drastic.

This drawing was titled Mental Mayhem. *It was a frequent style of my artwork, depicting the overwhelming chaos going on in my head.*

I was too petrified to even make the call to my insurance company to find out what our mental health benefits were, let alone schedule a counseling session. The representative who described my outpatient mental health benefits referred us to an outsourced organization that the insurance company contracted with. This group would assist me in locating a covered provider. On the phone I was asked what felt like a million questions, and the conversation went something like this:

Agent:	How old are you?
Cita:	Ummm
Hope:	Thirty
Agent:	Do you care if you see a man or a woman?
Cita:	Aaaa
Rim:	Woman
Agent:	What city?
Cita:	Everett
Agent:	Where in Everett?
Cita:	[Silence]
Agent:	Ma'am?
Hope:	Near the Everett Mall.
Agent:	What time of day works best?
Rim:	Nights
Agent:	What time of night?
Hope:	After 5 PM

Finally, WE were given a therapist's name and the date and time of an appointment.

By the time the day of our appointment arrived, I felt resentful and angry. I really didn't want to try therapy again and I believed deeply that I was a hopeless case. It was Hope that kept to our committed time by saying, "You need to do this for your life and for your husband." I agreed, but even so I felt like an angry cat being forced into a travel carrier. SHE, Rim, and I were hissing, spitting, and clawing all the way to my appointment. When WE walked into the reception area and checked in, I turned to look for a place to sit. There were probably five other people there and a few small children who were crying, tired of being held and just as miserable as WE were.

WE waited for about ten minutes, until a woman walked out and headed in our direction. I don't know exactly what caused me to react so strongly to just her look and mannerisms, but my gut response was

"No way!" I knew right then that if this woman did come for me, I would thank her, let her know I had changed my mind, then leave.

To my relief, she greeted the woman sitting next to us. With my heart clamoring in my ears and my hands shaking so badly that I was hiding them in my pockets, WE continued to wait. Another door opened and another woman came out. She began walking toward us. She was short, blonde, maybe ten years older than me. I could feel my fear but sensed no alarms going off to deter me from following her once she greeted us.

I can't remember much after that initial contact. This session and many to follow are just a blur, although I feel my anxiety rise even as I write these words. I just know that I could barely say a word to her; I was as frightened as a trapped rabbit.

Rim:

I remember just shooting these looks of sheer hatred toward Mariana. I hated her. I hated Cita and I hated myself. Cita just frickin' wimped and went comatose internally. Hope may have been out here and there, but I think the sheer energy behind Cita's fear and SHE's and my rage blocked Hope from participating.

SHE:

I knew Hope was pining for Cita to trust in Mariana. Hope wanted Cita to feel safe enough to spill her beans about all of us. I was not going to let that happen. I can't tell you why I was so adamant about not being exposed. I just felt rage toward Mariana and "Fuck her" were the words frequently racing through my mind.

Hope:

The anger levels that radiated between Rim, SHE, and Cita were so intense. I felt warning alarms triggering throughout Cita's body. However, I did not feel angry, only hopeful. Something about Mariana just pulled at me. Maybe it was knowing that this might be our last chance at getting Cita to see a therapist. Or it was just watching Mariana and feeling her love and compassion. Here sat a woman truly unknowing of the depths of hell of Cita's life and still she allowed her to just be. There was no demanding, no expectations, no threats. Mariana allowed Cita to just be, and that was beautiful.

So there WE sat. I was frozen in silence. Rim and SHE were mute with rage, with occasional spits of aggressive verbal explosions. It wasn't that Mariana ignored us, but she was really big on allowing silence. If WE sat frozen staring in one spot, Mariana might say, "You're safe here" or "Breathe, Chris." Other times she would sit and let the silence happen. It was important to her that WE feel safe in her presence, and she was willing to give us time and acceptance. To Mariana, WE presented ourselves as me, Christine (Cita). If Mariana knew she was dealing with additional personalities, she did not acknowledge it to us.

In time, Mariana introduced crayons and paper in hopes that WE might communicate better by drawing or writing. It was a blessing for me because slowly I could say on paper what I was too terrified to verbalize. Now I look at all the pictures I drew then and often can't recall drawing them. In fact, many were drawn by Rim and SHE, although again, the artwork outwardly appeared to have come from just one person—me. These pictures are often filled with gruesome violence and death. Some of them appear in this book, and many are disturbing to view.

It was hard to have only an hourlong session once a week. WE certainly weren't eager to be in therapy, but at last tiny cracks began to appear in our veneer. Intense sadness, fury, and pain found their way through to the surface. After leaving Mariana's office, we'd be in turmoil. WE would write and draw at home too. I have pages of journal entries crying out, *"Help me Mariana. Make it go away."* Another one dated May 3, 1995, shares:

IF I could crawl out of this body and mind, I honestly believe my
life would be better. I don't know how much more I can take. I
want these feelings to go away. I feel as though I've lost any con-
trol of myself… I keep trying to talk myself out of this mood, but
all I want to do is scream. I'm SORRY!!!!!!!!!! Oh please, please
make this pain go away. I'm so tired. I don't want this anymore.
Please, please, please. My head hurts, my eyes are tired and my
brain is too… Mariana, I sure hope you don't decide that you'd
rather not counsel me.

So much turmoil inside, and I had only just begun to skim the surface.

We continued seeing Mariana once a week. It was a year later that our visits increased to twice weekly, but with each passing year WE seemed to require more time in therapy.

One of my many drawings filled with self-hatred and loathing around my body image.

20

⟻◈◈⟼

Life as WE Knew It

OUR TIME IN COUNSELING BECAME so intense that WE were unable to prevent our unleashed emotions from spilling out to other areas in our lives. At this time WE were still working for that large medical insurance company. While WE managed to work full-time and maintain a rating of "Exceeds" or "Good" at each annual review, our success did not include high ratings in the attendance category, as WE missed a lot of work.

Rim:

Mornings were the worst for us. Why? Well back then, SHE was most active during the night. That was her prime time to torment Cita. Some nights she'd just spout off a constant barrage of insults.

SHE was never nice to me or to anyone other than tolerating Rim here and there. Her outbursts had no rhyme or reason. Some nights she'd yell profanities the minute she sensed I was drifting off to sleep. Other nights the affronts continued for hours on end. And at still other times she'd scream offenses every two hours until the wee morning hours.

SHE:

Yeah, I was a rude ho back in the day. Our going to Mariana just added fuel to my rage and it was one more topic to torment Cita with. I'd tell her, "You know Mariana's going to stop seeing us. She will realize how fucked up you are Cita and kick your ass to the door." Or the ongoing taunt of how much

Christopher really loved it when Rim was out more than when Cita was shifted out. This all in addition to the nasty, favorite phrases of mine: "You're a demon seed. You're ugly. No one likes you."

Yeah, I was a little ray of sunshine.

This hurtful jeering happened nightly, although Hope did try to intervene. Blocking SHE, however, is not easy. Of all of us, SHE is the strongest in putting up a shield that keeps us from interacting with one another. Our best guess as to why this happens comes from the sheer amount of energy that anger and fear produce. So even though Hope would block me from having to listen to SHE, her blocks were short in duration—maybe just an hour or two. Eventually, SHE was always able to break through and her merciless taunting would continue.

Even with SHE's bedtime banter, I would manage to sleep off and on throughout the night. My body desperately needed a respite. It's not easy juggling all of these people, let me tell ya! The upside to sleeping was that for short spells I could disconnect from my reality. I dissociated, so to speak, from the emotional upheaval that was my life. Starting counseling was a pivotal point in our lives as WE began the agonizing task of tearing down the walls of the protective fortress we'd spent a lifetime building. However, it created even more anxiety and stress in my life. Many mornings I woke up in tears. It was torturous simply trying to wake from slumber and face my day.

Hope:
Some mornings Cita was too emotionally unstable to even get out of bed. Rim or I would shift out and get us ready for work. I say "Rim" lightly as she was sporadic in her dependability. Once WE were on the clock, Cita might come out for an hour or two during the workday. It's important to note that up until this point in our lives and for several more years to follow even

on Cita's good days, she never went through the day without one or more of us shifting out and functioning on her behalf.

I remember once that Mariana gave me a package of small blue dot stickers. She was being creative and thinking of ways to help me decrease my anxiety. Mariana suggested that I stick these on anything that I might easily notice to remind myself to breathe. My house, car, and workstation became splattered with a plethora of these little blue dots, but they did help. Whenever I saw one, I'd pause, take a couple of deep *breaths, and then continue on with what I was doing. It was a small victory, but any* tactic that led toward self-healing versus self-harm was a step in the right direction.

Even with Hope's and Rim's support, on many days I was too emotionally ill and would call in sick or leave early from work. WE might do really well attendance-wise for a month or two and then I'd crash. This was a pattern in my work history time and time again.

Work wasn't the only area impacted by the emotional seepage that counseling was creating. Christopher was left feeling confused and helpless in our aftermath too.

Christopher:

I didn't have any understanding what a real relationship was back then. It's embarrassing to me now how oblivious I was. My immaturity kept me shielded from seeing and assessing relationship problems with any real depth. Like a stone skipping across the water, my ability to go deeper was simply nonexistent.

Here's an example: After an evening at the in-laws, we'd have about a twenty-five-minute drive home. While I drove we'd regularly discuss what wasn't working with her relationship with her parents, and Cita would shut down. I would then get anxious and try to motivate her by forcefully suggesting what she should do to change. I wasn't yelling. I was not an abuser.

Here is another illustration of my unawareness: I call it the Alka-Seltzer dance. When Cita was my girlfriend, we were once parked alongside the highway. I was tending to the truck, checking the oil and doing my thing. Cita was in the camper preparing lunch for us. When I opened the camper door, I saw Cita stomping a box of Alka-Seltzer to death. I *was* aware enough to know that this wasn't normal behavior. But before I could grasp the depth of the issues at hand, she covered her tracks with a smile and a trumped-up explanation. We would often reflect back on this incident with humor, but we never truly addressed the rage behind the dance.

Cita's episodes were always short-lived—a day or a weekend—and then she was on the upswing and life was back to what I perceived as "normal." Once again she became enthusiastic and I had something to believe in again.

A drawing done in January 2002. There are two knives resting beside me, with the words "Is the danger the knives? Or are the knives my protection?"

21

Continued Therapy

IF MARIANA HAD PREDICTED IN those first years of counseling that we'd still be seeing her seventeen years later, WE would have run for the hills. Therapy, while necessary, was a painfully slow process. There was no quick solution. Any time Mariana pushed just a little, especially with me, I'd shut down and regress to not talking. Mariana could guide, instruct, and coach all she wanted, but until WE were ready to talk, there was nothing she could do.

One topic that I adamantly refused to discuss at all was my parents. I would not talk about them, period. I wanted to get help with my current behaviors, and I did not want to drag my parents through the coals, regardless of any abusive history. After all, *I* was the one not coping, who needed help. It felt like a betrayal to speak negatively about them.

WE had been working with Mariana for close to four years before WE started sharing small snippets of the physical and verbal abuse inflicted by my dad. It took more than ten years for me to share about having MPD.

Rim:

Mariana still knew us as only one person (Christine), but when I was shifted out I would get so pissed at her rigidity. Mariana is very into keeping boundaries. There WE were pouring our frickin' guts out and when we'd ask a personal question, she'd say something like, "Let's focus on you. We're not here to talk about me." I know I'd tell her to take a flying leap, "Quid pro quo, man. I give, you give." Sometimes she would give us just a little nugget, but mostly it was no.

Rim would get pissed, Hope was respectful, and I would get my feelings hurt. It's funny because intellectually I knew the importance of her boundaries, but emotionally I was desperate for connection with her. I would call her work number ten times in a day and never leave a message. Whenever I was scared, I would chant her phone number over and over again. It turned into my own little mantra, as if somehow just saying her number would keep me safe. Through this maze of craziness, Mariana was able to plant seeds of trust. WE might not have been able to acknowledge that then, but WE know that it did happen.

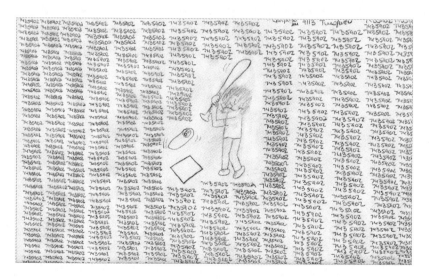

This drawing shows me playing baseball. The ball is a baby and surrounding them is Mariana's phone number written over and over again.

Learning to have a healthy relationship with someone can be an agonizing process. Learning to have a healthy relationship with yourself can be absolute hell, but WE kept trying, kept working, and kept seeing Mariana. With our emotions all over the map, WE found it very difficult to keep in contact with our friends or be around family. So WE began to withdraw. I was still way too frightened to be truthful to anyone about our MPD. (As well as many other things!) It was very difficult to tell people close to us that WE couldn't cope with life and needed to not see them. Instead we'd say WE didn't feel good or that WE had other plans.

Long-time friends were hurt, since they could not understand the battles I was waging. A few friends, although confused, did give me space. Christopher, lost in his own fear and confusion of what was happening to me, began to attend family and friend functions by himself.

Christopher:
I smoked weed, I drank some, and inundated myself with sports and work. The difficult issues concerning my wife interfered with my happy oblivion. I too was having issues with my relationships with family, friends, and coworkers. I remember sharing with one or two of my brothers that my wife inflicted injuries to herself. But I soon realized it was an uncomfortable topic and that I wasn't going to get the support that I wanted. I kept hoping that other people would step in and help, not realizing that it was my responsibility and no one was going to swoop in and save me.

It takes a lot of hard work to go from being a needy, insecure man with an emotionally unstable wife to an independent, responsible couple. And it was going to take a while to make that transition.

Cita starting counseling was a big step in the right direction. However, I soon began to resent how much money we were spending for her sessions. Cita had good medical benefits, but there were copays and a limit to the number of visits she could use per year. With her going three times a week, that maximum benefit capped fast. This left us paying over a thousand dollars every month for her mental health treatment. I was not part of Cita's sessions during those first few years, and after a while I really questioned Mariana's integrity. At that time, I felt she was taking advantage of my wife for her own financial gain.

Mariana:

Because of Christine's and Christopher's extreme dependency issues and their irresponsibility around work and finances, I continued to ask them to pay the full fee. During some of the most difficult times of the therapy, such as when the alter Lou was emerging, they were simply unable to pay. I did not charge for my time then for over two years. To suggest terminating the therapy simply because of their inability to pay would have been obscene. But I know that deeply rooted problems are so difficult to change that if people don't experience a severe enough crisis, they continue to escape facing what they are choosing to do. It took many months of hard work for Christopher to face the reality that he needed to find work with an employer who could pay for their health benefits instead of being self-employed. It was a huge relief for all when he did.

Christopher's tension over money and my sessions with Mariana only added to my already strained emotions. I was building a lifeline through Mariana and felt threatened that Christopher might ask me to stop seeing her. Instead, Mariana had Christopher come to the sessions with me, and he was able to work through his concerns directly with her. The cost of therapy and money in general continued to be a constant topic throughout the years we saw Mariana.

Another matter that was addressed in therapy dealt with honesty. When you're hiding something like seven additional personalities or withholding an entire abusive childhood, lying becomes as natural as breathing. At least for us it was. There were lies about how WE got a bruise or a broken bone, lies about being sick for work, lies about why WE couldn't get together with friends, and lies to cover up not remembering events that were lived by one of the alters and not me. WE lied about how much food WE ate or how often WE went to McDonald's.

Rim:

Sometimes WE just made shit up, anything to cover up the truth of how messed up our lives were. WE never believed that the truth was good enough—that *WE* were good enough.

Buried in food. If you look closely you'll see one hand next to a chicken leg, and another on top of the pizza. There is one foot sticking out by the T-bone steak and the other by a bag of Cheetos.

So Mariana instigated the honesty policy. The purpose of the policy was to reinforce that Mariana was not there to judge or scold as a parent would do. For her to help us, she needed to know our truths. It wasn't just lying but withholding too. If WE drove to the store at 2 AM and bought donuts, it was okay for me to share this with her. If WE spent four hours lost on the computer playing Solitare, she would want me to fill her in on it. It was the only way she could get a full understanding of how I was dealing with life. Granted, the ultimate goal was to get me to not lie at all, but this was a starting point, and Mariana wanted me to learn that her office was a safe space. The lying and withholding didn't stop automatically, but WE did begin to come clean with her, even if the deception had occurred months before. It wasn't even the lying or withholding itself that mattered so much, it was how WE related to Mariana that did.

WE eventually lied less and less, and our turnaround time in telling Mariana about a spoken falsehood shrank from months and weeks to within a twenty-four-hour period. More and more WE would acknowledge lies moments after the fib left our lips. To this day, there are still times when WE lie to Mariana, but WE quickly acknowledge it and then discuss why it occurred. Being honest decreases my baseline anxiety and improves our relationships in a way I never experienced until I was in my thirties.

Mariana also referred me to a medication management provider in the hope that I might find some reprieve from my constant, severe anxiety with a prescription drug. The therapist was a nurse practitioner with education and training in prescribing psychotropic medications. Mariana wanted me to see this particular practitioner because of her willingness to give the time necessary to work closely and be patient with me. The care provided was and continues to be spectacular, but trying to find a medicine that my body would react to favorably was a fiasco. As if WE weren't already suffering enough, WE soon discovered that my body tended to react the opposite to what a specific medication was designed to do.

Rim:

Trying to determine a medication that helps someone with anxiety or depression is really a type of crapshoot. I'm not saying that medical providers aren't trained in what these prescriptions can do, but until you actually start taking one, there is no guarantee that the drug will work for you. Oftentimes you have to take it for weeks before you notice even the slightest change. With our odd reactions, we'd be prescribed an antianxiety medicine and the next thing WE knew, WE were racing around like we'd taken speed. I was so lovin' the buzz.

I have to admit that I enjoyed it too. It felt as though the grey clouds had finally lifted from my mind and now I had all the desires and energy I ever wanted. It sounds great, I'm sure, but the reality was my mind was just racing. Our house was spotless; I lost weight, worked out daily, and rarely needed to sleep. But both Mariana and the medication doctor knew that I was going to crash and burn. There was no way that this was healthy, and with much fuss on our end, a new prescription was prescribed.

It took close to a year for us to find a combination of medications that allowed me to feel more grounded. That year was long and crazy. Sometimes WE were in a drug-induced fog for days, while other times our minds raced nonstop. My body bloated up on one drug, while another caused our food to taste like metal. WE were all over the map, and although I secretly hoped for some sort of happy pill, there was no miraculous cure awaiting us.

Prior to the new medication, my anxiety would have been twenty on a scale of one to ten. After the medicines began to work, I would rate myself closer to a six or seven. Anxiety, fear, and sadness were still there, but at least a necessary and consistent reprieve was experienced by all of us. Another key point to this process was the acceptance that the medicine was only an aid toward stability. WE needed to continue doing our relationship work with Mariana and with Christopher. It was going to be through our efforts in counseling that WE would find a calmer sense of peace within ourselves.

This drawing illustrates how terrified I felt. I drew myself as an adolescent hiding beside the couch and holding Mariana's hand.

22

Mom

THIS IS A DIFFICULT CHAPTER for me to write. As is most often the case, my anxiety increases and my mind goes blank—an all-too-common defense mechanism when it comes to discussing my past relationship with my mother. Growing up I would have said that I was closer to my mom than other girls were with their mothers. By having other personalities shifting out and taking responsibility for my life for hours or days on end, I hid signs of discontent that might have surfaced much earlier in my life.

My mom never knew her own mother, who passed away before Mom was even two years old. Not having maternal guidance left a negative imprint on my mom's life. She grew up very self-conscious and was acutely sensitive about her body image, even though weight wasn't a problem for her until she was in her thirties. Her fixation put my own weight under her radar for as long as I can remember. Now I realize that she was only trying to protect me from the challenges and social stigma that being overweight can bring.

However, her neurotic scrutiny fueled my own fragile sense of self. When the Gang and I look back at photographs of us in grade school and junior high, I can't believe how good I look. There was really nothing wrong with my body. I was not tiny or petite and at 5'11" tall, I would never be, but there wasn't anything fat about us. I feel really sad at how distorted my view of my body was then. In fact, it continues to be a topic of work in counseling to this day.

To her credit, my mom cherished my brother and me. She was warm, affectionate, and loving. However, she could also be obsessive and controlling. Although she denies awareness of Dad's physical abuse, she was completely conscious of his unpredictable fits of rage. Raising two young children with a husband so volatile added another dimension of hyperawareness in my mother. Part of her controlling ways came from making sure that my brother Chuck and I were always looking and acting our best so as not to set off Dad.

Rim:

People used to tell Mom and Dad how good their children were. "So well behaved!" In part, we were good kids, but fear of Father played an enormous factor in how we grew up. Also, Cita was excruciatingly sensitive and her need to not upset her mother also made a difference in how WE acted and the choices WE made.

My brother at age seven and me at age three.

I was six or seven when my parents sat my brother and me down and let us know that they were thinking of getting a divorce. It was very upsetting to me, but I think it's important to also share that I truly believed it was my fault for being such a bad child. In addition, I had never been able to handle my mother being sad or angry. During that time when my parents' relationship was even more troubled, I could feel Mom's pain emanating from her. I know that she tried to keep her mood light for us kids, but I became absorbed in her sorrow and was highly tuned into every sigh or pause that she displayed. I could detect any sign of her tears, and I felt completely helpless to stop her pain.

Hope:

Here is one memory that shows how emotionally entangled Cita was with her mother. I believe she would have been in second grade when a teacher asked her to be a crosswalk patrol guard. Cita really wanted to participate, but then she began to worry about the time she would be away from her mother. She asked me, "What if Mom needs me and I'm not there for her?" I don't think this is a normal reaction for a child her age. Even though I encouraged Cita to participate in the safety crossing program, she declined the offer.

Rim:

I recall a weekend when WE spent the night at a friend's. I'd say it was about the same time frame, first or second grade. WE were invited to go for a bike ride with this family. Cita was hesitant, always the worrier. I was the person in control of the body at that moment and I chose to go. I had a blast, but when WE returned WE found out that our mom had called in our absence. Cita flipped out. She saturated our system with a flood of guilt for not being there when her mother "might" have needed her. When Mom arrived to take us home, she explained that she had called only to see if WE wanted to go shopping with her. Cool, I thought, Cita will settle down now that she realizes there was no emergency, but oh no—she still felt that she had failed our mother somehow.

As a child of six or seven, I remember going shopping for school clothes in late summer with my mom. As we strolled down racks of fall-colored dresses, wool skirts, and soft warm sweaters, my mother would drape outfits over my arms to try on. It didn't matter to me what she selected; if she really thought an item was cute, I would agree with her. I truly believed that I'd hurt her feelings if I said, "I don't like that, Mommy." Rim was more verbal about her tastes, but she was rarely present for shopping matters.

I also always thought that with my mother, there is the right way to do things (her version) and then there are the less effective ways. Sometimes she was so dismayed if I chose not to follow her suggestions. She seemed to always know so much about everything and I often felt too intimidated and afraid to contradict her. I didn't know how to stand up for my own thoughts and opinions.

Rim:
It's hard to describe our mom in a fashion that gives the reader a clear and precise understanding of how difficult it was. Not everyone has to agree with someone else's suggestion. I get that, but keep in mind how oppressive it can be when you constantly bump up against someone else's absolute certainty.

Mom's assertive, often domineering manner overwhelmed me. Growing up, I never felt I could go against her views without a confrontation, which I spent all of my time trying to avoid. As a daughter, I should be able to tell my mother "no" if I don't want to do something. As an adult, I should be able to disagree with my mother's opinion and not be petrified that she would be mad at me. It may be hard to believe, but I didn't overcome that irrational thinking until I was in my forties.

There is no question that starting counseling impacted my relationship with my mother. Sometimes I felt a pull between the two of them: Mom's expectations of what I should be doing with my life and Mariana's insistence that there was a healthier way for me to live: that I could have a life where saying no to someone was okay. A life in which it was all right to be mad at someone and for them to be mad at me. Life wasn't going to end if confrontation was in it.

As I started to face my fears in counseling, I just wasn't able to function in a way that wasn't fear-based with my mom. I was a nervous wreck when I was with her, and I couldn't wait until it was time to leave. Then I began to move her into the category of obligation instead of enjoyment. These changes were quite apparent to her and I know it hurt her. One day we were standing in a Target parking lot when she pointedly said that she felt more like something that needed to be fit into my schedule versus a person I wanted to see. She was right. Our relationship only became more and more strained with each passing day.

Mariana constantly tried to get me to set healthy boundaries with my mother and I just wouldn't do it. Originally I had told Mom right away when I started counseling. But I know that she felt threatened by Mariana and didn't agree with some of her recommendations. Although I can't recall specific examples, I do remember not wanting to talk about my time in counseling with my mom anymore. It was easier than getting nonsupportive comments about the therapy that was quickly becoming a saving grace to me. Still, Mariana pushed me to make changes in my relationship with Mom.

It wasn't until 2003, a full eight years after I had started counseling, that I even allowed myself to consider making those changes. Mariana and I discussed many different types of limits for me to set with her, but whenever I tried to talk to my mom about what was happening inside me, I just froze, so fearful that she would be hurt or angry.

I believed that if I tried to tell her that I wanted her to do something as simple as call me before she stopped by, that she would raise a fuss and I would not feel strong enough to explain myself or enforce it. Not surprisingly, as Mariana and I delved even deeper into my relationship with my mother, I regressed. My anxiety consumed me, SHE's physical and verbal abuse increased, and my overall health declined to the point where WE could only work part-time.

❦

That same fall our father was diagnosed with terminal cancer, and he passed away early the following year. My company had a program called FMLA (Family Medical Leave Act), which enabled us to take time to go to Montana, where my father and his wife Pattee had been living.

Although my father's illness and death saddened me, I experienced a small reprieve from SHE while WE traveled back and forth to Montana. It wasn't anything WE discussed; SHE just seemed to call a short truce. It was because of this respite that I enjoyed being in Montana, even though I was still very unstable and continued to have phone sessions with Mariana almost daily.

During the last six weeks of my father's life, he fell into a deep depression and was silent almost all of the time. During one of my visits with him, I tried to tell him that I loved him and that I had forgiven him. Dad and I had never talked about the physical abuse he had unleashed onto me as a child, so how was it that I could forgive and forget so easily? First, it was hardly easy. Second, I myself had rarely felt the rage or anger at the abuse he inflicted. These emotions had been deflected to SHE, who absorbed them as her own.

Instead, during those last moments with Dad, I saw a broken-down man whose golden years were being robbed from him less than a year into his retirement. He had been an abusive father, but I still had some fond memories of my childhood, and as adults we had enjoyed each other tremendously. He and his wife Pattee enjoyed having Christopher and me over for weekend barbeques and lazy afternoons just watching sports together. Dad and Pattee didn't try to fix me or fill me up with their opinions. And at the time, it was truly a blessing to just be broken and have that be okay.

Later, as he sat dying of cancer, I could look him in the eyes and feel his anguish and sorrow over what he had done. But it was still hard for me to love him just as he was. I was keenly aware that my father had been emotionally unwell long before he got cancer. Unfortunately, he waited too long to get help with either condition.

After returning from Montana, I began to unravel and spiral out of control again. My depression was at an all-time low, and WE even left the insurance company WE had worked at for the past decade. Instead WE took a job just a few miles from our house working at a weight-loss center, hoping that this career change would decrease my stress levels. It did seem to make a difference for about a year. My weight went down to a new record low and I was in super physical health. After a year however, the cracks began to surface again as I faced having to make relationship choices with my mother. What made this relationship so damn toxic? Was I harboring some ill will toward her for not protecting me from the abusers in my life? That had to play a part, although I wasn't conscious of it at the time.

As layers of my hidden life began to peel away in counseling, I felt increasingly vulnerable and even less able to keep a healthy boundary. No matter how Mom tried, I continued to pull further and further away. It might have been my pulling away that caused her to push even harder into my personal space, and together we just shredded any remnants of a relationship.

I admitted to Mariana that I needed to take more drastic steps to separate myself from my mother. With her help, I wrote the first of many drafts of a letter to Mom asking to no longer have contact with her for an unknown amount of time. Mariana was quick to edit out any phrases where I expressed guilt for the choice I was making or if I appeared to be taking care of my mother. I painfully agreed, trusting in Mariana's own life experience and knowledge. I continued to write and rewrite, but I felt swallowed by intense fear that my mom wouldn't understand. I was so afraid of her anger. I had spent my entire life trying not to hurt her and now I knew this letter would do exactly that.

Ironically, it was a get-together with my mom on Mother's Day 2004 that pushed me to finally send her the letter. As I have mentioned before, our relationship was really just a vacant shell at that point. We didn't enjoy our time together; she would leave feeling hurt and confused and I would depart feeling disconnected and empty. Still, it was Mother's Day, and that meant I had to do something to honor her even if it would be miserable for all of us. Christopher and I went with her to an arts fair. I can't recall all the details of that day, just that at one point Mom pulled my shirt down to cover my bum when we were eating lunch at a café. She then launched into her typical diatribe that even though I'm large, it doesn't mean that I can't purchase clothes that actually fit. She then pointed out that if I bought clothes in several sizes, at least I'd always have something suitable to wear.

That did it for me. I went through the motions that got us done with our outing and then Christopher and I headed home. It was just a few days later when I mailed my finalized letter to my mom. But as I closed the envelope, I felt as though I were sealing my fate too. I was so consumed with panic that I even started smoking again that day, having stopped years before. I remember sitting idle in my car in front of the mailbox at the post office very late that night, playing with a brand-new cigarette in my mouth, the letter sitting on the front seat. My heart sounded like the roar of a waterfall in my ears. You would have thought that I was about to murder her, and yet all I was asking of her was for time.

Hope:

The letter was very brief. It was a direct request for her mom to give her time to do what was necessary in her life without any interference or contact from her mother. When Christopher read a copy of the letter later that night, he mentioned to Cita that it contained a small typo. Cita was appalled. Not only was she frightened to death over any possible confrontations that might ensue with her mother, but now she believed that her mom would read this letter and believe it was written carelessly.

We were surprised when there was no immediate response from my mom. Even so, I turned into a paranoid freak! Any noise that I heard outside my home, I feared it was my mother. If someone actually knocked on our door, I'd drop to the floor in sheer terror. Somehow I knew she wouldn't understand the peril I was in and give me space.

I was right. Within a week of mailing that letter, my mom showed up unannounced at my door. I was in such turmoil and had no idea what to say. I invited her in and we sat across from each other in the living room. She was hurt and started to cry. Then her pain came out in anger. I can't recall all that was said, but I know that she asked me if I thought she was really some kind of monster. All I wanted to do was cry out, "I'm sorry Mom—I didn't mean to send that damn letter. I was wrong and I just want you to love me." But as much as that was true, I also knew there was no other way for me to get well. I needed to shut her down, but instead I just sat frozen on the couch, not saying a word.

I remember my mom saying something like, "You could talk to me if you wanted, but you just choose not to." It was so apparent that she could never grasp what kind of hell I had been living. She blamed me for her own discomfort, and I couldn't get through to her that my life was literally in peril. She would never understand my needs and see my actions as anything but spiteful and hurtful. I don't think the visit was more than twenty minutes long, but my trauma lasted for weeks.

-◦⟨⊱⊰⟩◦-

In time my mom became less angry, but she still refused to respect the boundaries I set. Each unexpected appearance felt very violating, and I regressed after each visit. Mariana suggested I make it clear to my mom that she was not giving me the space I had asked for. The thought of having to ask this of her again made me sick with nerves, but I knew I had to stick to my guns if I was going to heal. When I actually did speak with her again, I lost confidence, but I did manage to tell her that I needed her to call first before coming over. I sighed with relief when she happily agreed.

I think that Mom was unable to separate herself from me and to realize that I had different needs than she did. She probably did not like being told that she couldn't see me or that she had to follow a guideline. She was so enmeshed in my life, and I don't think she had ever comprehended that her behavior was not healthy. Whatever the reason, she wouldn't or couldn't respect the necessity of the boundaries I asked for.

It took a year before I began to feel less frightened of her visits. She'd stay away for months at a time and then on a holiday or birthday she'd appear on my porch. "Well, I wasn't going to miss your birthday," she justified. It was aggressive behavior on her behalf no matter how good-willed she might have believed she was being. Again, it just showed her inability to realize the impact her unexpected visits had on me.

23

Breaking the MPD Silence

AFTER SETTING THE NO-CONTACT BOUNDARY with my mother, therapy became increasingly intense. The more I opened up to Mariana, the more frightened I was of the outside world. I began experiencing such panic attacks that even shopping for groceries became a traumatic event; oftentimes it was only with Mariana's encouragement that I was able to drive to the store, but getting there was only half the battle. More often than not, I would sit in my car just waiting to muster the courage to go inside and start shopping. Sometimes I never found the nerve to step out into the world, and I'd start my car back up and return home.

If I did actually begin my shopping expedition, I'd experience waves of anxiety and break into a sweat. My eyes wouldn't focus, my breathing became sporadic, and my ears would ring. Other customers' voices sounded warped and the store lighting seemed to penetrate right through my skull. With the help of Hope or Rim, I'd make it back to the car, having abandoned our cart in the middle of an aisle. SHE, Hope, or Rim would then drive us back home.

Not only did I have panic attacks but also something I call "noise terrors." Oftentimes sirens would trigger them, but other sounds did too. One night Christopher and I were sitting on the couch together; he was watching TV and I was trying to read. I don't know what instigated the terror, but the first sign that something was amiss came when the words in my book began to swim in front of me. I couldn't get my eyes to focus and then the TV volume increased tenfold in my ears. At the time Christopher was tapping a fingernail on the remote control. It was just a slight clicking noise, but it distorted into clanging cymbals in my head. The noise became all-consuming, as though my whole body had been transported to a distant place of only sound. The TV and the clicking on the remote were the only sounds I could identify.

When Christopher realized what was happening, he gently stroked my hand and softly called me back to him. These episodes lasted only seconds or minutes, but for me they felt endless. When I was finally able to calm myself down, I would lean against Christopher and sob. I was losing my grip on the last shreds of my sanity and had no idea if I was going to survive. I remember a coworker asked me once where I wanted to be in ten years, and my response was "Alive."

The deeper I worked in therapy, the closer I came to revealing our truth. Unfortunately, SHE had threatened me with more bodily harm if I said a word to Mariana. While Hope pleaded with me to fight for my life and not give up. One day I realized that SHE's threats frightened me less than my own thoughts of suicide.

I felt so sick walking through the doors to my counseling office that day. That's what I recall and not much more. I was forty-one years old. I'd been in counseling for over ten years, and for the first time in my life, I had found the courage to utter my terrifying truth:

"There is more than one of me."

Those seven words would launch a journey that would twist beyond any possible or imagined path—down and through the deepest darkest places in my mind and soul.

As I sat there, I waited for Mariana to ask me to leave her office. Certainly after hearing what I'd just shared, she would believe I was too bizarre for her to work with.

Instead, with tears in her eyes, she softly replied, "Yes, I already know."

That was not what WE had expected. Stunned by her response and ashamed of my admission, I said nothing. Internally, however, all was not quiet. Rim was shouting "What the hell?!" while SHE blasted out, "Why didn't she fucking say something?"

Angry and confused, I asked Mariana why she hadn't said anything to me before. She explained that in her opinion, it was crucial that WE be the first to speak of the MPD. Because some in the medical field question the legitimacy of multiple personality disorder and because of my extreme dependency on her, she believed I should be the one to bring this into the open, without any overt action on her part to lead us to such a conclusion.

At first WE couldn't understand what she meant. Here WE were, having dealt with multiples for an entire lifetime, and now she was informing us that some people might not think that MPD was even real? It upset us all, and again it triggered our lifelong fears of how WE could possibly be accepted by friends and family.

When I was finally able to find my voice again, I asked her when it had dawned on her that I might have alternate personalities. Mariana reflected back to the drawings I had done in my first years of working with her, when drawing was how I communicated because speaking was far too terrifying. At that time I frequently drew myself surrounded by the same characters. There was the angry person who wore a baseball hat (Rim), and another who was a boy (Tristan). There was a monster (SHE), a young child (Chrissy), the fat one (me), and a slender, long-haired girl (Hope). The consistency of these multiple people representing myself in my pictures, as well as my abrupt and often violent mood swings, had given Mariana the first hints of my condition several years before.

Now that I had finally shared my secret with her, the question of "Where do we go from here?" quickly came to the forefront. Mariana felt that it was extremely important for us to take our time, but she encouraged me to allow the Others to meet her. And of course, we'd need to share this news with Christopher in the near future. I wasn't yet ready to reveal the alters to him, so instead I considered the idea that they would shift out and talk to Mariana as themselves. (Of course, Hope, Rim, and SHE had shifted out in front of people many times before, but they had always been covering as me.)

SHE:

I had been adamant from the start that Cita not say anything about us alters. Cita's choice to go against my will was a psychological breakthrough for her, but it really pissed me off. I had absolutely no desire to hold hands and sing "Kumbaya" with Mariana.

Just recently Cita asked me if I had been fearful of Mariana. I really had to think on that. There has been very little in my life that I've feared. The alter Lou, whom WE talk about later, caused me fear, but Mariana? No. At the time she was just a new ripple of irritation like a mosquito that needed to be swatted. I was not afraid of Mariana, but I'm certain I felt she was a threat to my authority over the Gang and Cita.

Tristan:

I was stunned that Cita went against SHE's wishes and then pretty much just went into warrior mode, protecting the young 'uns from the wrath of SHE that was certainly going to rain down on us.

Sharing with Mariana about my multiple personalities was an enormous step in my life—in our lives. I felt exposed and vulnerable. My nerves were so thoroughly frayed and my emotions so out of control that holding down a job was no longer feasible. With encouragement from my work supervisor, husband, and therapist, I went on the Family Medical Leave Act (FMLA). I hoped that with some extra time off, I could work in more depth with Mariana to try to get myself back together.

My "extra time off" increased to short-term disability and to my surprise extended into longer-term disability. After all, I'd worked full-time since the age of sixteen and I just couldn't believe that I was becoming more unstable to the point of being unable to work.

When I qualified for state disability, I mired myself in even more shame. I felt as though instead of getting better after all those years of counseling, I'd somehow failed by getting worse. My husband and I took a huge hit financially, and in truth we've never quite recovered from that choice. Although "choice" is not quite the right word—the situation really could not have been avoided, and in time I came to accept it.

Being home full-time, however, left a lot to be desired. It sure wasn't like being on vacation. Instead, I now had more time with fewer distractions. My nerves were on red-alert. I couldn't do any needle-work or knit because my hands quivered nonstop. Nor could I calm my brain enough to focus on any books. I became afraid to leave my house, completely afraid to live my life. I often kept the lights off in the house and hid in my bedroom. Christopher was lucky if I was able to even wash a dish or do a load of laundry. When I woke up in the morning, I'd burst into tears, unable to face my day. I would go days without showering. When I did bathe, Christopher would have to sit in the bathroom to keep me company and make me feel safe. Some days my anxiety was so extreme that I'd drive to Mariana's office even if I didn't have an appointment. I'd sit in my car for hours just to be physically closer to her or in her lobby during office hours, feeling safe in her space.

The Others were getting restless inside my internal prison. Hope and Chrissy were eager to be out and meet Mariana, but my emotional instability made that a slow transition. SHE was ominously silent, like the calm before a storm. Tristan seemed more like a deer in the head-lights, just waiting to see which way to run. Rim, who was accustomed to shifting out and living my life, wasn't thrilled with being shut inside.

I wasn't blocking them, but my emotions were so out of control and my depression so massive that Rim felt stunted even when she was in control of my body.

Rim:

I was annoyed by Cita wrapping us up in a blanket of depression. I just wanted her to pick up the pieces and keep moving like we'd always done. I was confused and leery too. What would all this show-and-tell lead to? If Cita was able to talk about having MPD after all these years, how long before she mentioned more of our hidden past? I certainly didn't want to be pressured into getting in touch with my feelings. They were shut off for good reasons. Fuck anyone who tried to pry them open.

Rim and I were both emotionally unstable and at times it felt like
we just put on the face that people wanted.

24

⋅❦⋅

My Husband Learns of the Others

TWO MORE WEEKS PASSED BEFORE I told Christopher about the Others. I had no doubt in my mind that he'd go running toward the nearest door, never to return. Mariana did not agree; she felt certain that he'd be strong enough to work through this with me.

How did I finally tell him? I honestly can't remember. I know it was in a session with Mariana, and the silence that followed felt like an eternity. I was so ashamed. I felt as though I had betrayed him. He married me not knowing the woman he loved was fragmented into so many pieces. How would he ever forgive me?

Rim:

The commentators at the Olympics often state that the longer the judges take to rate a performance, the worse the score will be. I recall the silence that filled Mariana's office, and as the time kept ticking by, I thought to myself, "We're screwed!" There was no doubt in my mind that Cita telling Christopher the truth just put an end to the marriage.

Christopher:

I cannot truly recall the details of that session either, other than thinking, "What happens now?" What does it mean to me and to my relationship with Cita? I felt confused and angry that this was happening to her, to us. I know that it never crossed my mind that Cita had betrayed me. That wasn't the case, but I *was* a bit fearful of the unknown. When I reflect back on that time I'm amazed that I had no idea. I was married to her for a very long time and thought I knew everything about her. Cita was a master at keeping this to herself.

A few hours passed before Christopher's stunned silence turned into curiosity. He asked me if the Others had listened in on our conversations and wanted to know if they'd watched us when he and I had sex. He was furious at my parents, at having a fractured wife, and at his inability to fix me.

Christopher:

With my emotional floodgates now open, all sorts of feelings just started pouring out, including continued anger toward the changes we had experienced in our finances once Cita left the insurance industry. We were now seeing Mariana three to five times a week and sometimes more. Now my wife was in serious need of long-term medical care. Was she going to be admitted to inpatient care? How in the hell were we going to pay for this? I felt myself drowning and overwhelmed.

It was apparent that Christopher needed support as much as WE did. Mariana quickly involved him in our therapy sessions, which at that time were daily, including Saturdays and over the phone. Mariana assured us both that she would work with us regarding payment and would not stop seeing us if and when the time came that we could no longer afford treatment. As for admitting me into a psych ward, Mariana felt that as long as I was able to keep myself safe, we would strive to keep my care on an outpatient basis.

⊰◈◈◈⊱

It was within that same week that Christopher met an alter for the first time. Hope was more than happy to shift out and finally meet our husband.

Hope:

I felt only excitement to finally meet Christopher as myself. Remember, I had interacted with him for years, but always under the pretense of being Cita. Now I got to share my admiration of this man from my own heart. I kept wondering how odd it must feel for him to see his wife's face but hear a different woman talking to him. I don't know how it would have been if our roles had been reversed, but I only hope I could have dealt with the circumstances in the same loving manner he showed.

Christopher:

What I remember most about meeting Hope was her calm and regal manner. Hope held me in such high regard and it gave me a sense of strength and encouragement. With Mariana's and Hope's stability, I felt my fear lessen a bit.

I had always drawn my security through Hope, and this continued as Christopher and Mariana met the rest of my internal family.

If memory serves us correctly, it was the alter Chrissy who came forward next. She desperately wanted to be seen and to finally talk with these two people whom she'd seen from afar for so very long. Christopher's most vivid memories around his first interactions with Chrissy occurred not in Mariana's office, but in the car.

Christopher:

Chrissy first began shifting out while I was driving, specifically when I would go through yellow lights. She would come out to reprimand me with great fervor.

A special bond quickly formed between them that grew stronger each and every day. At night Christopher loved for us to shift Chrissy out, so he could watch her sleep.

Christopher:

I learned that Chrissy always talked in her sleep to some unknown person. Once Cita shifted her out and I could hear her jabbering away. Chrissy will appear to be sound asleep and talking as if she's in the company of friends. She's answering questions, asked by who knows who, and I hear only half the details of some conversation or story she's sharing. Sometimes she makes sense, but other times it's just a child's gibberish play-talk. If I gently touch her arm, she'll continue to sleep, but then she quietly says, "That's my Christopher." If I tickle her, she busts a gut laughing. She won't wake up and I'm warmed by her own special giggle. I feel as close to her then as if I'm sitting right next to her in her internal bedroom. Chrissy has an extraordinary ability to touch my heartstrings, the high pitches and low tones that no one else can play.

But he also had to work extremely hard on his patience:

Christopher:

I was now a first-time father and I had to learn to reach her at her own level. Chrissy's feelings were easily hurt and there were times when I would accidentally squish them. I was learning how to be around a small child. I became aware of how frightened she became when I sounded too harsh or used profanity. At first when this occurred, she'd suddenly shift back to her safe internal home and either Cita or Hope would shift out in her place.

Chrissy:

I remember I wanted him to love me so much and I was afraid he would hate me like cita did and that Mariana would tell me he couldn't be my dad. I didn't want to be told I had to stay inside and not get to come out and be with him. when cita and Hope did let me come out I didn't like how loud the outside was and I would run back internal even though christopher was so nice to me.

Chrissy was so full of youthful energy. She was longing for attention from Christopher and Mariana, but she was still very frightened of the external world. Once, in her sheer excitement of getting to be the one to talk to Mariana in a session, she wet our pants. She was so mortified that she began to cry. From that point on WE began to carry spare clothes with us, just in case, though the nervous wetting did not turn out to be a consistent issue. Thank goodness!

With great patience, Christopher proved his love to her, and a beautiful relationship began to emerge between them. The same was true with the trust that was growing between Chrissy and Mariana.

⋯⊰❁❁⊱⋯

Rim was definitely not eager to speak with either Mariana or Christopher. She disliked Mariana's probing questions during our therapy sessions, and in those early days, Rim didn't offer any details unless Mariana or Christopher asked to speak with her directly. Rim's disconnect and serious attitude intimidated Christopher.

Christopher:

I knew Rim as a woman rough around the edges—a tomboy who lived dangerously. It's taken more time for me to separate Rim from past judgments. Given her life experiences, I feel bad that she is imprisoned in Cita's body. When Cita was younger, Rim ran wild, had sex when she wanted, and partied hard. Rim knows she can't do that now; in a way she is under house arrest.

Rim:

If truth be told, I would really prefer to be left alone and not coerced into writing about shit that is best left unsaid. But as Tristan has stated time and time again, "Take one for the team Rim. Our story isn't complete without your side." So now that I'm done bitching, I'll add my two cents…

It's difficult to write about the transition from "us" being a secret to now coming out as ourselves. I mean, let's think about this a little further. Cita, Hope, and I were the main characters in the life that was Cita. This was true even after she came out about having MPD. I mean, she didn't just all of a sudden stop needing us and start living her life like a normal healthy person. Cita still shifted internally and WE still functioned as Cita that first year. Part of her work in counseling was to rely on us less and less, but it took time.

So with that said, it has been stated frequently enough that I was the sex kitten and party girl of the group. I won't deny that. With that in mind and knowing that I was an active participant as Cita, then it wouldn't be a large leap to assume that yes, I had sex with Christopher as Cita on more than one occasion. That can't be a shock to anyone. I was Cita too. Do you get that? Cita might have been the first to sleep with him, but she still shifted back and forth and there were times when duty called and I stepped up to the plate.

So, tell me, how do you think it was for me to meet Christopher as myself? "Hey, hi dude, you may not know me as Rim, but remember that time we screwed on top of that old washing machine that shook the house like a rocket taking off? Well anyway, yeah that was me, nice to 'officially' meet you."

That's pretty much all I have to say.

⋯◈◈⋯

Whereas Rim was cautious and resistant, Tristan was both excited and petrified to meet Christopher and Mariana. After all, this was his very first time to shift out and be external as well. In addition, Christopher represented his first male contact.

Tristan:

It was really difficult for me at first. Everything was so different on the outside. It was brighter and louder and busy. Mariana had difficulty hearing me because I talked so quietly. Oh, what they wouldn't give for that sweet innocent voice now! I was insecure about how to be in this new wonderful place. I may have been sixteen, but I was naïve in the ways of the world.

Mariana was just about the nicest person I had known, other than Hope. Right now I can hear Rim and SHE laughing in the background over my comment of Mariana being the nicest person. Mariana herself will probably laugh too, but in many ways she really is one of the most wonderful people I know. Mariana gave us a gift of time, love, and life. In this lifetime I couldn't thank her enough. She also worked with me on my self-confidence and self-worth. By talking with her each week, I could share with her all of my frustrations, fear, and pain regarding this new way of living. I shared internal frustrations too, because even though I got to shift out now, I still remained inside the majority of the time. Believe me, one guy and the rest chicks … yeah, I had some issues to talk out with Mariana.

Another relationship Mariana helped me with was with Christopher. I had never talked to another boy, let alone a man. I seemed to get my feelings hurt so often by Christopher, and he wasn't necessarily doing anything wrong. I would wait inside, just hoping he'd ask for me to shift externally and be with him. I waited and waited and some days he didn't even ask about me. I'd be crushed. But he himself was going through a ton of changes in his own life, and he'd spent a lot of years just being oblivious to all that was happening around him. Now he had a wife with MPD and instead of it being the two of them, there were now eight of us. I'd go into session with Mariana and find myself gushing tears of anger and frustration. I was depressed and suicidal—all over learning to have relationships.

Christopher was just in the beginning stages of his own therapy when he began to build relationships with the alters. He needed a lot of coaching on how to relate to people himself. When Tristan became disappointed at not getting the attention he wanted from Christopher, I sat down and talked with Christopher. As loving and giving as my husband is, his focus can often be self-oriented and a bit immature. I'd listen to Christopher say that Tristan did this or didn't do that, or Tristan said this or didn't say that. In the beginning, I constantly had to remind Christopher that he was the adult and Tristan was just sixteen. Yes, Tristan really was wise for his years, but totally inexperienced regarding life itself.

I remember an instance when Tristan was working on a three-dimensional wood puzzle of a goat. It was Christopher's first Christmas knowing all of us, and Tristan wanted to make this for him. When Tristan had his time to be external, he worked determinedly on this goat. Tristan had to sand the pieces, put it together like a puzzle, and then paint it. He had wanted to do this project all by himself, but it became too complex, plus he really needed to use some of Christopher's power tools. However, the Gang and I were not familiar with how to correctly use them.

Even though Tristan wanted to give the goat as a surprise Christmas gift, I still suggested that he ask Christopher for help. My husband is a contractor and has built homes and other wood projects since he was fifteen. I knew they could put this darn goat together. Tristan did finally ask Christopher, who said he would be glad to help him. However, neither one set any actual dates or times to work on it, and Tristan went back to waiting for Christopher to offer assistance. Days passed with Christopher doing his own things. He'd still have loving conversations with Tristan, but neither one actually mentioned the goat project. Tristan took this as a sign of Christopher's lack of caring and soon he began to withdraw.

Tristan's infamous goat.

When I realized that Tristan was spending increasing time back in his internal home, I suggested that he discuss his feelings with Mariana at our next session. I was happy that Tristan agreed to do just that.

Tristan:

I really let myself get totally hurt by Christopher's lack of enthusiasm, not just to work on the goat, but to also be with me. Mariana explained that Christopher was a good man who would sometimes get lost in his own needs. She told me that if I wanted something from him, I needed to ask until I got what I wanted. I pouted and responded that if he really loved me, he'd ask to be with me on his own and he'd remember to help me on my goat task. But instead of stepping up and working through my problems, I just harbored anger toward Christopher, although outwardly I acted like nothing was bothering me.

We laugh about that experience now when we look back on it. Tristan may not have confided with Christopher about his feelings, but he did get back at him for not helping him with his goat. That year for Christmas, Christopher got a box of painted wooden goat parts.

Christopher:

I was shocked and thought, *Oh my God, I didn't help him.* I'm so selfish with my time. Tristan only has me to count on and I totally botched it. This was one of those giant neon signs in the sky for me to pay attention to how my actions match my words, or how they didn't in this case.

Tristan:

I remember when Christopher and I had our first guys' night out together. I got to pick where we ate for dinner and as we waited for our teriyaki to be served, I asked Christopher if he thought there would ever be a time when I was shifted out that he could look at his wife but actually see me. His answer brought tears to my eyes as he responded with, "I already can."

Christopher and the Gang ran the full gamut of emotions while getting to know one another and adjusting to living cohesively internally and externally, but none of them were more challenging for him than SHE.

> **Christopher:**
> I was completely mortified, totally intimidated and frightened by her. When SHE came out during a session, she would toy with me because she perceived me as weak. I quickly determined that it wasn't that she didn't like me in particular, but men in general. It was almost futile to try to talk with her.

This relationship was complicated in part because I was just beginning my own work with SHE. I was still very terrified of her myself and thus couldn't offer Christopher support. During a session, he might share with Mariana how concerned he was over an incident where SHE inflicted self-harm on me by burning my arm. Seconds later, SHE was out telling him to "Fucking mind his own business." When Christopher would try to respond and say that I was his business and that his concern for our welfare was legitimate, SHE would just laugh at him. In every way, SHE was condescending, vengeful, and downright scary.

> **SHE:**
> Yeah, those were the days when everyone kowtowed to me! Seriously though, back then my pleasure came from the discomfort and fear that others experienced, whether I was the cause of it or not. And yes, I was not fond of the male species in general, but it wasn't just Christopher. However, he was the pest in my life at that time. I wasn't about to let some Y-chromosomal dork tell me what to do. I loved to put him in his place and watch him sputter trying to figure out how to protect himself from me!

Christopher continued to feel extremely confused, angry, and frustrated with the self-harm that SHE was inflicting onto my body.

Christopher:
Several times a week I would come home and Cita would either tell me about or I would notice another burn, cut, or a new bruise. I couldn't grasp the amount of control that SHE and Rim had over these injuries, and I'd instead get mad at Cita for not stopping herself.

As time went on and with Mariana's help, he began to better understand these dynamics. But his frustration and fears continued to surface, and they often came out sideways. Sometimes he'd disconnect from me after an injury occurred, blaming me for not stopping SHE. While he never went so far as to give me the silent treatment, a palpable tension always ensued. Christopher and I are pretty touchy and lovey with each other, but when he's frustrated, he doesn't hold my hand and he gets quieter than usual. If one of the Others shifts out, he's warm and friendly with them but not so with me.

Whenever he displayed this distance, I felt even more frightened and again became concerned he would leave me. Fortunately, we were still having daily contact with Mariana and were able to talk through any issues that needed to be addressed. The sessions didn't take away our problems, but they did give us a safe outlet to be heard along with a professional to help us understand each other and ourselves better.

Christopher:
My actions reflected my resistance to believe anything other than we were normal people, even though Mariana would warn me of difficult times ahead.

‑◈‑

No words could ever possibly express my love for Christopher. Even though our path has been riddled with incredible obstacles, we've stayed true to each other and to our special family.

Christopher:
When Cita began revealing her hidden gang to me, I made up my mind that my mission, out of my love for her, was to provide unconditional support. I felt lucky to be included and was amazed at her mind's extraordinary ability to protect and adapt.

Christopher met each of my existing alters—SHE, Rim, Hope, Tristan, and Chrissy—within a week of first learning about my MPD. From that point on, the alters became a part of his daily life too.

The fear of being seen, and feeling like I'm self-destructing.
Drawn shortly before telling Christopher about my MPD.

25

⁓◈◈◈⁓

Adjustments and Support

THAT FIRST YEAR WITH THE alters participating in my life externally was complete and utter mayhem for Christopher, the Gang, family,
friends, and of course me. But there was an enormous sense of relief at
having finally talked about it—in addition to an absolute vulnerability.

All my life Hope, Rim, and I had functioned as one cohesive person.
However, as our sessions progressed, Mariana began to ask me to no
longer use the alters as a means of escaping. Before, if I got scared, the
shifting transition was as natural as breathing, but now I needed to start
facing life on my own. We knew this wasn't going to happen overnight,
but even the thought of having to be in complete control of my life was a
foreign concept to me. Each time I got frightened in session and shifted
internally, Mariana would call my name and ask me to come back out.

This happened not just for me, but for Hope and Rim too. They
were so in tune to my emotions that once they felt my nerves increasing
to a level of concern, they'd shift out and take control of the situation.
It was like having my own internal warning system. However, Mariana
continued to reassure us that the dangers that originally caused my
mind to split were no longer a threat to us. Even so, I began to wonder
if sharing about my MPD was a bad decision.

Not only did I continue to pine for Hope and Rim when I was
frightened, which seemed to be every moment of every day, I also began to resent the alters spending more and more of my time in sessions. I was envious of the loving interactions they were having with
Mariana and Christopher. Increasingly I began to fear that Mariana
and Christopher liked them better than they did me.

At home I found that I spent less and less time with Christopher too. The Others were now acquiring a taste for external living and wanted to be out more often, seeing, doing, and learning. Mariana and Christopher genuinely enjoyed their time with the Gang and strong bonds were developing. I would share my fear of being loved less to Mariana and she might reply that she loved us all the same. To this I would retort that I had been out with her the longest and she should love me more. Mariana would warmly reply that these alters were all a part of me and that she would not and could not say that she loved one over another. This included SHE, which enraged me further. How could Mariana love SHE the same as me? SHE who beat and abused me? SHE, who had always been the devil reincarnate, is now loved the same, is now equal to me? I understand the importance of these boundaries now, but back then my feelings were frequently hurt.

There was another change that I noticed with my husband that added to my squished psyche. He treated the Others differently than he would me. For example, let's say Chrissy was out and playing with her stuffed animals. The tone in his voice was filled with such tenderness and love, but when I shifted out he might be short or terse. I'd demand to know why he wasn't expressing that love and joy in our conversations. I didn't connect the logic that, for one, Chrissy was a six-year-old child and that the relationship they were developing was one of father and daughter. I only knew that I wasn't the one being showered with patience and kindness all the time, but that's the irrationality that comes with jealousy.

Honesty was another battle I had to continue to work on. Mostly I just withheld information and would not share something that needed to be dealt with. I had worked on this for years with Mariana and Christopher, but withholding information was still a form of "control" that I hung on to. However, Rim and I were the honesty exceptions, as the

Others were naturally quite truthful. This caused rifts with SHE and me specifically, because often SHE would share things about my life that I chose not to.

SHE:

Anything I could do to mess with Cita was high on my to-do list. Cita was a compulsive spender and if she bought a new purse, I was quick to bring it up in counseling. If she and Christopher were making plans to go out of town, I was right on her, treating our sessions like some Catholic confessional.

Man, SHE pissed me off. I so viewed it as SHE tattling on me. Mariana was quick to stop SHE if she felt that her disclosures were purely vindictive. These moments of truth occurred with the Others too. If Chrissy was talking, she might mention that I had cried a lot that morning or that Christopher and I had taken them out to eat. Dining out isn't a bad thing, but we didn't have the money to be spending it so frivolously. Mariana would remind me that anything they brought up was worthy of discussion, especially in a counseling session.

Another person whom the alters were building a relationship with was my stepsister Jennifer. She grew up in the Seattle area but moved to Arizona over fourteen years ago. I consider her my best friend, but even so, she did not know about the alters until after I shared with Mariana and Christopher.

Jennifer:

I never would have wished MPD on Cita and I'm amazed every time we're together. She's so brave and I can't imagine what it must be like. The first time I met the Gang, I felt awkward and didn't know how to act. It was like being at a party and not knowing anybody.

During that first visit Chrissy asked to play a board game, so Jennifer, Tristan, Chrissy, and I began playing. My sister cusses, as do several of us. WE have had the benefit of learning to be kid-friendly, but my sister hadn't quite adapted to this way of thinking yet. When my sister's game piece was knocked back or she didn't get the card number she wanted, she'd drop a verbal "F-bomb." Later when I asked Chrissy if she wanted to play another game with us, I was surprised when she told me no.

Chrissy:
Jennifer is mean. It is not fun to play with her when she gets so mad.

It took a couple different visits for Jennifer to practice being a better sport and for Chrissy to learn how to be around her competitive nature. However, WE did make sure there was ample noncensored adult time too.

Another incident involving Jennifer and Chrissy happened while we were eating dinner. As Christopher came to sit down at the table, he accidentally stepped on our dog Dixie's tail. Dixie yelped and cried out in pain, startling Chrissy, who then began to cry herself. In the next instant, Jennifer picked up a green bean from her plate and tossed it at Chrissy. It smacked her right in the face. Jennifer's purpose was to get her to stop crying and it worked. Chrissy was so stunned that she sat frozen with her jaw hanging open. Internally I was encouraging Chrissy to realize that Jennifer was just playing with her, that the flinging of the bean was all in fun. I could hear Chrissy trying to laugh, but it sounded false. It wasn't long, though, before Chrissy was genuinely laughing with all of us.

It is probably quite obvious by now that my sister is not comfortable with children. Jennifer feels helpless when she is around a child who is crying or having a tantrum. She would rather be anywhere than in the same room as a "junior mint." Jennifer and Rim are quite similar in that way, although they have both managed to grow quite fond of our two kids and I'm grateful for that.

Jennifer:

Of all the things to deal with, kids are not on my list of favorites. As a matter of fact, I think I'd rather have a Pap smear than spend an afternoon with kids. Of all the alters, I resented Chrissy the most. I would get to spend so little time with my sister and I didn't want to share my vacation time with a child. For the most part though, Chrissy's turned out pretty cool. It's soothing to spend time together coloring or dying Easter eggs—artsy stuff I wouldn't normally be doing at home.

Tristan and Jennifer, however, hit it off right from the start.

Tristan:

I thought she was a flippin' hoot. We'd work on puzzles for hours, cracking jokes and laughing at each other. She liked to make fun of me, calling me a man-child. She might have been older than I, but I felt like we could relate. It was fun to hang out together. She gave me the nickname of Nilla.

Jennifer:

I've always had more rapport with men, and I think of all the alters I've spent the most time with Tristan. We have the best laughs together! He's incredibly smart and sensitive, but don't tell him I said nice things about him. I don't think his scrawny little body could support a bigger ego.

As for Rim, she was not keen toward Jennifer. Later I realized that she was jealous of the time that Tristan was spending with my sister.

Jennifer:

Rim is the quietest alter and doesn't come out much around me. That's been okay with me as I get more time to be with my sister, but I *am* curious about her. When I think back on some of the fun (as in naughty and illegal) things I did with my sister, I realize it was probably Rim. She came out a lot during my last visit in July of 2012 and I loved getting to know this most elusive alter.

SHE, on the other hand, has a tendency to be assertive and sometimes inappropriate. With that said, SHE is also comfortable with her lesbian sexuality, and her forwardness can take people time to adjust to as well.

SHE:

I wasn't the little social butterfly then. Jennifer was a spoiled brat at times—moody and just another annoyance. It wasn't until her second trip to see us and a year of counseling under my own belt that I was able to appreciate her. We actually play well together now. She has a wicked and demented sense of humor that I quite enjoy.

Jennifer:

It's a fulfilling evening during my visits when SHE and I are eating a healthy dinner of cheese puffs and Cadbury Mini Eggs and picking on Tristan. SHE likes to freak me out with her sexual innuendos and sometimes it works, but I know she's teasing. SHE wants to be all tough, but I know there's a soft spot in there. I love ya, SHE, just not in the way you would really like!

⊰⦂⊱

I didn't talk about having MPD with anyone else for almost another year. People close to me knew something was amiss, but they had no idea of the journey Christopher, the Gang, and I were on and I didn't have the energy or desire at the time to try and help people understand.

For Christopher, respecting my need for some sort of control on who was told and who wasn't was a boundary he struggled with. I would find out during a session that he had spoken with a neighbor or a person he worked with about my MPD and I would get upset.

Christopher:

There was a time I found myself opening up to other people as an attempt to solicit support, get attention, and to receive feedback. This turned out to be a bit clumsy, as I only managed to confuse the hell out of people. Getting support from outsiders is a tricky deal.

When he tried to share with some of his family members, he felt hurt by their lack of support.

Christopher:

I wanted to share details about the courageous work my wife was doing. It was powerful to me and I wanted to talk to people about it. This was such a huge deal and I was at a place where I needed big-time support: money, meals, hanging-out time. There were moments I was freaking out because I was sharing with others and in doing so was freaking them out too. No one knew what to do, and I didn't know how to ask for what I needed.

It's difficult to know how to help someone who is experiencing a trauma of any kind in his or her life. I believe that what made this even more complex was our lack of understanding of what was even happening to us. I was pushing friends and family away and barely able to focus on taking a shower, let alone holding a conversation with someone to tell them how I was doing. On the other hand, Christopher desperately wanted connection and someone to share all these new exciting and confusing experiences with.

For some people, not knowing what to do is a common experience. All WE can say is ask questions. Ask, read, and ask some more. The only way you can learn about MPD and the unique experiences that occur for those with this condition is to ask. Becoming involved is the best way to be supportive and to learn. Don't be afraid to meet the alters, although do keep in mind that our situation could be quite different from that of another person who has been diagnosed with MPD. Remember that you can also help financially with gift cards for groceries, or offer to pay a bill or fill the car with gas. Cook a meal and drop it off. Remember that you don't have to stay if you're not comfortable. Drop a note or even call, but don't be hurt if the phone conversation is short or if the person going through the hardship doesn't respond exactly how you hoped.

And if you are fortunate enough to meet someone who lives with MPD, remember that the alters are their own unique selves and should be respected and treated as such.

Tristan:

I wanted to meet people and I wanted them to know me. I was keenly aware of people who continued to say "she" or "her" after talking with me for a length of time versus those who made attempts at remembering to say "he" or "him." It made me feel more connected to them, as though they could accept me for who I was.

Rim:

I just wanted to add this: I would shake my head when someone would start talking to us who obviously did not care or think about who they were talking to. Like if Chrissy is out drawing and someone starts talking about a person at their workplace that really pissed them off. As if Chrissy needs to hear that. Chrissy will stop the conversation and nicely ask them who it is that they want to talk to. It's a gentle reminder of our situation and keeps people focused on the fact that some considerations need to be made before they address us as a "generic" personality.

We've since made new friends, reunited with old friends, and lost other friends along the way. One interesting discovery is that although we have had people not want to be friends with us because of the MPD, it's really not the norm. And when we've lost friends, more often than not it is because of a conflict of one of our personalities with theirs. Just as with anyone else, it is more of a case of, "Hey, you know what? You're just not my cup of tea; see ya later." It's rarely due to the diagnosis itself.

SHE having a smoke in 2006.

‐◅◈◈▻‐

26

The Loss of an Alter

PRIOR TO COMING OUT ABOUT MPD, my relationship with SHE went something like this: I'd first plead with her to stop whatever form of torture she was inflicting on me. If SHE was particularly pissed off, SHE'd start in on a marathon barrage of vile labels: "Fat bitch, stupid cunt, worthless piece of shit." This bombardment could last for one hour or continue for twenty-four. As a survivor of physical and sexual abuse, I lived in a continual state of "victim mode" and never dared to stop her. On rare occasions Rim might say, "SHE, that's enough, let's blow." Otherwise, Hope had been my only saving grace, but even Hope was unable to stop SHE all of the time. SHE is unique among the alters in that she can block all of us.

SHE is brutal. SHE has used my face, arms, legs, and hands as a carving board; she's smashed a picture frame over my head and broken several bones. As I have mentioned before, SHE has had me self-inflict injuries hundreds of times through the years. I would be so petrified of what would happen to me if I refused her that I did her bidding, regardless of the pain or consequences. I've cut and burned myself, sometimes severely. The resulting fear-fueled adrenaline would fill my body and act as a sedative, so I rarely felt the immense pain these actions caused at the time. These experiences were a form of dissociation too, and it was hours later before I felt the full physical reactions from the injuries. My body tells a tortured story by the scars I bear.

I remember sitting in Mariana's office and steeling myself to talk directly to SHE for the first time. My fear level was off the charts, my heart pounding and ears ringing. I could hardly breathe. Mariana and Hope were speaking softly to encourage me, but their words sounded distorted. Soon my eyes were blurry and the room began to spin. Then I couldn't breathe at all. I remember grabbing at my throat as though I were being strangled; then the room stopped moving and my body began shaking. Soon tears streamed down my face as Mariana informed me that SHE had been out for almost thirteen minutes. SHE had come and gone. I felt vile, like SHE had left some sort of evil residue inside me.

Our work together was slow and agonizing. Often I was so physically stressed from my encounters with SHE that I'd be sick for days afterward. Outside of Mariana's office, I'd remain passive while SHE continued her aggressive behaviors. The fact that Mariana was calling SHE out in our sessions added to her agitation, and for months her rage increased to daily tormenting versus sporadic weekly abuse. Not only was Mariana trying to bring awareness to SHE, but she often told me that SHE just wanted to be loved, like the rest of us. I didn't believe that for a minute.

I wasn't alone in the abuse SHE dished out. Mariana felt the brunt of SHE's verbal attacks too. The difference was that Mariana told SHE that her behavior was not acceptable. Mariana stated that she would not continue to speak with her unless SHE could control herself in a responsible manner.

SHE:

I think that below the surface of my rage and abusive behavior was the same primal desire for survival. I absorbed Cita's rage and expressed it as repetitive destruction, but I was never homicidal toward her. When Mariana presented new ways of acting and being, it inflamed my fury. I was pissed off being told what to do, but I slowly inched my way in a healthier direction.

The following is a journal entry I wrote regarding an actual conversation SHE and I had following one of our counseling sessions. The entry is dated July 6, 2006:

SHE: *What does she mean she won't talk to me?*

Me: *She wants to talk to you. Mariana has questions and wants to hear what you have to say, but you can't threaten her anymore.*

SHE: *Fuck that! I want to fucking smash her face in. She can listen to the sound of my fist in her angelic face!*

Me: *That's exactly how you can't communicate to her, SHE!*

SHE: *Shut the fuck up, Chris. You're marked by the devil, you worthless piece of shit. Mariana's just too afraid to talk to me. No one tells me what to do. Tonight in your sleep you will see your blood spilled and your dog lapping it up.*

At the very end of this journal entry I wrote,

"Well Mariana, at least this time all SHE's anger wasn't directed totally at me."

Regardless of how nasty SHE was being, Mariana continued her endorsement to love SHE. In other words, "kill her with kindness." Mariana certainly didn't want anyone literally killed, but she did want us to prove to SHE that no matter what, SHE was loved unconditionally. That was oftentimes easier said than done!

Mariana:

To be clear, I was not all sweetness and light with SHE. Christine refers frequently to my loving kindness, and although I *was* kind, mostly I was very matter-of-fact and often stern with my message to SHE. The message was that SHE had to stop being abusive and become open to other possibilities in life.

Despite the level of individuation in Christine's alters, I have viewed them as part of one system with Christine as the primary person. Being consistently calm and rational in my message that SHE was not a random manifestation of evil, but a part of Christine who had served an important function and now needed to adapt to the reality of Christine's adult life helped SHE—over some considerable time!—start trusting me and the direction I was pointing her in.

I took seriously her threats to harm me and was adamant that I was not going to tolerate violence directed at me. I made it clear that I would involve the police and end the therapy if SHE didn't control herself. Although Christine acted helpless in the face of SHE's presence, I also refused to accept that Christine was powerless. I challenged her repeatedly to enlist the entire system to exert influence and control over SHE when necessary.

⊰⦿⦿⊱

I had just started building my courage and confidence up to work with SHE when I began to notice some physical changes in Hope. Earlier I mentioned that Hope and I had the ability to hear each other's thoughts. This was a bond that I did not share with the rest of the Gang. You might again ask why this was and again I'd have to say I don't know the answer.

Regardless, I started to notice that during certain moments Hope would not answer me. I knew she wasn't ignoring me, which left me realizing that Hope couldn't hear my thoughts anymore. I didn't say anything right away, as I didn't want to scare anyone, but my stomach knotted up with dread whenever this happened. A few weeks later, Hope's image started to fluctuate in its clarity. I could still see her internal image, but it was like seeing a low-definition version of her. The knot in my stomach turned into an electrical current of fear as these changes could mean only one thing: Hope was starting to fade. ("Fading" is a term the Gang and I use to describe the phenomenon of an alter dying. It is not a universal MPD term, and I doubt WE are the first to use it in relation to integration.) When the significance of these transformations came to light for me, the grief that consumed me was beyond anything I had ever experienced. The thought of Hope leaving me was inconceivable, and I was unable or unwilling to accept or even acknowledge the possibility of losing her.

I continued to keep this information to myself. The Others did not seem to notice any changes and frankly, I truly did not know what to do or say. I felt completely paralyzed. However, I was able to keep myself in silent misery for only a few days when Hope finally approached me.

Hope:

I recall how odd it was to me that Cita was not responding when I'd send her questions telepathically. That was so much a part of our way of communicating that we often went days without speaking to each other in any other way. Cita had been going through so many changes and I thought it was possible that she just needed some privacy to sort through her emotions. It had happened in the past often enough, especially when she was getting ready to make a choice that she knew I wouldn't agree with, but the silence would last only a few hours at a time. At the end of the second day, I told myself that if Cita didn't respond to my mental inquiries by morning, I'd have to find out what was wrong.

When Hope did broach the topic with me, I broke down in tears. Hope took the information stoically, as she did with everything.

Hope:

I've been there for Cita most of her life. We never doubted each other's love or that we'd be there for each other. Now the realization that I was leaving her was unbearable to her. I kept encouraging her to talk to Mariana and Christopher, but her resistance was so strong. I felt it was important for Cita to share this information, so I gave her time.

Instead of feeling relieved by having talked with Hope about it, I felt myself spiraling into a deep depression.

It was close to a week later when I let Mariana and Christopher know that Hope was fading. I was completely baffled at why, of all the alters, Hope was fading at that time in my life. If Hope had originated from desperation at my own mental plight when I was just a baby, then why now, when I still needed her? At the time we had no answers. What I do recall is that once I verbally sputtered out those words, my emotional floodgates opened and for weeks afterward, I was pounded by an angry tornado. Then, as quickly as it had descended upon me, the black funnel of emotions simply evaporated and took with it the thunderous winds that had threatened to destroy all that dared to stand in its path. In return, I shut down and pushed away from feeling anything. I went through months in this numb state, slowly watching and waiting for Hope to fade. But instead of handling this knowledge responsibly by discussing my feelings in counseling with the Others or even with Christopher, I pushed everyone away.

As the months passed, I began to slowly ease back into myself. As my resistance lessened, my feelings began to flicker back on. Suddenly an onslaught of anger came on so swiftly that it took my breath away. I was mad at Hope for leaving me, and I was also pissed at Mariana. I believed that if I had not shared about my MPD in the first place, then Hope would not be fading. But in actuality, we had no way of knowing what truly triggered Hope's integration.

Hope [to Cita]:
I know you're angry with me for leaving you. I hope in time you'll realize that it's okay to feel that way. I'm certain Mariana will agree, if she hasn't already, that it's a normal part of the grieving process. You are not hurting my feelings, baby. You are being human! In fact, as Mariana has stated time and time again, people in healthy relationships get angry at each other. No hostages are taken, no lives are threatened, no physical harm is done, and no blood is shed. Anger happens on a regular basis and not just when someone special is dying.

In all my life I had never allowed myself to be mad at Hope. I think I never wanted to do anything that might make her want to leave me. In fact, I can't ever remember experiencing aggressive thoughts or emotions toward Hope until the last months of her existence. Hope's fading and the anger it triggered was a new experience for me, one I would have gladly done without.

In addition to my pain, the Gang was trying to process theirs as well. They felt their own grief, but they also wondered if this was the start for all of them to fade away. If Hope was fading, then how long did they have? It was just a few days after the Gang learned of Hope's condition that Chrissy started wetting the bed. This wasn't just an internal experience for her; if she was the one shifted out sleeping, then she'd wet the bed WE shared with Christopher too.

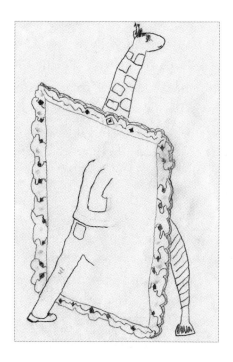

This is one of my favorite of Tristan's drawings. It's clever and fun just like he is.

Chrissy cried frequently and was extremely needy for Hope and her brother Tristan. Hope had been the only real mother figure in Chrissy's life. Chrissy's and my relationship was not a healthy one then, and I'm certain her fear of losing Hope and being left with me did not help matters for her. Rim, who was guarded anyway, became even more withdrawn. If she did speak, her words were snarky and filled with rage. Tristan was even quieter, but I believe he stayed strong for Chrissy. As for SHE, we called an unofficial truce. SHE kept to herself and refrained from being abusive or intrusive.

As for myself, I was not available to support anyone, not even my husband. During these months, Christopher was helpless to be of any comfort to me, and he relied on Mariana for his own emotional support as well.

Christopher:

Having known Hope and the Gang for less than a year, I was unable to realize the impact Hope's integrating would have on Cita. Who can empathize or relate to a person losing an alternate personality? This was all so new to me, but what I could grasp was that Hope was dying and the pain the Gang and Cita were experiencing was real. They needed me. I wanted to be there for them. That was enough for me.

Six months passed from the time when Hope and I told everyone our fears of her fading … six months that we were waiting and wondering when her time would come. In early September, Hope's condition took a turn for the worse. In addition to her image warping further and our inability to communicate, Hope began experiencing physical ailments as well. Each day she grew weaker and weaker. Some moments I had to force myself to look her in the eyes when I was talking to her. Her body became just an outline, really. When she held me, there was a fleeting moment that I could detect her touch. I'd sense a slight flutter or sensation across my skin, but it didn't last. There was no radiant warmth or Hope's lingering scent. At times, my glance even passed over her—I did not even realize she was there. And where I had once sensed her presence with me at all times, I could no longer feel the caress of her spirit.

Shortly before her passing, Hope had a private conversation with Christopher.

Christopher:

Hope sat me down for an hour or so on her deathbed, so to speak. She held herself with elegance and grace, but she was clearly incapacitated. I don't remember her exact words, but her message was powerfully inspiring. She encouraged me to stay on course, to love Cita, to trust the bond Cita and I had, and stay strong.

We didn't know how much longer we had with Hope. Days, weeks? I was trying to keep my grief in perspective, but my pain was utterly overwhelming at times. Sometimes it felt at any moment as though I'd be consumed by my agony, never to return.

I think there must be some sort of hideous monster that ascends from the depths of our suffering in these times. It is at that point when we can no longer remember anything in our life that brings us joy; our only point of reference is our grief. There is no recollection of my husband's embrace, or the way his blue eyes shine like the sky when he laughs. There are no thoughts of the way our pets so often make us laugh or how their ears feel like rich velvet to the touch. Images of my favorite holiday or shopping with my sister are miles away. The dearest support groups or closest sponsor have somehow become unfamiliar. The call of ocean waves are drowned out but for the one and only demand in my mind—my grief.

It is then that we are willing to turn away from everyone and everything and walk hand-in-hand with that monster. However, even at the most painful of times, the monster has never been able to walk with me forever. The pain eventually subsides. Like an ebbing tide, the throbbing slowly eases and where my mind was once beyond my grasp, I again begin to sense the reality of my surroundings and return. It is the coming back that I have to continue to do, no matter how petrified, tired, and sad I am.

⊰⊱

Even in her incapacitated state, Hope often felt my profound hopelessness and constantly encouraged me to keep on going. One particular night she sensed a particularly deep despair inside of me and feared that I might take my life. Hope thought of the Others and then felt a flash of anger.

Hope:
I remember almost shouting at Cita, "You can and WILL go on without me—don't you dare give up now!"

When I shared this incident with Mariana, she asked if I had wanted to die. To my surprise, I hesitated only for a moment, then replied, "No." I left that session feeling stronger than I had in months. Now I had a passion to give Hope's life meaning to other people. I needed to share her with the world. From this, I began to write, and from these writings I was able to create this book.

I drew strength from my writing and encouraged the Others, Christopher, and Hope to write too.

Hope [to Cita]:
Right now I'm at a point where I can hardly recognize myself. I'm a mere shadow. It takes all of your energy to allow me to write. I've pushed us hard to get these words down. I fear that if I don't do this right now, time will pass, and I will no longer have the strength to even write.

Soon I'll no longer be beside you, as I have all these years. I have never been for want, Cita. I hope you know that, other than a brief time of jealousy over Mariana, which you and I have discussed and can laugh at now. I feel that my life has been full of love and purpose.

You are such a treasure and truly the most incredible individual I have ever known. I'll continue to pray that you will soon see the love that surrounds you every day and learn to let it in. I'm so sorry that I will be one of those people who leaves you. If I had a choice, I would stay for always, but this is your time now. It might not feel like it, but you are ready to take care of yourself. You're able to take care of the Others and they are able to help too.

Oh Cita, this is so hard. Promise me you won't give up. Before I fade and can no longer hear you, I need to ask one thing from you. I need to hear you promise me you won't give up. Give that to me, and I can go with a full heart, knowing you are in good hands. I love you, sweetheart, with all that I am.

These words continue to fill me with Hope's love to this day.

Just prior to Hope fading, my husband and I made a special dinner in her honor. Christopher prepared all the makings of teriyaki kabobs, which turned out fabulous. We all took turns assembling them, even SHE. We had our choice of cherry tomatoes, mushrooms, chicken, bell peppers, and freshly sliced pineapple. Hope would visit for short durations, rest, then come and visit some more, but it was clear to me how fast she was fading.

Christopher:
Hope's going-away party was very moving. In addition to the joy we all experienced in honoring Hope, it was the first time I remember that we all, including SHE, participated in a family evening together.

That dinner was on a Saturday evening. By Monday I wasn't certain if she would be with us through the night. The past week had been exhausting. I had been taking Imitrex once or twice a month for an occasional migraine and was now taking it one, two, even three times a day. I didn't want to sleep for fear I'd wake up and Hope would be gone.

I could feel her life force slipping away from me, and there wasn't one thing I could do to change that fact. I wished so desperately to feel her loving hands embrace me one more time, but it wasn't to be.

⋯⊰⊱⋯

On Tuesday, September 25, 2007, I was standing next to Hope when I closed my eyes. I had a vision of her as I'd always known her. I looked in her eyes, promising that I would not give up on my life. When I opened them, there was a brief moment where her true image stayed. Then it shimmered away, leaving a sickly remnant. I sat down next to her and listened to her sporadic breathing. I tried to hold her hand, but I felt nothing between my fingers.

Late that afternoon I felt a small tickling sensation and looked up at Hope. She was smiling at me. For a brief moment I felt her inside me, just like I always had. Then I could see and feel her no more. Hope had faded. I called her name. No answer. I cried her name louder, still no answer. I screamed it even louder, crumpling to the ground. Still no answer. Rim, Tristan, Chrissy, and SHE all gathered around me. Rim, Tristan, and Chrissy all clung together in grief. It wasn't as if WE hadn't known this was going to happen, but the absolute nothingness that now filled the air was more than WE could bear.

Christopher:

The day that Hope passed was unforgettable. The impact on Cita and its finality was immense. This was a death in the family and it was real. There was so much grief, and everybody struggled so mightily to fill the void. So much fear hung in the air about who was next and where this was going. Clearly a matriarch had just vanished.

Five years later, Hope is immortalized in our daily lives. We have mementos and colorful artwork by Chrissy that are displayed around the house. Much of her art shows Hope represented as a bird, and we have inspirational knickknacks with the word "Hope" on it. As a small child, I didn't know my grandmother well, but I heard stories about her and felt that I knew her from the heartfelt sharing I experienced through my family. It's the same with Hope. Cita and the Gang paint beautiful memories of her, and she is not forgotten.

Chrissy drew this after having a dream. The sun was huge and golden.
Hope was a beautiful multicolored bird, and she had Mariana and I tucked safely away
in her wing. Christopher is the bear and he too was looking protectively toward us.
Chrissy always laughs at drawing Christopher's cute bear bum.

27

Picking Up the Pieces

I STILL FEEL THE LOSS of Hope each and every day, but now I understand that losing her was necessary. It forced me to take charge of my own life. I needed to learn to step through my fears and walk on my own. After all, the dangers I experienced as a child are not my reality now. If Hope had continued to exist within me, it would have been in her nature to assist, as it was her very purpose for existence—to care for and nurture me. I now know that she would have hindered my healing and growth process. That being said, losing her was still the most painful experience of my life.

I was in bad shape after Hope's passing. I had little patience and felt angry all the time. Whenever Mariana or my husband told me how proud they were of me, I just wanted to tell them, "SHUT UP! I'm not doing well—can't you see that?" I felt like a failure. All these years in counseling and here I was, nowhere close to handling Hope's death like a mature adult. The Others seemed to draw strength from one another, but I could find no solace.

Christopher once told me he wished I had a better support group or a close friend I could talk to about Hope, other than himself or Mariana. I know he meant well, but all that ran through my mind was, "I had a close friend and her name was Hope!"

I was inconsolable. Each time I thought of her, I'd get an intense cramp across the left side of my tummy and waves of nausea ran through me. I kept telling myself, "This cannot be real."

Each morning I woke up feeling lost and scattered. I would drive to Mariana's office and just sit in my car for hours. I could no longer bear to be at home. I needed to be near Mariana, where I felt safe and loved. The Others tried to be patient, but they felt restless and were eager to continue shifting out and living in the external world.

Tristan:
WE felt like hostages. Up until Hope's passing, we'd been free to explore living in this fantastic world. Each of us received time to be out reading, watching TV, coloring, playing outside, and even learning to drive. I missed my conversations with Christopher. Each day I felt Cita's pain. It was like a poison seeping through all of us. Don't get me wrong, I don't mean that to be insensitive, because I cried many tears for the loss of Hope, but Cita was in such a deep depression that it impacted us all.

Two weeks after losing Hope, I wrote a journal entry about an incident between my husband and me.

As I stepped from the shower, he came to me and gently wrapped his arms around me. He cautiously pressed his hands against my bare back, smiling as I flinched at their coolness against my skin. He slipped the towel I held from my grasp and did one final once-over, ensuring I hadn't left any areas of dampness on myself, then kissed me goodbye. It was time for him to leave for work. He embraced me once more and gently said, "Yes, Babe, I have my lunch, wallet, phone, and water."

It's my ritual morning chant to him, although yesterday I hadn't gone through it and lo and behold, he had left his phone at home. We said we loved each other and he headed out the door.

What he didn't know was just before my shower, I had eaten two 3-Musketeers candy bars. Nor would he have known that as soon as he had walked out the front door, I raced to put some clothes on so that I could wave goodbye to him on the front porch. But I don't believe he saw me. More so, he couldn't possibly know that I sat down on our porch bench and burst into tears. He was gone and I was there without him. I knew that this day was going to bring more pain and more shame. My promise to Hope reverberated in my head—"Don't give up!"

⌇

Any effort toward taking care of myself now seemed to be lost along with Hope. I was acting out by eating junk food, spending money, and smoking again. I feared that my body would give out from this self-destructive behavior, but I still did nothing to change my circumstances. My thoughts were filled with questions: Does Hope still feel me? Can Hope possibly know the pain I feel without her in my life? I used Hope's loss as an excuse to not face my fears and live. I told myself over and over again that this is what happens from speaking the truth, and soon all of the Others would leave me too.

Whenever the Gang or Christopher asked Mariana for guidance, she advised them to continue to give me time. Mariana did not want to see me avoid life by shifting internally and letting the Others function for me, but she also felt that I needed to go through the grieving process.

The first month went by in a blur. I don't recall even brushing my teeth or bathing, although I know that I did it with the help of the Others. I never made a lunch for my husband or listened to how he was doing when he told me. Rim or Tristan shifted out to do the laundry. Meals were put together slapdash, unless Christopher did the cooking himself.

Well into the second month, I finally felt a slight turn in the storm clouds surrounding me. I was able to start giving and receiving loving embraces from my husband. I relaxed my hold over the Others and they began spending more time out and about. We shared mealtimes together and started playing games and watching movies again.

December was now upon us, and this would be Tristan's and Chrissy's first Christmas with us. Chrissy had experienced the holidays from afar, but now she was beside herself with enthusiasm. Every decoration was revered and displayed with newfound joy by Chrissy. Individual stockings were hung, and Chrissy even wrote her first letter to Santa.

Chrissy's exuberant drawing for Christopher during her first Christmas out.

Tristan is much older than Chrissy, but he was equally enthusiastic and hypnotized by the holiday spirit. Rim was still moody and SHE continued to behave, but even SHE was touched upon receiving her first Christmas gift, although SHE would never have admitted it then. In fact, SHE opened her gift during the night when we were all sleeping. Then SHE rewrapped the box and it appeared that it hadn't even been touched. It wasn't until we lifted up the box that we noticed it was empty. We never asked her about it—we just smiled and let it be.

SHE:

I'd never received a gift in my life. The whole thing about people caring about one another and being nice and thoughtful just wasn't my style. I think I felt embarrassed about having a gift under the tree for the first time ever, let alone being expected to open it up in front of everyone. All the "oooohs" and "aaahhhhs" and "Gee thanks—it's everything I ever wanted" made me want to vomit.

⋯❖⋯

As the New Year dawned, I was still living one day at a time, but I was starting to feel the love for Hope more than the grief of losing her. With my healing in progress, we were able to focus more on issues arising with the Others during counseling sessions. Tristan and Chrissy shared feelings of hurt toward Christopher, who allowed the TV to hinder his ability to communicate with them. Christopher agreed to limit the amount of time he watched it. The changes were immediately positive and after a few days, Christopher found that he rarely missed it.

The aggression in Rim's and Tristan's sexual encounters was addressed too. Mariana confronted Rim about it, and soon it stopped. For Tristan, though, this caused even more problems.

Tristan:

Rim then ignored me like the plague. I know it was her way of trying to keep herself under control, but it was really hard to go from all of that attention and immense emotions that come from a sexual relationship to nothing. I felt I was getting screwed either way, so to speak.

Tristan and Rim continued to discuss their feelings in session. It was a big step for Rim and possibly the first time that Rim shared truthfully about her emotions. It wasn't long before they came to a sort of comfortable companionship and learned to enjoy each other without sex.

Each of the alters spent time with Mariana. Those first eight months were crazy for all of us. Chrissy wanted to be out talking with Mariana at every session, but with five of us and Christopher, all having issues to address, it wasn't always possible and Chrissy had to learn to share. Tristan had his challenges with Mariana too. At times Tristan is very wise and mature for his years, and yet he can be very naïve to the ways of external living. Mariana sometimes scolded him when he was goofing off and told him to act his age. Tristan would be hurt and he'd sulk off to his internal room, slamming his door shut. When I told Mariana this, she would state that it was a good sign that Tristan was expressing being angry.

Just before the New Year, Mariana also suggested that it might be time for SHE and I to continue the work we were doing on our relationship just before Hope became sick. That sat with me like a gulp of sour milk, but even with the curdling sensation spreading through my stomach, Mariana would not be ignored. Only through the pain and over the obstacles would I find the pieces of my shattered world coming together.

28

—◆◆◆—

You Can Teach an Old Dog New Tricks

My journal entry dated January 8, 2008:

> *I don't want to work with SHE. It won't work for me. I will die Mariana! SHE will eat me up and spit me out. I already feel myself shrinking with each passing day as SHE gets stronger. I don't believe I can coexist with her as an active participant in my life. I don't have the desire or the strength. I don't think I'm going to survive this.*

I bucked and moaned, cringed and cried all through my work with SHE. Any steps I made during counseling prior seemed to vanish overnight. Having to face SHE without Hope felt like my undoing. But still, SHE and I did make progress.

SHE:
Cita did indeed buck and moan while I just bitched and threatened. At one session I shared about a dream I had where I shape-shifted into a wolf and attacked Mariana while she was leaving work. I believe I tore out her neck in one vicious bite. Subtle little comments like that.

One suggestion Mariana had for SHE was to write down her thoughts and feelings. It just so happened that the gift we had given her at Christmas was a journal. However, SHE didn't race to put pen on paper. Eventually SHE did write in it, but only after asking Mariana if

SHE could keep the journal at her office. SHE did not trust us; more specifically, SHE wanted no chance that we might stumble upon it and read her private thoughts. Mariana said that at some point allowing at least me into her thoughts would be the better route, but until SHE was ready for that step, Mariana was more than happy to let SHE leave her journal at her office.

In time, SHE was not only writing but also sharing her journal entries with Mariana. In an entry dated January 7, 2008, SHE had drawn a picture of herself in the form of a wolf smashing through a window. Above the window she had written, "Integration is a Myth." In another entry, she drew the back end of a horse taking a dump on a crucified figure. That figure is supposed to be me. Beneath the picture she wrote, "Dear Father who art in heaven, forgive us our sins Motherfucker." It continues like that for the first part of her journal.

We also found that SHE began participating more and more during family gatherings. (When I say "family," I'm referring to Christopher and the Gang, not outside relatives.) SHE was still short-tempered, foul, and abusive on occasion, but her anger was rapidly decreasing. SHE was finally finding herself in a place of beginning to care, and that pissed her off even more. In addition, Mariana made it almost impossible for SHE to continue hurting me by opening her heart to her. Mariana encouraged her writing and asked that SHE call her at any point when she felt she was going to hurt me. Much to my surprise, SHE did call Mariana at least three times to inform her of an injury that SHE had inflicted, something WE don't recall her ever doing beforehand.

SHE:

I agree with Cita, but I only remember calling Mariana once. It was the time I carved the letters "333" onto your shoulder with a knife.

Yes, that one I recall too. WE had come home from another emotion-ally intense counseling session with a deep desire to sleep. Three hours later, I woke up and I stepped into the shower. I instantly felt a stinging sensation on my upper left shoulder. When I looked down, I saw the numbers "333" gouged into my skin. I yelled, "Oh my God!" These numbers were a take-off of the evil 666, but I was only half-evil, appar-ently. When I called Mariana, she let me know that SHE had already called her about this.

Throughout this tumultuous time, Rim had remained close to SHE and was a big support to her as SHE found a new way of being. SHE could vent up a storm to Rim, who never felt threatened, and she could tell SHE straight up on how things were. SHE could even tell Rim to fuck off and Rim would reply in the same way. It was a win-win for SHE and it helped to keep her rage away from the rest of us.

⋯⋯

I was really amazed at the transformation from SHE the adversary to SHE the protector. This entry from her journal, dated April 6, 2008, shows her concern toward me. Her caring about me in any way still felt foreign to us both:

> *This is fucking retarded!!!!!!!! Is anybody out there fucking paying attention? Jesus Christ, do you all need a bloody map? Hmmmm, Christina weighs over 300 lbs, she's spending mon-ey again, eating like crap, and withholding—Hello—anybody home?—BIG PROBLEMO people…*

Previously WE shared that SHE had been tattling on me in sessions, telling Christopher and Mariana when I withheld pertinent informa-tion from them. At some point, SHE's intention around this changed and even though SHE still brought incidences to their attention, her actions became more helpful versus hurtful. I still got infuriated when SHE'd start to say something in session, but it didn't take long for me to stop her in mid-sentence by saying, "Enough, I can talk about this myself!" I was finally being pushed into integrity. It was an incredibly important step as half-truths in session certainly weren't aiding my healing process.

In time I began to notice sides of SHE I never knew, although to be honest, I'm not certain SHE had been aware of them either. The Others greeted her with open arms and forgave so very easily. SHE has a great sense of humor and is actually full of fun. SHE is honest, assertive, and much to my surprise, quite dependable. I was not as quick to shower her with warmth, but we created a mutual tolerance.

Christopher too created a friendship with her in which he felt admiration toward her. Their process was amazing to watch unfold. SHE might respond to Christopher in her short, curt way and he'd reply, "Tone SHE, watch your tone." This would make her laugh and SHE even thanked him for his feedback. One time Christopher was driving us to an appointment and SHE once again tested his patience. SHE asked Christopher to pull over prior to arriving to the facility (which is located on a nonsmoking campus) so that she could have a cigarette. SHE, Rim, and I were all smokers then, but I rarely smoked in the car when Christopher was in it and SHE knew that. Once they were curbside, SHE grabbed her lighter, the unlit cigarette already between her lips. Then SHE patiently waited. There was a long silence as the two of them sat looking at each other, until finally SHE exclaimed, "Are you gonna get out of the car so I can have my smoke?" We all just cracked up. SHE was smoking whether he liked it or not and SHE wasn't going to be the one to stand outside. It took a few situations like those for SHE to adjust to the concept of being courteous.

I have one particularly fond memory of the time that Tristan asked me if I had seen Chrissy. He had looked throughout their internal home and could not locate her.

Tristan:

As Cita said, I'd looked all over our internal home for Chrissy and was unable to find her. Keep in mind that WE don't have a lot of places WE can hide. As alters, if one of us just disappears from sight, it's a little unnerving. It had been less than a year since Hope's passing and I was filled with dread at the thought that Chrissy might have faded. I couldn't find her anywhere! I had looked under beds and in the closet, but there was no sign of her.

Rim and Tristan continued to search for her. A few moments later they both came to me with looks of shock and it was then that I felt a tremor of fear. "What? What is it? Is Chrissy okay?" I gasped. Rim walked over to me and said, "You are not going to believe this!" Apparently, when Tristan left, he noticed that SHE's bedroom door was open a crack. (SHE has always kept her door completely closed.) In anguish Tristan said, "Rim, you don't think Chrissy went in there?" (As if by going into SHE's room, one might not ever return.) Rim, having visited there many times before, strolled down the hall and then quietly peeked in. SHE was sound asleep, and curled up at the end of the bed was a napping Chrissy. When they shared this with me, I was filled with wonder. SHE has never been someone I would have run to for security and yet Chrissy so trustingly sought SHE out. It touched me beyond words.

Tristan:

I think that Mariana's continued coaching about SHE wanting to be loved like everyone else might have fallen on partially deaf ears for Cita. With their past history, who can blame her? However, Chrissy wanted and needed to feel safe. I think Chrissy began to believe that SHE was just an angry person, but still a very lovable one. With Cita unable to provide Chrissy with a sense of security, Chrissy went to where the strength was, and at the time, she found it with SHE. Believe me, I was as floored as anyone.

–◦◦◦–

Not all of SHE's choices during this transitional phase were wise ones. Once WE were shopping at Target. I was still suffering anxiety outside our home, so SHE offered to shift out and be the one shopping. Unfortunately, the store was in the middle of some sort of inventory check and people with little scanner machines were lined up and down all the aisles. Because of the chaos and obstacles, SHE left our cart at the end of an aisle and just walked down to get the item that WE needed. This was a great idea, but SHE soon discovered that our cart was not where SHE'd left it. Instead, the same employee was continuing to do inventory on the end displays, and our cart had been moved to another aisle.

After the third occurrence of our cart being moved, SHE's patience evaporated. She strolled up to one employee and casually stated, "If you touch my cart again, I'm going to shove it up your ass." With that, SHE grabbed our cart and WE headed on our way. SHE was lucky that the startled girl didn't report her and WE weren't banned from the store.

Progress was being made, but SHE's social skills were still lacking a bit. Obviously it was not a perfect process.

29

❦

A Friend Reunited

In addition to the work SHE and I were doing, I was also reunited with a dear friend. Sandy had been my supervisor when WE worked at the weight-loss center. She had encouraged me to pursue getting on short-term disability compensation when my emotions began impacting my job performance; however, Sandy was unaware of my MPD. After I left the company Sandy called frequently to see how I was doing. I rarely answered the phone, nor did I often return her calls. Sandy was not deterred by my lack of reciprocation, however, and she never let more than a few weeks go by without checking in with me. Finally, the December after losing Hope, Sandy left a message for me that went something like, "How can you ignore me when it's Christmas!!!!"

Her ploy of using my favorite holiday as a tool to get me to call her worked. From that point on, I tried to meet Sandy for lunch and if my anxiety was high, she would come to the house. She came for dinners and got to know Christopher better. The Others stayed inside and allowed me time to be with Sandy.

I knew at some point I needed to share about the MPD with her. It didn't seem fair to allow the two of us to build a friendship on a premise that was less than honest, but I needed more time. One evening, Christopher and I invited her over for dinner with the express purpose of sharing about my MPD. I chickened out. Over dinner, Sandy could tell I was anxious about something and told me that when I was more comfortable, she'd be there to listen. I replied that I was afraid that she would never return once I shared my secret, but she said that would not happen. It was later that same week when we were on a drive together that I finally told her. Sandy didn't say much at first. She stayed relatively quiet, but I could tell she was trying to grasp the situation. She asked great questions, though, and didn't go screaming off into the sunset.

For the most part throughout this book, I've been referred to as "Cita." In Sandy's reflections below, she calls me "Christine."

Sandy:

I think I took it well, at least outwardly. I was kind of freaking out inside, but I certainly didn't want her to see that. I asked a lot of questions, although I don't remember a lot about the actual conversation. I was too busy trying not to let her see that this was really freaking me out!

The hour-long drive was beautiful, and Christopher was excited to show us all the work he had been doing on a custom 10,000-square-foot house.

Sandy:

When we arrived at the house, Christopher greeted us and took us on a tour. When we got to the library, Christine ran in and started jumping up and down and twirling around. Christopher laughed and commented that this was "her" favorite room. It was another awkward moment for me. When we left, Christine told me that Chrissy, the six-year-old, wanted to meet me really bad. I asked if it was Chrissy whom I had seen in the library and Christine confirmed that it had been. Then Chrissy came out and said hello. She told me about what she remembered of Christine and me working together. She liked that I had written "Missy Chrissy" on the schedule. However, I was unaware of Chrissy at the time—it was just a nickname I called Christine. Chrissy wasn't out for long. I think I also met Tristan and Rim briefly that same day.

⊰⟨⟩⊱

Afterward, I was so nervous and uncertain about whether or not I'd see Sandy again. Another part of me was very grateful for her presence and her seeming reassurance that she was not going to abandon me. What I interpreted as going smoothly, though, was not what was happening behind the scenes for Sandy.

Sandy:
I had a hard time sleeping that night. I'm a prayerful, faithful Christian, so I prayed for Christine a lot that night. I prayed for the Lord to show me how to handle all of this new information about my dear friend. I was scared and I needed direction. When I finally did fall asleep, I had a dream that the Lord was in a classroom at the dry-erase board being my teacher. I was the student sitting at a desk as He was writing my lesson on the board. He wrote:

<u>C</u>hrissy
<u>H</u>ope
<u>R</u>im
<u>I</u> (as in "I, self, Christine")
<u>S</u>HE
<u>T</u>ristan

He was able to show me that even though she was fragmented, it was still Christine and that He was there for her in all of the fragments. I wasn't to be afraid; I was there to love them all.

When I got up the next morning I wasn't afraid, but I was still unsure of what to expect, kind of like walking out of the sunshine into a dark room and not knowing the furniture layout. What am I possibly going to run into next? I know it was just before Easter, because I went out and bought Easter candy for both Tristan and Chrissy. [Q was not part of the Gang then.] Chrissy loves chocolate but really didn't want to bite the heads off the little chocolate lambs I bought. I think she even named them. From that point on, we all became closer and closer. Chrissy brought out all of her toys and stuffed animals. I felt very trusted and loved. It was easy to see that this really was a six-year-old in a grown-up body. What a trip!

Chrissy:

I thought Sandy was so funny. She was always bringing us things. Like fun little pens and paper. She always made time to talk with me and even play games. Sandy was my first external friend and I really really love her.

SHE:

I remembered her from work, though I was never out in her presence then. At that time in my life, I just wanted to be left alone.

Sandy was patient and kind. She'd bring little gifts for Chrissy, work on puzzles with Tristan, and went out of her way to love us all. It might have taken her a bit longer to love SHE, but that was still during the time when SHE was just beginning to learn to play well with others.

Sandy:

I still hadn't met SHE, but I had heard plenty of stories. It was okay with me if I didn't get to know her. I do remember exactly when I met her for the first time. Tristan and I were going into a video store to get *Finding Nemo* for Chrissy and me to watch, and Tristan said something about SHE being mean or scary. Without any warning SHE came out spurting profanities at

Tristan. I know my eyes got big and I'm surprised Tristan didn't wet his pants. I asked if it was SHE, although I was pretty sure it was, since I knew and liked everyone else. SHE wasn't very nice, but SHE did tell me who she was and then SHE was gone. I started to laugh, but Tristan was careful about what he said the rest of the night.

⊰◈◈⊱

Sandy came to visit often and would take us out occasionally when I felt up to it. On each visit, she got to know more about each alter.

Sandy:

Rim seems to keep to herself a little more than Chrissy, Tristan, or Q. I enjoy Rim's sense of humor and personality. Rim seems to be more of a tomboy type who likes to watch football and talks a little tougher than Christine. Rim can also confuse me because she sounds like Christine a lot. One day I was coming over for a barbecue and asked Christopher if he wanted me to pick anything up. He thought a beer would be nice and some ice cream for dessert. Christine had been sitting with us talking, so I thought it was she who asked me to bring back a wine cooler. I bought something that I thought she would like, but when I brought it out to her, she looked confused and thanked me for the thought but said she couldn't have alcohol because of the meds she was on. Rim came out laughing and told me I was too easy to mess with. It was a good laugh and now I pay closer attention to their sarcastic ways.

Rim:

I remember Sandy quite well, as WE all worked together with her under the guise of Cita. I liked her well enough; she was a great supervisor, but I wasn't in the right mindset to feel like bonding with anyone at that time. I liked to come out and flip her shit now and then, but that really was it.

Sandy:

I have a different relationship with each of the personalities. I love each of them in a different way, kind of like how you love your children, equally but different. I felt like I was watching a one-man band. Christine must be exhausted all the time being the one body with so many performers! I was exhausted just visiting.

It didn't take Sandy long to adapt to our unique lifestyle and I'm so grateful for her friendship. WE all are.

Sandy:

Now it's all very different for me. I can recognize each of them quickly and easily and it has become a very relaxing relationship. Chrissy and Tristan always come out to see me when I'm there. Rim and SHE visit with me most of the time, but not every time. They all know that I love them for who they are and I know they love me for who I am. When I leave, they usually all come out individually to say goodbye and give me a hug. It's very much like visiting a good-sized family. Christine and Christopher just don't have to pay for all of the clothes and college educations, although Tristan and Q want to go to college. They are both incredibly talented. Tristan is a great storyteller and writer and Q creates beautiful jewelry. Like any teenager, neither of them is completely content. They have hopes and dreams, and thankfully they have a wonderful (although different) family life.

⤛⟨◈⟩⤜

30

The Alter Q

IN THE MIDST OF REUNITING with my friend Sandy and working on my relationship with SHE, Tristan mentioned feeling a new presence within our internal home. I checked with the Others, but he was the only one sensing a new Alter.

> **Tristan:**
>
> I didn't experience the sensation frequently, but it was enough to cause me concern. Sometimes the presence felt angry and it scared me a bit; other times it was neither friendly nor mean. I have always been very perceptive to the emotional vibrations of the Others. For example, if SHE was extremely pissed about something, I would always feel her negative energy before she ever came out for a confrontation. Maybe it's a third eye or a sixth sense. All I do know is that the energy I felt was not from any of us who currently resided within our internal home.

In previous counseling sessions, Mariana had discussed with us the possibility of other alters emerging, an idea I adamantly rejected. It became clear, however, that one or more new alters were stirring inside of me. Sometimes Mariana would see a change on my face. She'd be looking at me, but who was staring back was not me or any of the Others. A few times this presence pierced her with intense, angry stares, and then it quickly disappeared. Other times the stare was softer, more quizzical. When the softer alter was shifted out, it would look around the room or out of the window, but then it quickly shifted back inside. Inside to where? WE are not certain. This calmer personality never spoke when it was out. It wasn't animated, nor did it appear at all aggressive in nature.

⟿⟨⟨⟩⟩⟾

These minor incidents continued into the months following Hope's passing and through the following January. It was very difficult for me, because when this alter shifted out, I "lost time," meaning that I did not know that he or she had been out or how much time had passed. The Gang was aware when the new alter was shifted out, but they found themselves unable to communicate with it and were confused on how to reach this new personality.

As the shifting with this entity became more frequent, my stress rose. I did not want another personality. I did not like this sensation of losing time, and I felt unable to control the situation. Mariana tried to reassure us all and advised that WE not resist. Whoever was trying to surface was going to come whether WE wanted them to or not. Fighting it was not helping anyone. I tried to be patient, but each time I lost time, I felt my resentment toward this new alter building.

Similarly, each alter experienced trepidation. Not knowing if this new one was going to be nice or mean added stress to us all. However, its arrival brought mixed feelings.

Chrissy:
I wanted a younger sister to play with on the inside and to color with and watch movies with me externally.

Rim:
I couldn't care less. As long as it left me alone, I would be fine.

Tristan:

I tried to stay open-minded and have a come-what-may attitude. I felt WE needed to make the best of the situation. I don't
recall wanting or hoping that this new alter would be male or
young or old, just that she or he would be friendly and fit in
well with all of us.

SHE:

I would be lying if I didn't say I thought it would be nice if it
was a cute babe who happened to be lesbian too. Yeah, that
would have worked well for me. As for being afraid, nah; it was
just another person I had to try and play nicely with.

One day while WE were grocery shopping with Christopher, I headed down the dairy aisle to get a carton of two-percent milk. The next
moment an alarmed Christopher was gripping my arm and looking
at me with deep concern. I had no idea that the unfamiliar alter had
presented itself right then and there in the dairy aisle.

Christopher:

I just remember standing by the cheese display and suddenly this strange look came over my wife's face. Clearly a new
personality had shifted out. It was so startled to be out in the
external world that it literally fell over. As I reached to catch
my wife's body, it had this look of stunned amazement.

Within seconds the unknown alter had shifted back in and I was out
again, my bum chilling on some pepper jack cheese.

It was a few days afterward on February 4, 2008, when Q arrived on the scene to stay. This occurred while WE sat in the reception area of Mariana's office. We don't know why Q opted to shift out externally right then and there. We've asked her, but she doesn't know either. It is possible that Mariana's office is such a safe place that I felt more secure there, which therefore made it easier for Q to come out and explore.

What I do remember about that incident was that one moment I was there and the next I found myself sitting in our therapist's office with only fifteen minutes left in our session. I felt disoriented and confused. I could recall nothing. Mariana shared that she had entered the reception room to collect me for our session and all she saw was my purse sitting on the floor. Mariana glanced in the bathrooms, all the while thinking it was odd that I would have abandoned my purse, but I was nowhere to be found. Her concern rising, it dawned on her that this new alter might have shifted out and left the building.

Sure enough, Mariana found us walking up the office driveway, not far from a public road. After she calmly called my name several times, the new alter turned to look at her. Mariana could tell from her facial expressions that this was not me, but someone new. Then she coaxed the new alter back inside and into her office.

SHE:

During this particular instance, the other alters and I knew that something was up. WE were calling out to Cita, but she wasn't answering. In addition, when WE looked out of Cita's eyes, WE were unable to see externally like WE normally can. I'm the strongest at blocking and undoing blocks, but I couldn't bust a move on what WE all guessed was the new alter. After swiftly surveying our internal home, I was quick to deduce that this new alter was not residing in our internal home. Where were they? WE did not know…

Tristan:

WE downplayed the situation so as not to upset Chrissy. WE just said that Cita wanted some alone time with Mariana and that WE were all being blocked to allow her privacy. Inside though, my rather nonchalant attitude toward this unknown alter became more alarmed as I pondered what changes were in store for us.

This alter was unable to verbally communicate, although we are not certain why that was. Because she was so quiet, Mariana began to call her the Quiet One. Tristan shortened her name to just Q, like the character "007" in the James Bond movies.

For months Q was unable to get words from her brain out through my mouth. That changed over time, but even so, she still speaks with a slight impediment. In the following from Q, I have tried not to change her writing unless I felt her meaning was unclear; then you'll see my corrections in brackets. Also, when she was first talking about herself, Q would refer to herself as "Q" versus using the words "I" or "me."

Q:

Q remember standing in Mariana room [lobby]. No one else there. I want see what outside Q never been before. It felt nice have new kind air touching skin. I hear birds sing songs, dog bark, and different noises I not know what is. I walk to side building and see pond. I touch water and feel first time wet. I look at windows and people talking to other people. I walk back to front and go up driveway. I see cars driving street, fast and loud. Don't know how long out when hear woman talking me. It Mariana, but I not know her then. I can't remember what she say, but know she trying get Q back inside. First she scare me, but remember see her when shift out other times. She take me to her room and Q sit down. Q don't feel right in Cita's body, like body know I should not be there and won't work right for me. Hard lift arms and not know how mouth works. Mariana ask me name, tell me her name, ask many questions. I know words, [but] not able speak. Mariana ask Q to go back in and let Cita out. Mariana say Q come back different time. I go. I not hear Cita and Cita not hear me.

When I first heard that Q had actually roamed to the back of Mariana's building, I was mortified. Other therapists work in this building whose offices have a view of the back pond. This meant that they saw my outward body, not realizing it was Q, staring into their offices while they were having confidential conversations with their clients. Mariana only laughed, but we made sure that it didn't happen again.

Many of the sessions afterward were spent with Q as our primary focus. Mariana teased me that I would do anything to get out of having to focus on my own relationship with SHE, even to the extent of having a new alter appear. We can't confirm or deny the possible truth of that, but it was indeed food for thought. Mariana worked hard to learn more about Q, but with her inability to speak, they could only get so far. What we did discover was that Q was female. Age was difficult, and our initial guesstimate was nine or ten years old.

I still resented this new alter. Even though I now knew a bit more about her, I was angry that I couldn't control my brain. I told Mariana that I was trying to be patient and kind, but in reality I wanted to know why I was splitting again. What had caused another alter to surface now? Was I going to get new alters every year like someone else might get new shoes? I felt panicked and incapacitated, and I was still mourning Hope.

After further examination and thought, Mariana and I came to the conclusion that Q already existed for as far back as my preteen years, maybe even further. She had just not surfaced or completely fractured off because there had been no need to—until now. But the stress of los-

ing Hope and then my establishing a healthier relationship with SHE
was enough trauma to force Q to emerge completely.

⤛⬧⤜

The brunt of communicating with Q landed on Christopher and Mariana, as they were the only ones who could actually hear her. Christopher suggested we create symbols for her to draw or gestures for her to
do with her hands—our version of sign language. He in particular was
really challenged by her.

> **Christopher:**
> I'd come home from a long day at work and there would be my
> wife, the Gang, and our newest Q, all eager to spend time with
> me. I knew Q's isolation from the Others made her especially
> lonely and desperate to connect with someone. Often I was
> unable to understand what she was trying to say to me, and I'd
> get frustrated. Nonetheless, Q was relentless in her attempts
> to reach me.

Soon tension was growing between Christopher and Q. She began to
retreat more from him, and she tried to communicate in Mariana's office instead. Mariana worked hard at helping Q try to gain verbal skills.

> **Q:**
> Mariana ask Q practice make sound. Since all by self, had lots
> time practice noises. Q practice all time; still words from head
> don't come out mouth. Christopher and I try hard commu-
> nicate. Sometime he want me slow down. I go too fast, but I
> want say so much. I think both frustrated. Think [I] taught
> Christopher more patience and me too.

The Gang and I brainstormed ways that WE could help Q to come up with a solution. She would make hand movements and write down the symbols she'd learned, then shift back in. Christopher would show the rest of us what she had done. Together we would all try to crack Q's codes. This added a deeper sense of unity, and it triggered more creative thoughts to help Christopher decipher what Q was trying to say. The process also allowed all of us to get to know Q better.

During one particular counseling session, I shifted back out to find my eyes wet with tears and my nose stuffed up from crying. I asked Mariana what had happened and if Q was okay. Mariana shared with me that Q had made an arm gesture of holding an infant. Q wanted to know if she could have a baby. Since I had already had a hysterectomy, the odds were not in Q's favor! She later shared how painful it was for her to know that she would never have a baby of her own. It was during moments like these, however, that we realized our original guess at Q's age had fallen short; she was at least in her late teens, if not older.

Chrissy:
I was sad that she was not my age. I wuld love a friend the same age as me. I was happy she liked workbooks that helped you learn to spell and write. I did those to and we would take turns shifting back and forth doing them. I also was sad that she didnt get to live with us in our internal home. I dont no where she was but I had wanted her to live in Hopes old room becaus she would be right across the hall from me.

Just when Mariana, Christopher, the Gang, and I discussed that we might want to start learning official sign language versus reinventing the wheel, Q began to make verbal sounds that soon became recognizable words. We still have no idea why she was unable to speak early on. It shows that there is so much about our mind and MPD that we just don't know and that is still beyond our full comprehension.

Christopher's initial drawing of Q (with bigger breasts than she was comfortable with).

It was especially difficult for Q to be isolated. As we've mentioned before, she does not live with the Others. From what she describes, she lives in a tunnel of some sort. It's long and white. The walls give a little if you push on them. You couldn't bend them in two, but they do have some sort of flexibility. At one time when we were replacing our kitchen floor, Christopher had painter's plastic draped from the ceiling to the floor to keep the dust out of the other rooms. After it was first hung and Q shifted out, she looked rather stunned and told Christopher that this was how it was where she internally lived—like looking through thick plastic. Q sleeps on the ground, has no bed, and doesn't even have shoes. Christopher once tried to draw a picture of Q based strictly from her answers to questions he asked her. His picture shows her complete with bare feet. Q found much humor at the breasts that Christopher had drawn for her, as they were much larger than she felt they should be!

As she began to shift out more and more, it became harder for her to be back inside. She started to experience boredom for the first time. Prior to her external arrival, she never realized that an entire world existed outside of the one she had known internally. At first she wasn't familiar with the emotions that we experience each and every day. But her time out in the real world enabled her to experience joy, to have her feelings hurt, and to know the desire of wanting more.

One day Christopher came home from work with two balloons, a pink one for Chrissy and a green one for Q, who had said that she loved that color. When Christopher gave Q the balloon, she began to cry. She expressed feeling so happy that someone would think warm thoughts about her even when she wasn't with them.

Now that Q was spending increasing time with Christopher and the Others, it was not surprising that I began to feel left out again. Not only from my own time with him, but with time getting to know Q herself, who paradoxically was living, breathing, laughing, and crying inside of me while I was unable to see, hear, or talk to her. Everything I heard about Q's new experiences was all secondhand from Mariana or Christopher.

But as I began to know her better, any reservations or agitation I had about having yet another personality gradually dissipated. Instead, I longed to know Q more. When she cried for the first time, Christopher was there to share it. When she'd make a funny face over something she did not like the taste of, he saw it. He and Mariana got to be with her for everything.

⋆⟐⋆

Q has surprised us all with her wonderful sense of humor. She is very literal, too. When we are playing a board game, someone might apologize for knocking an opponent back to the start of the game, and Q asks, "Why apologize for that?" After all, if people are voluntarily playing a game, the object of the game is to get from A to B, and it's in the rules that if you land on the same square as another player, they have to return to home. So why apologize? Rules are important to Q. They provide guidelines for her to follow, which help her to understand what she can and cannot do. What she doesn't agree with, she'll ask about.

One day she asked Christopher why some people laugh when someone farts. (Q calls them "belly bubbles.") Christopher tried to explain common etiquette, but that didn't satisfy her. She then asked him, "Who are 'they' that make these rules? Everyone get belly bubble, why problem?" Q also finds it odd that some people act so sensitive around the topic of sex. With humor we reply, "Because 'they' say so." She'll laugh and exclaim that someday she wants to meet 'they' and tell them what she thinks about their silly rules.

When it comes to learning, she is anxious and often impatient. There's a whole world of knowledge out there, and she soaks it in like a sponge. Tristan started calling her "QY" because she asks questions all of the time. For Christmas one year we got her some books that just answer random questions: Why do beavers build dams? Why do thimbles have holes? Why does orange juice taste awful after brushing your teeth? She has three entire books filled with these "imponderables."

Another way she has learned is by watching what I do. Q can see out through my eyes, just as the Others can. At first, she would watch me unload the dishwasher to see where our dishes went. We made sure she knew where the fire extinguishers and the first-aid kit were stored. When I'd knit, she would watch me create a few rows, then shift out and do some knitting herself. Then I'd shift back out and check her work. When she saw me give her a thumbs-up, she knew she could come back out and knit some more. If she saw me point at her work, Q would watch the corrections I made so she'd see what she did wrong.

One time, Q was helping me bake a cake. I pointed to the directions on the box, and she measured the water and oil and put them in the bowl. It was her first time cracking eggs.

Q:

I try first one and much shell fall in. Cita come out help clean shell out. Then I shift and try again. I did one good. [The third] egg slip from finger and land in cake mix. Cita shift out and no way tell her whole egg under batter. Cita start beating and see whole egg bobbing. I laughing inside and she laughing outside.

In time, Q began to shift out consistently when we'd say her name or even if we were laughing at something in particular. We thought she was starting to hear us and in a way she was, but it was not quite in the way we had hoped. Q told us that she could hear sounds, but only as vibrations when we were talking or making noise. She even started to recognize individual words by the particular vibrations they made, including the one for her own name. If we laughed, she recognized that vibration too. Other words, activities, and sayings made specific vibrations that helped us communicate with her.

One day I was sorting out a closet when WE discovered a large box full of beads and beading supplies. Early in my marriage, I had had a major surgery and a friend had given me all these beads. She thought it might be a relaxing activity while I recuperated. Unfortunately, I found it to be tedious, irritating, and far from relaxing, so the beads ended up tucked away in the back of the closet.

Q was enthralled and asked if she could use them. Of course I said yes. Whereas Q is impatient when it comes to wanting more and more knowledge, she is almost reverently patient when it comes to beading. Her first project was a "light catcher" that she made as a surprise for me. Q used fishing line and sewed tiny beads on the front and back of a plastic circle. She attached a small metal fishing lure, which allows the sun catcher to spin in the wind, although we hang it in our dining room window rather than outside. It still gets plenty of sun and all the glass beads sparkle like magical gems. With that one craft project, Q got hooked on beading and has become the "Queen Beader." She has a natural ability to envision a piece of work or jewelry and brings it beautifully to life with beads.

Prior to her speaking, she took a liking to watching baseball with Christopher. They are both big Seattle Mariner fans. Rim had always been our sports gal, but as long as she got to keep watching football, she was willing to share baseball with Q. It was a great bonding experience for Q and Christopher, who is a wonderful teacher of the game, and Q quickly learned all of the players' names.

This was all happening in the spring of 2008. I was still uncomfortable being out in public, not just because of the MPD, but because of my own anxiety disorder. So we did not take Q to any games that season. Christopher, however, contacted Mariner's Care, a charitable foundation that is affiliated with our local Major League Baseball team, the Seattle Mariners. They sent an Ichiro Mariner cap to Q for free! She was ecstatic. When we finally took her to a game, it was a priceless experience for us all. It was not only Q's first time to the stadium, but Chrissy's and Tristan's too!

Q in 2009 with her creations at Salon Retro.

※◈◈◈※

Q was my first personality to split while I was an adult. Many dark days and painful nights passed with us not knowing who this new person was. Would she be more like Chrissy, would it be another male, or would she be mean to the Others or me? So many fears had raced through all of our minds. In the end, we were all blessed with a genuine, endearing, and very special young woman.

Q:

Every day excited for new thing happen. It not easy have share Cita body to be out. Would be better all out as WE are, but I think Q, I mean me, very lucky and special [to] live even little bit.

31

⋘⟡⟡⟡

Adapting

IT IS COMMON FOR A primary or main personality to dominate throughout the life of someone with multiple personalities. In some situations,
the main personality might even switch out between different alters.
As for us, I was born Christine Louise and it was under this title that
WE were identified by others in the external world.

However, for as far back as my memory takes me, I have never
experienced being just me for an entire day without the support of
alters in one way or another. In my youth, Hope would actually have
been the main alternate personality, with the role shared between Rim
and me. But with Mariana's gentle guidance, I was encouraged to start
taking more control of my own life.

WE were all still working through our grief of losing Hope and
adapting to the new alter Q while generally trying to create a lifestyle
that allowed all of us to have our own personal time in the outside
world. One constant challenge was equalizing the time that each alter
spent shifted out while still allowing Christopher and me time to ourselves. After several group discussions and counseling sessions, WE
agreed to put together a daily schedule and give that a try. It looked
something like this:

SHE	9–10 AM
Cita	10–12 PM
Chrissy	12–1 PM
Lunch	1–2 PM
Q	2–3 PM

| Tristan | 3–4 PM |
| Rim | 4-5 PM |

The first day of our schedule was far from organized and efficient. The night prior, SHE had been up until 2:30 in the morning, so SHE opted to take her time later in the day so she could sleep. Chrissy was eager for her time so she swapped with SHE. I fell asleep during my time and WE let my body rest for three hours. Shortly afterward, my sister called and we talked for twenty minutes. Q beaded for her hour, but then Christopher called and asked if WE could pick up a prescription for him. While WE were out, WE grocery shopped. Well, it was SHE who shopped as I ended up having a panic attack right next to the seafood counter, leaving my cart in the aisle as I staggered back to our car. Once home, WE had less than thirty minutes until our phone session with Mariana. Christopher arrived home from work an hour later.

I'm certain you understand how ineffective this schedule was for us. Following it was just too exhausting, and it actually caused my anxiety to soar even higher and was obviously not realistic for our needs.

What did work was all of us simply working harder at being conscious of one another. When I was out, I would usually be writing. I'd set a timer and make sure that I stopped after an hour and let Chrissy draw and color. Once she was done with her picture, she'd ask if someone else wanted to be out. SHE might surf the Internet, or Rim would read. WE often worked on jigsaw puzzles and several of us might work on that together, rotating back and forth in putting together the pieces.

SHE:
It's funny, I had pretty much lived internally for most of my existence, give or take moments of wreaking havoc on Cita. But once I started doing more things externally, it became harder to just stay in our internal home. WE all got the fever of being external, with the exception of Cita and Rim.

Rim:

Yeah, well take away the sex and booze and it just wasn't that big of a deal to me. I'd get out and breathe. I love reading, so I'd enjoy a book here and there, work on bills, and watch a game, but I wasn't pushing to be out daily. I could take it or leave it.

Another person WE needed to include in our newfound consciousness of one another was Christopher. WE would allow him some time to walk in the front door and get settled for the evening before WE bombarded him with our wants and needs. Then Christopher, Q, and Tristan would focus on cooking dinner. (I'd try, but I've always been domestically challenged. Christopher actually enjoys cooking and wants to make the meals.) Once we sat down to eat, anyone could come out and say hello and visit with him. We'd shift back and forth, each of us adding our own two cents worth.

Christopher:

It was literally like sitting down to eat with a family of seven. There may have been just two physical bodies present, but I was talking with a group of people. It was exhausting at first, keeping track of who was coming and going, but it didn't take long for it to be the norm. Now I love dinner time! That first year, I learned a lot about each of the alters just from our supper conversations.

WE continued to allot Q with additional time with Christopher because of her isolation from the rest of us, but there were just so many hours in a day. Often one or more of us felt left out. Heck, that happens even now, but for the most part we were learning to balance our unique family life quite well.

Chrissy:

I really wanted to be with Christopher. I loved to cuddle with him and listen to him read to me and even if he sometimes fall asleep right in the middle of the story. That little rascal.

It was snuggling close in bed that Christopher and I claimed as our own private time. After settling everyone down, we would hold each other, talk, laugh, and cry, secure in our love for one another.

In January of 2008, just four months after Hope faded, WE experienced another unusual phenomenon. Tristan, who usually awakens later than the rest of us, woke up one morning feeling awfully sick. He was experiencing sweats and chills, head congestion, and fatigue. What made this odd was that none of us were experiencing these symptoms except for Tristan. In the past when I have been ill, the alters may or may not have been sick too. It's common that when an alter shifts out externally, they experience the physical health that my body is undergoing at the time, but when they stay internal, they might not at all, or the effects lessen in severity. This was the first time that an alter was sick and not me, excluding the time when Hope was fading.

When I took my temperature, my numbers were normal. When Tristan shifted out, he was running a temperature in excess of 102 degrees. Uncertain as to how to help him, I made a doctor's appointment for the very next day. But I had not talked to this doctor regarding our MPD. Not certain how to handle it, I just had Tristan be "Christine" and he stayed shifted out for the appointment. WE left with an antibiotic prescription in hand and an over-the-counter decongestant recommendation.

When WE got home, I immediately took the initial two-pill dose. I took another that afternoon and a third before bed. The next day, the routine was the same, but Tristan was not improving. At a session with Mariana, she asked if Tristan was taking the pills or if I was. Duh! Of course, I had been, so at the next dose WE had Tristan take the antibiotic. He started feeling stronger the very next day and once he was the one taking the medication, he recovered within the week.

Shortly after this incident, we talked with a friend who said she had heard of something similar in an article she read. I do not know who the author was or what she had read, but a man with MPD had an alter with diabetes, while he himself did not. So odd and yet amazing!

⤜⧫⤛

As a family, we worked hard at adapting to a life with MPD. Every day we experienced growing pains, be it normal daily problems that other families may have or our own individual MPD-specific issues. Regardless, we stayed committed to each other and to our special family.

Tristan, the boy on the left, with his trademark grin in 2006.

32

❧

Lou

REMEMBER WHEN Q FIRST BEGAN to appear and Tristan had sensed two different personalities? One was quizzical and calm, which later turned out to be the alter Q. However, the second presence was far more aggressive in nature. By August, that alter began to appear more regularly and it quickly eliminated any sense of stability we had created.

It was early August 2008 when I began losing short periods of time again, like I had experienced with Q. When I returned from these episodes, I felt disoriented and scared. If these instances occurred when Christopher and Mariana were present, they were quick to reassure me and share what this new alter did or said.

Right from the start, this alter rubbed me the wrong way. When Mariana asked this new personality what its name was, it replied "Chris." My reaction was intense and selfish—I would not share my name. *I* was Chris, and she couldn't have my name, period. Mariana suggested to the new alter that it pick a different name, but it refused. I realized that I was not being very considerate toward this new person, but I had no empathy toward it. I felt determined to hold on to some piece of my own existence. The Gang frequently called me Cita, but Chris is my true name. And I shared the same name as my husband. My mom had also thought my name sounded like that of a fashion designer when she named me at birth: Christine Louise Fashions! My name was mine, and mine alone.

Rim suggested that we call the new alter "Lou." It is still personal, as it is part of my middle name, but it's not nearly so invasive to me. It took only a few more sessions before this alter agreed to the new name.

"It's just a name, what does it matter?" was Lou's final comment on the subject.

⋯⊰◈◈⊱⋯

Lou's story began when I was a small child, although WE never knew of her until she appeared that August of 2008. As difficult as her emergence was for me, Lou was equally frustrated. She blamed me for instigating her arrival, and in a way, that was true. WE had been doing years of intensive therapy and at some point I stripped away the layer of my life that held Lou beneath it. Had I known what WE were in store for, I might have just left that layer alone.

Lou was in an utter state of hopelessness, with absolutely no desire to be living. It was soon apparent that she was obsessed with dying and had no concern about taking the Others and me with her.

Christopher:
I had a belief that in time, Lou would begin to soften and change for the better. I hoped Lou would learn to be more civil, but my optimism was quickly dashed after only a few encounters with her.

Tristan:
My attitude was less optimistic. I was filled with dread at the fragility of Cita's life—our lives.

Lou's behavior literally threatened our lives. She became acutely aware of where knives, scissors, or anything sharp was located. Lou never came out and said, "Hey, I'm going to stab us with the large screwdriver that's lying on the floor of the truck." Instead, she spoke in cryptic sayings that caused Mariana or Christopher to guess at what threat she was implying. For example, Lou would say, "Chris (Cita) is going to join me now and we're going to go to Route 66." After Christopher checked in with me, we discovered a small Swiss army knife in a purse I had in the closet. "Route 66" referred to the printed design on the material the purse was made from.

Another example might be Lou saying, "My grandfather was in the army. He was in the Swiss army." Our grandfathers were never actually in the Swiss army, but collectively we would hunt for another Swiss army knife and find it—an old one of Christopher's located in a junk drawer.

All scissors, kitchen knives, metal nail files, and the BB gun were moved out of the house and stored in the garage, and only Christopher and SHE had access to enter. From that point on, each time Lou mentioned "Joining the army," they knew that she had seen or knew of a sharp object somewhere, and we needed to locate it and get rid of it as quickly as possible.

In addition to her fixation with sharp weapons, Lou had the ability to mimic our voices. She was eerily accurate at imitating Tristan's and Chrissy's.

Christopher:
One night I was at the computer and Chrissy was next to me coloring when she looked over and asked me for a pair of scissors. As I headed to the garage to get them, SHE hollered to me that we didn't need them. When I came back inside, SHE told me that it had been Lou asking for them, not Chrissy.

Chrissy:
One time at marianas Lou talked sounding like me and told mariana she was going to go potty. Mariana is tricky and new it was lou and not me and told lou that she would go with her to the potty. Lou got so mad cause she just wanted to hurt us and I am glad mariana got her.

What would have happened if Lou had gotten us to the restroom? We can only speculate. There are glass framed prints and a mirror hanging in there, and these items could have been smashed or used to kill ourselves. Since the front door isn't monitored, Lou could have walked us out into the busy street. I'm just grateful that we didn't have to find out what would have occurred.

⊰⊹⊱

Another issue that raised the stakes for all of us was the occurrence of uncontrolled shifts between Lou and me. If I was speaking with Mariana, it was literally less than a minute before Lou shifted out and interrupted my conversation. A minute later I would reappear, and back and forth we'd go. We were unable to stop shifting and it crippled my ability to do anything.

A simple conversation with my husband would turn into a series of one-minute spasmodic intervals. If I was holding his hand when Lou shifted out, she would yank free of his clutch and glare at him. When I came back out, we'd rush to finish our conversation and then moments later, Lou would be back. This went on nonstop, twenty-four hours a day, seven days a week.

We found relief only when I shifted to the Gang's internal home and stayed there. Mentally Lou and I were still entwined, and I started experienced waves of her emotions pouring through me. It was like standing on the edge of a bottomless pit and knowing that in the next breath, you'd jump. No joy existed, only anguish. Her only purpose was to end her and our lives. But the longer she was around all of us, the more rage, despair, and agony she experienced at her very existence. In addition, when I was internal, I began to sporadically hear Lou telepathically and she the same with me. None of the other alters were impacted by Lou to the same extreme way I was.

Because of my inability to stop shifting with Lou, as well as her unhealthy and dangerous state of mind, Christopher, Mariana, the

Gang, and I made a drastic decision. We bravely decided I would stay internal and allow the other alters to function for me full-time. I would shift out only for brief moments with Christopher and Mariana. This was not meant as a permanent solution but a temporary reprieve until we could have time to see where this experience was taking us.

The relationship between Lou and me was not only emotionally draining, but it took its toll on me physically as well. Only days after submitting to staying internal, I experienced a physical fatigue that rendered me internally bed-bound. I lay wrapped in Hope's blankets, imagining that I was in her warm embrace, but the solace lasted mere moments. I was a prisoner inside my own mind.

I guess you could say that in some ways, I always have been.

⸻◈◈⸻

I may have been trapped internally, but SHE, Rim, Tristan, Q, and Chrissy were able to function in our internal home and could continue shifting out just like before.

SHE:

It was frickin' chaos. Cita may have been limited as to what she was capable of prior to Lou's arrival, but she *had* been our center. Funny coming from me, but it was true. There was manic discord among the Others, but I pushed them to do what was needed to be done to support Christopher. I think it made a difference having something other than Lou and Cita to focus on. The Gang assigned themselves to specific chores to help alleviate the demands on Christopher. Chrissy emptied the recycle bins. I made sure that Christopher's lunches were ready, as well as grocery shopped and got us to and from appointments. Q helped with dinner planning and preparation while

Tristan took on the laundry. Rim, who has always been quick with numbers, continued working on our bills and finances.

Rim:

Christopher and Cita had a very poor accounting system. For Christopher it was a don't-ask-and-we-won't-tell system. This worked well for Cita, as her style of budgeting was anything but black and white. For instance, she once wrote "groceries from Albertson's" in the checking ledger when the expenditure was actually for a $150 leather purse! If they wanted to eat out for dinner, they went. There was never a check or balance. If a bill was due, it would be set aside until additional funds came forth. We experienced years of financial hardship because of their irresponsibility with money.

Shortly after my confinement with Lou began, SHE started journaling again. SHE tracked any progress, setbacks, and comic relief. One of these entries related to a morning that Tristan was getting us dressed.

SHE:

I was still half asleep, but I could hear Tristan and our fashion-conscious Chrissy in a heated conversation. Chrissy was crying out in dismay, "Well, WE can't not wear a bra, Tristan!" Tristan responded, "I suppose both bras are in the laundry? Guys aren't supposed to worry about putting bras on, just how to take them off!"

With my exposure to the outside world limited and my emotional state unstable at best, I would often be inconsolable. If an alter was not shifted out to manage my body, they would sit with me in Hope's room. Often Tristan would tell a story, which he is incredibly talented at, or Chrissy would snuggle next to me as I rested. Other times we'd play the alphabet game. Someone would select a topic, like animals or food. Starting with the letter "A," we'd take turns naming animals or food that began with that letter: apples, apricots, antelope, apes. We'd continue through the entire alphabet or until I fell asleep.

In the meantime, Rim or SHE kept me informed on the comings and goings of my life, including phone calls or emails that WE received. They'd let me know what was happening for them, share concerns, and try to keep me up-to-date.

⋯⟡⋯

But the extreme peril continued with Lou, and it soon was apparent that we needed to implement some sort of surveillance over her. So the Gang and Christopher began the "Lou Watch" security program.

Tristan:

The three oldest took on shifts to monitor our safety. Rim had the day shift, Christopher the evenings, and SHE the night-time. Since Lou frequently spoke in Chrissy's and my voice, I was not included in the Lou Watch schedule.

SHE:

We never doubted the seriousness of Lou's threats. However, our Lou Watch wasn't foolproof. It was three weeks into what we refer to as "Lou Time" when I woke up one morning around 1:30. WE were standing in the rain, barefoot and in our pajamas, at the backyard gate. Tristan was out and fumbling with the gate latch. I asked him what was up and he replied, in a Lou version of Tristan, "I'm trying to find my route." This again pertained to the knife in Cita's previously confiscated Route 66 purse. I quickly shifted out and herded us back inside. In the process, I saw a pair of short-handled garden scissors resting in a flowerbox and quickly tossed them over the fence. I woke up Christopher and told him what had occurred. From that moment on, the house was deadbolted and the keys were rigged with bells to alert us if someone was using them.

After each such incident, we all gained additional wisdom and aware- ness, which helped prevent future mishaps. But still we could never let our guard down, even for a moment.

33

-◦◦◦-

Secrets Revealed

WHILE I WAS IN THIS state of captivity, I began to regress. I started having negative thoughts and beliefs about myself that I had already worked through with Mariana years prior, which had Christopher constantly trying to keep me focused in reality. If I said to him, "Maybe I truly am evil and that's why this is happening," he'd gently reply, "Come on, honey. I love you. You know that you're not an evil person. That's just nonsense talk."

Other times I became so engulfed in Lou's emotions that my despair stretched beyond comprehension. When this happened, Mariana's tone would turn stern. "Cita, this is just Lou's emotions moving through you. You need to stay focused on what is real. These feelings are from long ago." In spite of her and Christopher's encouragement, staying present and forcing myself to distinguish my own emotions versus Lou's became harder as the days limped on.

To add to our tension, Lou hated the moments when I was out with Mariana or Christopher. She didn't like bright lights or noise, and compared to internal living, the outside world was intense and loud. Lou also did not like being touched. If Christopher was holding me, he learned to let go before Lou arrived.

Christopher:
To maintain a sense of calm, I learned quickly to make sure the lights were down, the TV or radio off, and phones muted prior to having my time with Cita. Even the Gang would quiet down internally to help lessen Lou's agitation.

I had to work on my empathy toward Lou, too. At first I was filled with anger. Screw her for trying to take out my wife, but with Mariana's help I was able to keep Lou in perspective. Lou was a fractured part of my wife's mind; Lou *was* actually a part of my wife. That doesn't mean that Lou didn't still piss me off, but I was able to learn to care about her needs too.

Rim:

During a particularly harsh session spent Lou-bashing and bitching about how much WE wanted her gone, Mariana said to us, "Sometimes the hardest people to love are the ones that need loving the most."

SHE:

Hey, I think Mariana spouted that crap to Cita when WE first started doing work together. Pretty certain I told them both that it sounded like a bunch of crap then too.

⚜

Because of the irritation it caused for Lou to be out when we were shifting, I started speaking to Christopher less and less. Some days I would talk with him a mere twenty minutes. And that was twenty minutes of shifting back and forth; my actual talk time would have been only ten minutes. Believe me, that did not help lift my spirits.

Christopher:

Cita was my center. She made everything better. I missed her smile and the support she provided me on a daily basis. Cita had always made me laugh, but she rarely laughed now. Each day I felt terror at the possibility of losing her. There was just so much about this situation that we had no answers for. I had to tell Cita and myself to be brave, and together we'd get through this.

⸙

More changes occurred after the fourth week with Lou. During a session, Lou spoke in a voice that we did not recognize. It was the sound of a young girl, but not Chrissy. Mariana began to refer to this child as young Lou or Little Lou. Sometimes this youthful voice would say, "I don't want to swim." Or she'd say that she was afraid to be in the pool by herself. Initially we were unclear on what she was referring to, but Little Lou used these sayings repetitively like a mantra whenever she was stressed or afraid. It was Rim who finally put it together.

Rim:

I guess that WE would have been six or seven. Our parents had bought us a good-sized kiddie pool. It was maybe three feet high and approximately six feet in diameter with an aqua blue inset. It was set up in our side yard below the dining room window. I can't remember the fun times (although you gotta think WE had them), but I do remember this one particularly shitty moment. WE were playing in the pool alone, but Mom had the window open above so she could look down and keep an eye on us while ironing. One of the rules WE had been told while playing in the pool was not to hang onto its sides, because its frame was made with thin metal sheeting that could easily collapse. In spite of this, I vaguely remember leaning against the side and hooking my arms around the top. That way I was able to float on my back and kick my legs. That's all I remember … until I saw Cita standing in the middle of the collapsed pool hollering as water flooded out of it.

What Big Lou shared mirrored Rim's memory, except that Lou filled in the missing pieces. Lou remembered us using the side of the pool to help us float on our back, but that shortly after WE started kicking, she heard a loud sound of crushing metal and then water gushing out onto the lawn. My mother, I'm certain, had been so startled by the sound of the pool breaking and us screaming that she was convinced that I must be near death. None of us remember anything further until Dad came home from work and reprimanded me verbally about how irresponsible I had been. WE can't summon any memory of further punishment, which is fine by me. However, what WE can gather from this incident is that Lou had been with us since the first or second grade.

With Mariana's guidance, Lou realized that if she shared more of our memories, maybe she would integrate and no longer have to exist. It was a relief to have her focus on something other than killing us. However, as Big Lou and Little Lou continued sharing, Rim and I began to experience more agitation. At one point, young Lou started talking about a childhood friend whom Rim and I knew. Immediately I tried blocking Lou and asked SHE to shift me back out, declaring to Mariana that our session was over even though WE still had over thirty minutes left. No one knew what memories the Lous were delving into, but as they spoke, Rim and I both experienced subconscious warning alarms, and I frequently told them to SHUT UP!

In one session, Lou began talking about an experience related to this same friend. Lou stated that the friend's bedroom had holes in the ceiling. Then Lou would talk in riddles, saying, "He'd stick it out" or "I don't want to play anymore." With increasing agitation, Lou would fall back to her mantra of joining the army or going on Route 66.

Throughout all of this, Lou and I continued shifting back and forth. With each piece of information shared, memories started to re-form.

I never had any "Aha" moments like, "Oh my God, I was raped and never knew it!" But the high walls I'd built around those traumatic experiences were slowly crumbling as I started recalling what both Lous were describing.

They revealed memories of terror and abuse by a sick and demented man who was the stepfather of our neighborhood girlfriend. The graphic details that unraveled during those weeks in counseling were filled with incest, torture, sodomy, and rape. What began as two seven-year-old girls having to touch and fondle each other by knife-point while my friend's stepfather masturbated over the top of us progressed to our forced participation in witnessing the rape of our friend.

These memories were especially difficult for Rim as we learned how much guilt and responsibility she carried about these rapes. My own body was very typical of an adolescent. I did not have overly developed breasts or extra curves. I was cute, but really, I was only seven! Even so, when this man began coming for us, Rim turned herself into the pursuer. In her mind, she refused to be a victim and acted on his advances instead of cowering from them. As he approached us, Rim stepped forward to meet him. She pressed our naked body against his, all the while trying to convince herself that if she pursued him and kept in control, then it wouldn't be rape. Our youth was already filled with physical abuse from our father, and it isn't uncommon for a battered child to attract attention from other types of predators. Sometimes the pleasure a young child experiences at being noticed, even if it's inappropriate attention, can be appealing and hard to resist.

At first the stepfather was taken aback by her unexpected assertiveness, but his eyes were soon gleaming with perverted sexual desire. Rim posed herself on the ground, provoking him and mentally preparing herself for what was to come. Rim, however, did not plan on him flipping her onto her stomach and raping us anally. Kicking and screaming, she twisted us around and reached out for his balls, pinching them with all her might. He shoved us, yelling, "You stupid bitch!" He then fell back in pain and Rim kicked him in the stomach. "You try that again, motherfucker, and I'll kill you!" she threatened. He only laughed at her as he pulled his jeans back up and left the room, leaving my friend and I to slowly clean us up and erase any visual trace of his attacks.

⊰◈◈⊱

Just as I stayed silent regarding my internal family and the physical abuse from our dad, WE spoke to no one regarding the rapes. Why? It was a combination of fear, shame, and threats made from this vile man to go after my brother. One summer night, Rim and I woke up to find this man standing in front of our second-floor bedroom window. Rim's memory is that he remained at the window flashing his knife at us; my own includes him crawling through it and holding that knife to our throat: "You say a word and your brother will be next."

Who's to say which memory is the truth, but just knowing that he had crawled up onto our porch roof to scare us even further was more than enough. In addition, WE felt WE were responsible for everything happening to us. Rim believed she'd brought it on, and I already knew I was bad and deserving of all the abuse.

SHE, Rim, and I have talked at length about what prevented SHE from stepping in and protecting us. WE can't be certain, but to start with, SHE and I didn't have a relationship when I was that young. And SHE was my abuser too. I can envision her feeding off the terror and rage flowing through us during these rapes, like a bloodthirsty vampire.

SHE:
Cita is right in a sense as I have years of abusive history. However, I never remembered the rapes. In all the sessions with Lou, Rim, and Cita sharing, I did not recall one moment of them. WE know I existed then, but where was I? One account

we've discussed is based from the limited memories I have from that time frame or earlier. It's possible that I was a "presence" in the same way that Q and Lou were prior to their official arrival into our lives. The rapes might have actually caused my presence to fully fracture, thus giving rise to my existence as WE currently know it. It's our best guess.

After Rim lashed out at our friend's stepfather, he stopped attempting to rape us. But WE still participated in vile acts and watched helplessly as he raped his stepdaughter. This went on for two years, until our family moved out of the city.

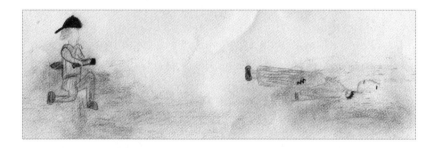

Rim on the left expressing anger toward therapy, our secrets,
and life in general as she kills Mariana and herself in this drawing.

34

⟨⟨⟩⟩

Fighting for Our Lives

I HAD BEEN LIVING ALMOST entirely inside my mind for thirty days when Lou, Rim, and I first began speaking in therapy about the rapes. It had been emotional hell, with countless tears and nearly unfathomable pain. After each session, I remained quiet and filled with shame. I wanted to talk to no one, and I decided to cut myself off from shedding even one more tear. Rim, too, felt isolated, but she was also consumed with rage.

Rim:

I was so fucking pissed at the world. I was angry that Cita had started counseling. That she had led Mariana down the yellow brick road that led to Lou, who internally exposed a part of my life I never wanted to think of again. I was ticked at Mariana and Christopher for their patronizing sympathy and outraged at our parents for the parts I held them responsible for—like not protecting us. On top of all that fury, I was feeling a graphic impulse to find that man right then and there and kill him. I had this white-hot heat racing through me for revenge, and homicide sounded like a great way to release this energy. Instead I stayed in my internal room and slept, ignoring everyone.

⟨⟨⟩⟩

Lou and I continued to shift back and forth, but in time the length between our switching continued to slowly increase. It was a small celebration when I could talk for two minutes externally without Lou appearing. Even with these slight wins, my depression hung over me like a heavy gray cloud. When Christopher came home from work, he'd ask to talk to me, and I'd barely give him a few moments before I'd slip back into Hope's internal bedroom. The overall mood for us all was solemn, and any effort to be cheery felt strained.

To make matters worse, Lou's agitation increased. She had believed that once she'd shared her secrets, she would quickly integrate and cease to exist. This had not occurred and now her threats of killing us began again. I didn't know how much longer I would be able to hold on, and sometimes Lou's threats now sounded actually inviting.

 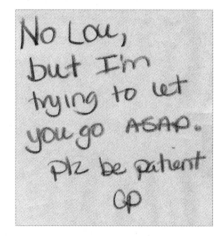

Drawing by Lou in counseling, expressing how desperate she was to no longer exist and my attempt to get her to hang on a bit longer.

Christopher:

We all were ready for Lou to be gone. Cita and I spent so little time together now, and she was continuing to push me away. I wanted to hold her in my arms and tell her to stay strong. I didn't know what I would do if she gave up. All of us relied heavily on Mariana for our own support and courage to stay positive.

During my sixth week of captivity, my tears started to fall once again. I was in session, still not talking much, but Lou and I had now reached about three minutes between our shifting. Lou asked Mariana, "Why did WE have to come to session when Cita's silence is an obvious expression of her desire to be left alone?"

Mariana replied, "Cita needs to be with people and not alone."

Thirty minutes of constant shifting with Lou had left me despondent. A few times I shifted myself internally on purpose, not wanting to be in a relationship with anyone. Mariana, aware of my avoidance tactics, would have SHE shift me back out. Another antic I pulled was mentally calling for SHE, who would shift right out, believing Mariana wanted to talk to her. SHE'd take one look at Mariana, realize what I had done, and again shift me back out. When SHE heard me mentally scream her name yet again, SHE would shift out to speak with Mariana.

> **SHE:**
> I told Mariana that there was such panic in Cita's voice that I felt it was important for me to prove to Cita that I would be there for her. Cita had never trusted me and with good reason. Now she needed me. This was a huge transition of my role in her life.

An hour into our fifty-minute session, my emotional dam broke. I fought every tear from falling, but to no avail; emotional surgery is the only term I can use to describe that moment. As this tormented crying continued between shifts with Lou, I melted further and further into the couch. Then I covered my face completely. It was all I could do to be seen. Mariana continued to reassure me by letting me know that I had nothing to be ashamed of. Soon I was barely able to keep my eyes open. Mariana, who had always kept her physical touching boundaries in place, was at my side, gently holding my hand. Moments later I had fallen asleep, and SHE got us home safely.

Christopher woke me up later that evening. I had much better eye contact with him and I held his hand, but still I did not say much more than hello.

Christopher:
I told her how much I missed touching her and sharing my life with her. With tears in my eyes, I told her how proud I was of her and that I loved her with all my heart.

That night just as Christopher was falling asleep, I shifted out. In between shifts with Lou, who was sleeping, I just watched Christopher resting. It was beautiful to feel his warmth and hear his breathing. As I drifted off to sleep, our night guard SHE shifted out and kept vigil over us until the morning.

For the next few weeks, additional repressed memories of the events involving my friend's stepfather continued to surface, including more distorted and monstrous games that he had tormented us with. But the difference in sharing this time was that I was doing the talking while Lou remained relatively quiet.

Meanwhile, her misery at her continued existence was expressed in each anguished breath she took. Mariana and Christopher tried to give Lou reasons to want to live.

Christopher:
During one of Cita's phone check-ins with Mariana, our black Labrador Dixie jumped up on the couch and curled up next to them. I waited, not certain how Lou would take to being snuggled by a dog. With relief, I spied Lou petting her, and it actually seemed to calm her some.

From that night on we tried to include Dixie in on our phone check-ins and had her up on the bed next to us as we slept at night. Dixie was not at all burdened by the extra attention!

In an attempt to draw Lou out, Mariana asked her if she would sketch a picture during one session. With some resistance, Lou agreed. My memory of this is quite foggy, but I know that we each took turns drawing on the same sheet of paper as we shifted back and forth. However, Lou strongly reacted to having me draw on her picture. Before we could correct the activity and get separate sheets, Lou lost her patience and stopped the process altogether.

One night, Lou experienced her first dream. She shared it at our next session:

> **Lou:**
> I was staring in a mirror. Our eyes changed, depending on which one of us was out. When she [Cita] was out, her eyes were normal and when I was out, they were red-and-white-striped. At one point I picked up a knife and stabbed her reflection in the mirror. The next time I was out and looking in the mirror, my face was cracked, bleeding, and starting to melt.

After telling Mariana about her dream, Lou started to mimic my voice. She told her that I wanted fewer sessions and phone check-ins. However, Mariana knew that it was Lou saying this, and she just let her talk. While she acknowledged Lou's request to change the frequency of our contact, she advised that this was not the time to make any changes.

Christopher often attended our sessions, and he mentioned to Mariana that Lou seemed to enjoy our dog. Lou joined in the conversation and even laughed a little when Mariana shared a cute story about her German Shepherd. Afterward Christopher asked Lou if she wanted a puppy.

Lou:

No thank you. No amount of dog kisses or the bonding I might be doing with you and Mariana are going to make me want to live. I respect your efforts in persuading me to go on, but I have done my living and believe me, have experienced more than enough.

That night during our phone check-in, Lou continued to share. She expressed anger at the thought that she might remain part of our internal family and not fade. After all, there were no guarantees of what the outcome would be. Lou made it perfectly clear that not one ounce of her wanted to be alive. Mariana said that there had to be a way to work this out for the good of all.

As our phone call continued, I addressed fears of being stuck inside my mind forever or even the possibility that I might be the one to integrate versus Lou. I was also afraid of re-entering my own life, and that Christopher had been without me for so long that his initial joy at my return would quickly dissipate. While the Others were a pleasure to be around, entertaining and joyful, I was just their stupid host. Mariana's response was that I had no realization of what a joy I was and what I contributed to the Others and Christopher. I ended the call in more tears, but that night I was far more affectionate with Christopher than I had been in over a month.

By this time, Lou and I had been struggling for eight weeks. Lou was as pissed as ever at still existing. She was done cooperating and felt there were no other options but to die—and take us all with her.

It might have been a survival reaction, but at this point I began to focus on my own thoughts. I would not let Lou bring me down, and I knew that something had to change in our situation and quickly. I began catching my negative thoughts and rephrasing them into something positive. Instead of anger and resentment toward Lou, I would tell myself that this wasn't Lou's fault. I sent positive and loving thoughts Lou's way. I might think, "Lou, you are loved." I would empathize with her and acknowledge that it must have been horrendous for her too. I apologized to her for all her suffering and told her that together we would get through this. Sometimes it took every ounce of my strength to feel love toward Lou, but I opened my heart to include room for her, too.

I had been practicing my optimistic thinking less than forty-eight hours when Lou angrily shouted, "Mariana, tell her to shut the fuck up." It wasn't immediately obvious what was upsetting her. After some discussion, we concluded that Lou could hear my positive messages and that my words were really ticking her off. It had not been my intention for her to be bombarded with my actual words. Instead, I now tried to keep myself positive but not direct thoughts toward Lou. To this day, we don't know if that made a difference for her; she never said one way or another.

In yet another session, SHE took some time to talk to Mariana about the toll this process was taking on her.

SHE:
Fifty-seven all-night vigils on Lou Watch and sporadic rest during the day—sheer exhaustion was taking over. I was also resenting Rim, who was still blockaded in her room. I felt she should be taking some responsibility in the Lou Watch too.

Mariana replied that Rim was doing a good job just keeping herself together. She was a victim too and needed time. After listening to Mariana, I remember telling her how humbling it was to be reminded, yet again, to work on my compassion.

I can't recall being worried myself about being admitted into a hospital while I was sick with Lou. My own external existence was such a distant concern in comparison to the hell of being enmeshed with Lou twenty-four hours a day, seven days a week. However, I did recognize the toll it was taking on everyone—SHE and Christopher, specifically.

> *SHE:*
> Throughout this adventure, we all knew that there was a possibility that Cita might have to be hospitalized. I told Mariana that I didn't want us to end up being admitted, but there was only so much I could do.

Mariana encouraged SHE, complimenting her on her amazing efforts thus far. She told her that it would not be failure if a time came when admission was necessary. At this point, WE needed to continue to take life one day at a time.

I had been in captivity close to nine weeks when Christopher began to notice that some mornings I was able to stay out up to seven minutes before Lou and I would start our shifting dance. Our best guess as to why this occurred was that while Lou was sleeping, my mind experienced less resistance, which enabled me to be out for longer periods.

For the next few days after Christopher's observation, Lou's anger and despair continued to rise. Lou begged Mariana for mercy to end her life. Her breathing was agitated, coming in fast and forceful breaths. Lou often hung up the phone during our check-ins and even threw it across the room. Christopher sometimes had to hold the phone up to my ear and remove it abruptly when Lou shifted back out, and Lou would often strike out at Christopher with her fist or foot. It was certainly not funny, but in their way of coping, Christopher and the Others would sometimes joke about how skilled he was at dodging her blows. Sometimes humor was truly the best way to endure.

At still another session, SHE asked for more information regarding hospitalization.

SHE:

It wasn't that I had given up, but I felt so fuckin' responsible for all of us. With my fatigue, I pondered if spending time in a hospital wouldn't be a safer bet. So I asked Mariana to provide more details about inpatient care.

Mariana filled her in on three local facilities that WE could choose from, and together they worked out a plan. If it turned out that WE needed to be admitted, SHE would advise the admitting staff that WE could no longer keep ourselves safe. SHE would provide them with a list of our medications, the name of our medication management physician, and our long-term care plan. SHE would need to have our medical insurance information available for them as well. If WE were not in a psychotic state, WE would simply be placed in a monitored safe room. And when WE did feel that WE could keep ourselves safe, we'd be released. Mariana assured SHE that these were good facilities and that we'd be well taken care of.

Mariana:

I stayed in very close contact with Christine and all the alters. We were talking every day, sometimes two to three times per day, and I knew Christine so well that I had a clear read on the danger levels. I enlisted all of the alters to help monitor and keep Lou from harming Christine. This was successful because of the progression of the alters' emergence. If Lou had come out much earlier on before we had time to develop relationships with the other alters, Christine probably would have had to be hospitalized. I knew that under that chaos and despair was a woman (and her other alters) who wanted to live.

Also, not every therapist has the time or willingness to be that available. These are personal and professional choices people differ on. At that time in my life I could offer a high level of constant contact, so it worked for all of us.

SHE:

I assured Mariana that I was just data-building at this point and that I was going to verify what our medical insurance benefits were too. I just felt better if WE were prepared.

Lou's emotions changed with the tides, but we did start to notice her demeanor becoming slightly more calm. She was still angry and a bit jumpy, spouting off about wanting to kill us all, but she didn't physically fight as much. In fact, Lou began to speak less and less. When I was shifted out, I shared that I felt drugged, even though WE had not taken any sedating or new medications. I expressed how I felt I had come to terms with the possibility of never returning to my outside world. I wasn't surrendering by any means, but just adjusting to the possibility of an integration process that didn't include me as the primary personality.

At the beginning of the tenth week, we had another Lou incident.

Christopher:

SHE and I were on the couch watching TV. SHE was on Lou Watch and must have dozed off, letting her guard down. All of a sudden Lou was gripping the front of my shirt. She had latched on so tight I thought she would tear it off my back. I immediately called out to SHE, who woke abruptly and shifted Lou back in. An hour later I was calling SHE out again. This time Lou had shifted out, but she had not threatened me or herself. Instead, she was tensed up and had drawn her knees up to her belly. She kept moaning and begging and crying for us to let her go: "Please just let me die!"

Acknowledging SHE's exhaustion, Christopher stayed up and told SHE to sleep for a few extra hours. SHE was going to be worthless without at least a power nap. After three hours SHE woke up.

SHE:
I didn't even remember my head touching my pillow. I had been down for the count, but when I woke up, I felt much more alert and ready to take on my nightly duties. Bring on Lou!

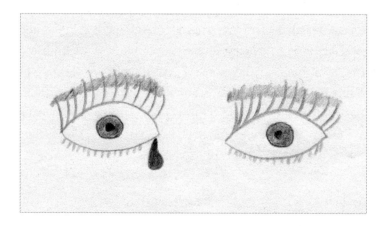

The tear is blood and my pain is trying to escape.

-◦◦◦◦-

35

The Integration of Lou

By the end of the second month, an idea began to form in my weary brain. Off and on throughout this captivity, Lou and I had experienced moments of enmeshment where there was no distinction between my own thoughts and Lou's. I would become so lost in her despair that I felt tempted to just end our lives instead of continuing to fight. It felt as if her thoughts were my own and we were just floating together in my mental abyss. There was no clear distinction between the two of us. It happened often enough that we began to call this form of bonding "melding."

My idea was simple. Why couldn't we meld on a permanent basis? Could we control which one of us actually integrated? It seemed very plausible to me and for the first time in months, I began to feel my spirit fill with joy at this possibility.

After talking about it to Mariana, WE presented the idea to Lou. She was less than enthusiastic.

Lou:

So basically, I need to open myself to you with no guarantee how it's going to end? I could get stuck inside you and become one of the paper dolls in the playhouse?

Needless to say, this wasn't the response I had wanted. But regardless of Lou's resistance, I continued to bring up the subject of melding in our sessions.

As the days blurred by, I could feel myself getting discouraged once again. One particular morning, Chrissy was taking a bath. I came out for a short time to enjoy the touch of the warm water caressing my skin. Lou and I were shifting frequently that morning in about fifty-second intervals. However, we soon realized that this was Lou's first bath, and she found it very soothing. It was such a rare moment to enjoy pleasure with Lou.

A quick moment was all it was. Later that day in session, Lou's sense of calm vaporized as she cringed and shouted that bugs were crawling all over her. "Get them OFF!" she cried. No one else was having this same experience, and WE felt at a total loss as to how to help her. At home Lou was still twitching and groaning while I fell in and out of a restless sleep.

Christopher and I celebrated our twenty-year wedding anniversary on November 5, 2008. I was still trapped inside and immensely frustrated at not being able to spend time with my husband without shifting back and forth with Lou; being out for any length of time was more stressful than enjoyable. Everyone tried hard to make our day special. It wasn't the most romantic celebration of my life, but it certainly was memorable. Christopher was wonderful, and his words of love gave me a piece of security that I needed.

Christopher:
I could tell that Lou and Cita were getting weaker, and I felt helpless to improve their situation. That night I had strong waves of intuition that Cita was going to get her life back and soon. I told Cita I wasn't going anywhere and was in it for the long haul.

It was just a few days later that I was able to stay out for a little over eight minutes between shifting. It was such a treat to actually have a conversation with my husband. I missed being with him so much. I was now starting to be out longer than Lou and more often. This change was exactly what I needed to restore more confidence and a more positive outlook. It was on this day that Lou actually agreed to try melding with me. I mentioned to her that I didn't expect her to match my emotions; that would not have been successful, so I would match hers. Given what we'd been experiencing, I didn't feel that it would be that hard for me to mirror her despondent state.

We waited for our next counseling appointment to experiment. For about two minutes, I no longer felt Lou's existence. Then, in an assault to my senses, her rage and despair washed over me again. It had worked, though! It might have been for an extremely short time, but nevertheless the melding had actually worked.

During future sessions and attempts, it was hard not to keep myself from thinking, "This time it will work for good!" I tried convincing myself that these were only trial runs so that my disappointment upon Lou's return didn't swallow me whole.

Melding was such a tumultuous exercise that the Gang and I found our emotions scattered all over the place. I remember snapping at SHE for rescheduling a phone session I had later in the week without asking me first. The Gang (and SHE specifically) had been responsible for our schedule since Lou arrived on the scene and with limited input from me. However, I felt as though I were living minute to minute, and when I realized that my phone time got pushed to four hours later than usual, I panicked. Mariana's connection was such a lifeline for me.

On a more positive note, my overblown reaction to that schedule change also indicated a clearing of my mind of sorts, as well as a reflection of my desire to once again be in control of my own life. Some of the Others had more mixed feelings, however.

Tristan:

With Cita locked away inside, I really enjoyed having so much external time hanging out with Christopher, doing stuff around the house, and being included in daily decision making. I was excited at the prospect that Lou might finally integrate and we'd have Cita back once and for all. However, I can't help but think that part of my crankiness dealt with my own selfish thoughts on how Cita's return would impact my external time. Would I have to relinquish my current role in our household? Would I be stuck back inside with only limited external visitation? After having these thoughts, I'd fill up with guilt. My focus should be on Cita's health, not how much play time I was allowed.

Lou and I continued to practice melding. Each attempt left us feeling exhausted and disappointed. Lou was still experiencing painful leg twitches even though the rest of us were not. SHE spent time doing stretching exercises in hopes that it might help Lou. It didn't.

During one phone session, Lou asked Mariana how much time was left on the call and was told ten minutes. Lou said, "How about five?" Mariana checked in with me, and together we agreed to cut the session short and allow Lou a small reprieve.

One evening I got a phone call from my brother. It was the first time I was actually able to carry on a conversation with him in two months. We were both thrilled to hear each other's voice, and I was able to stay out for almost nine minutes between shifts with Lou, at which point Christopher would talk to him. My brother confided how uncertain he had been as to whether it was okay to call or not, since he hadn't met the Others and this was all new to him. What if one of the other alters had answered when he called?

Christopher:

I told Chuck that calling was good and that Cita and I both needed his connection. In fact, I asked him to call more often. I also assured him that if one of the other alters answered, he just needed to ask for me or Cita.

During the next day's session, Mariana and Christopher spent quite a bit of time talking about his fears and concerns.

Christopher:

Frankly, I wanted my wife back and I was scared. What if I lost her during this unknown melding attempt? I wanted support from my brothers but didn't ask for it. Other than Cita, the Gang, and Mariana, I was going through this alone, and I was angry.

As Christopher spoke with Mariana, I shifted back and forth, trying to participate as much as possible in their conversation. At one point I was out for up to ten minutes and was thrilled. When Lou was out, she was quiet and miserable. As the conversation progressed, Christopher's voice became louder and more animated. Lou reacted by moaning and covering her ears. Christopher and Mariana quickly stopped talking and tried to reassure her that everything was fine. Christopher covered her with a blanket and Mariana tried to soothe her by telling Lou that she was safe. This seemed to help calm her down, but by that time Lou's sadness had completely engulfed me, and I began to cry.

On November 10, 2008, WE got out of the house and Christopher took us for a drive. That autumn day was gorgeous and the landscape still bore beautiful fall colors from the changing seasons. It was ecstasy to feel the wind licking my face from the open window, and the fresh air was heavenly.

Later back at home, something unusual happened. SHE and Christopher were preparing dinner when suddenly I shifted out and found myself standing next to him. "Hi!" I said to Christopher, and then I felt my legs buckling. SHE shifted back out in a flash and we all stood there in stunned silence. It had been two and a half months since I'd stood in the kitchen and actually spoken to my hubby.

This event, however momentary, lightened everyone's mood with thoughts of possible changes to come—that is, except for Lou, who remained eerily quiet.

The next day I shared the following dream with the Gang:

I was standing in the kitchen. It was dark out, although I don't know if it was the middle of the night or early morning. Regardless, some toast had popped up in the toaster and I was spreading peanut butter on it. Then I dipped the butter knife into some strawberry jam and as I eased it out of the jar, a big glob of sticky jam landed on our countertop. I spread the rest of the jam on my toast and was about to take a bite when I awoke. I could still smell the melted peanut butter and had been so disappointed to awaken before that delicious bite.

When I was through sharing, I could hear SHE laughing from within.

SHE:
I woke up in the middle of the night, wanting a little nibble. This is not uncommon for me. I remember one moment I was putting the toast in the toaster and then the next it was covered in yummy peanut butter waiting for me to take a bite.

I hadn't been dreaming. I had actually been making toast. In fact, I had done all the work and SHE got to eat it. How RUDE!

--<<·<>·>>--

In yet another session, Lou actually laughed a little when Mariana shared a funny about her new dog she'd rescued. Her laughter was short, but sweet. Lou and I tried to meld again, and this time it lasted for almost twelve minutes. But the high of sheer hope followed by the letdown of Lou's return exhausted us both. Although Mariana would not have agreed that it was a failure, Lou still remained present, so to us, it was.

We were too tired to meld daily, and rarely did we try to do it more than once in a day. Even through this fatigue, I started to resent Lou's refusal to try to meld more often. In the midst of this tug-of-war, Rim shared with me that she was ready to fade herself. I looked at her in total disbelief—as if I could handle much more. "What are you talking about?" I cried in alarm.

Rim:
At that time, I wasn't in the healthiest state of mind either. I felt that all my shit had been aired, and frankly, I didn't want to be around to process the aftermath of the rapes. I knew that Cita was an emotional train wreck, but I just wanted a permanent escape myself. I knew integrating wasn't a science. We really had no clue how to initiate an integration, but with Cita's and Lou's attempts I felt I might get to participate, too.

Rim believed that with the exposure of the rapes, her purpose was served and therefore she had a right to leave. "Fade-on-demand" was a nice concept, but it hadn't been working that way for us. I acknowledged Rim's feelings but replied that I did not agree with her desire to fade and that I couldn't imagine my life without her. Then I started to cry. Rim sighed heavily and said she was strong enough to hang tight and that we could address this after WE survived Lou. I was so relieved; I just wasn't able to handle anything more than Lou.

As we continued trying to meld, Lou became increasingly agitated after each attempt.

Lou:
Each time we melded for those few moments, I literally no longer existed. I felt nothing, thought nothing, and was nothing. When I returned, it was like being assaulted over and over again. The sounds, light, and sensations just pummeled me—it was so very painful both physically and mentally.

And I was not exactly feeling empathetic toward her. Shaking with anger, I was mentally screaming, "I don't care what you're feeling! I want my life back. Please go away!"

In the young Lou's voice, she cried, "Christine doesn't love me."

During our phone session that evening, Little Lou continued sharing to Mariana, "Sometimes he loaded blanks" or "He hurts me." Or "He thinks I'm beautiful. He only does this to bad girls. I was a bad girl from birth."

Mariana immediately replied, "No, that's not true. No baby is bad."

The next day's session brought more resistance from Lou. WE were all so tired and agreed to give Lou the rest of the day off, but first thing tomorrow we were going to try and meld again. She retorted with, "You can't do it without me, so I'll let you know when I'm ready." Then I started crying even more.

We were all profoundly exhausted and frustrated. We couldn't figure out why Lou hadn't melded, and the sickening thought that she might be here to stay kept haunting our minds. Mariana wasn't as certain; she believed that Lou's continued presence meant there were still more memories to share. I was beside myself. How could there possibly be more?

There were …

On day sixty-eight, young Lou confided in more detail about additional rapes by the stepfather. This time he used the shaft of his gun to repeatedly violate us in the anus. With that final detail spoken, we never heard from young Lou again.

On day seventy-one, Lou asked Christopher to call Mariana so she could talk with her. Lou had never asked for unscheduled time before, and Mariana was quick to accommodate. During this session, Lou told Mariana that she wanted to say goodbye. Lou was feeling herself become weaker and believed that this was a sign that her time with us was finally ending. Lou also shared an insight about herself and how she saw people in color:

Lou:
When I see Mariana, she is lit in orange hues and Christopher pale blue.

We believe she was talking about auras, but we don't know for sure. Lou also shared that her own color was red. Then she asked Mariana and Christopher to think of her when they saw something red.

On my seventy-fifth day of internal captivity, Christopher and I were sitting in Mariana's office. Lou and I didn't hesitate this time, and we started the melding process as soon as the session began. It wasn't difficult to lower my mood to meet Lou's. I thought about my mom, and I quickly filled with deep sadness at the unresolved issues I still had with her. My fears about returning to my external life also engulfed me. As I swam in this isolation and despair, Lou and I melded. I sat there, not certain of what to expect. Did I dare let myself believe that it would work this time?

Minutes passed. Two minutes became five, then ten, and soon thirty minutes had passed and still Lou did not appear. I sat and talked with my husband and Mariana for thirty solid minutes. Joy started spreading through me, and I began to bawl. It had been such an overwhelming experience that I was flooded with profound relief and sorrow. As the time continued to increase, I cried harder. Mariana, Christopher, and most of the Gang were crying with me and for me. Let's just say it was one sloppy session, but one I wouldn't trade for the world.

By the time it was over, there was still no sign of Lou. The Gang was cheering as we headed to the car.

A drawing I did after allowing myself a moment to imagine what it would be like to no longer have any alternate personalities. It seems peaceful; I'm hugging my husband and our dogs are playing at the beach. However, below the surface Hope, Tristan, Chrissy, Q, and Cyndi are all drowning. In addition, SHE the monster has been harpooned on the far right.

36

⤞⟐⟐⤝

Lou-Free

DAYS PASSED AND WE WERE still Lou-free. I wasn't yet strong enough to get right back into the pace and pressures of daily living, so the Others continued to manage my external life. I often had nightmares of Lou returning and me retreating back into my internal prison. When I was out and talking to Christopher or Mariana, I often spoke quickly, still anticipating minute-to-minute shifting—I just wanted to get everything out that I needed to say before I had to shift back in again.

With each passing day and week, I gained strength to take more control over my life. The Gang was so happy that I was safely back. No doubt joy was experienced by all, but as expected it was especially difficult for Chrissy, Q, and Tristan to spend more time back in their internal homes. SHE and Rim seemed all too happy to step back from being caretakers and the responsible party. I also noticed that the Others continued to go directly to Christopher when they had problems or questions, which hurt my feelings. I then began answering the questions they asked my husband before he had a chance to respond; I wanted to remind them that I was better and could help too.

By now, both Chrissy and Tristan felt quite jealous at the time I was spending out.

Chrissy:

I felt bad that I wanted Cita to stay back inside for part of the time so that I could play my Webkinz and be with Christopher more. It felt icky in my tummy to feel that way because I was so happy Cita was back and sad that I wasnt getting all Christophers attention.

Tristan:
I truly couldn't have been happier to have Cita back, healthier and happier than in a long, long time. And yet, it sucked too. Getting to be external, reading, learning, seeing, and doing— that was way cooler than living in our internal home. I had grown so much these past few months and now I had to relinquish my freedom. I had to chew on that for some time before I was able accept the change.

We were all adapting to being free of Lou when I discovered that something wonderful had happened while I was living internally. Somewhere along the way, we had grown into a cohesive family unit, and this made the transition of having me back go much more smoothly. WE were now all more conscious of one another and our needs. For instance, it was easy to let Tristan out for an hour, and then he'd shift in for SHE to be out. Tristan continued to do the laundry, SHE made lunches, Rim kept up with the bills, and Chrissy took out the recycle bins. WE made time for each of us to be out doing our own things, too. It wasn't an effort; it just worked out, with occasional moans and groans.

⚜

I was treated to another wonderful surprise that the Gang and Christopher had been working on while I was internal. Chrissy had the idea of holding a celebration of my return. Focusing on not *if*, but *when* I returned, the Gang decided to plan a small get-together for me. They called it the Life Party. Q came up with the name, and Tristan suggested to Christopher that they paint a full-size mural on our kitchen wall.

With me trapped internally, they were able to block off this section of the dining room so that even if I was out for a few minutes at a time, I could not see their project. They worked on their Life Party vision for weeks, and if I inquired, they would just tell me, "Never you mind. It's a surprise."

From the top to the bottom of this wall stretched an enormous painted waterfall, its rapids rushing down and gushing forth toward the floor. The painting also continued up onto the ceiling, and throughout its length it depicted rocks, ponds, and lush forests. Tristan had Christopher build a platform at the base of the mural, where rocks that Tristan made from papier-mâché lined the ground. A homemade pond was crafted from a small plastic fountain pool, and its bottom was painted blue and covered with tiny blue aquarium gravel. The whole thing was filled with water and plastic sea creatures. Chrissy also had made brightly colored fish, an octopus, crab, and mermaid from Perler beads (the kind you arrange in patterns and use a heating iron to melt and fuse them).

They also brought in a cut birch tree that stood about six feet tall. It had been fully dried, with all its leaves stripped off the branches and pretty white bark peeling off its two-inch-thick trunk. Tristan created more papier-mâché rocks and combined them with real rocks and cattails at the base of the tree and around the pond. Once Christopher added lighting, the effect was magnificent.

In addition, everyone had created items to hang from the tree limbs. Fairies, small plaques, butterflies, birds, and nests frolicked and abounded. Moments after my return to the house, the Gang and Christopher led me to sit on a kitchen chair with my eyes closed. Then Christopher told me to open my eyes, and before me was a beautiful work of art. The fairies glittered, the fountain trickled, and everywhere I looked were lovely artworks that someone had hand-made. Even Rim and SHE had been coerced into making something after hearing Chrissy's pleas.

The artistry created for the Life Party by Christopher, Tristan, and the Gang.

I was simply without words as each piece was brought to me for further viewing. With tears running down my face, I sat in awe at what they had created and the love it represented.

Their beautiful creation wasn't the only surprise they had for me. In honor of my return, the Gang also organized a small get-together with specially selected guests—only people who were familiar with the ordeal we had all gone through. I know their intentions were heartfelt, but the thought of socializing with anyone at that point overwhelmed me. Having been secluded for the past seventy-five days, I was scared, and wasn't accustomed to how active each of the alters had become in my external life. Nor did I feel prepared to have a meet-and-greet with anyone. Even prior to Lou's external arrival, I had kept myself, and therefore the Gang, quite isolated. After being informed that the invitations had already been sent and the date set, I had to reach deep inside myself to follow through with their upcoming event.

Tristan:

I felt bad that our sheer joy of Cita's return overrode some common sense on our behalf. In hindsight, I could see how we might have given her more time to get reacquainted with her life. On the other hand, I'm not certain waiting would have made a difference. Our push might have been the necessary course of action.

In December 2008, less than a month after returning from the trauma with Lou, the Life Party Celebration commenced.

This get-together turned out to be a great success, with fewer than eight people present at any given moment (in addition to all of us). For the Gang, this was more people than they'd ever visited with in one setting. Q seemed to handle it with ease, having met several of the guests prior through her beadwork.

Q:

I had much fun being with many people at one time. Each person radiated love toward Cita and us all. People want to learn how we live, what like for us, and they ask many good question. Only way they learn is by asking and we all glad to share our lives with them.

Chrissy wanted so badly to greet everyone but found herself acting bashful. At first, she focused only on Christopher and our dear friend Sandy, looking to them for reassurance. With some coaching, she was soon asked about her love of Webkinz and that was all it took. Shortly afterward, everyone was meeting her entire stuffed animal collection and the ever-present Sarefino the reindeer.

SHE:

I came out here and there. I had met a few of the friends prior to the gathering. I was still honing my people skills then and trying to keep it a PG-13 party. I also sensed additional tension from Cita anytime I was out chatting. I may have done my share of bonding with Christopher and the Others during the Lou experience, but Cita still had visions of me as the enemy. With that in mind, I tried to be discreet, which is not something I do often—it was just to lessen her stress.

Of all the alters, Rim was the only person who chose to stay internal during the Life Party.

Rim:

I was thrilled that Cita was back out, but I'm not into banners and balloons. Frankly, I'd had more external exposure in the last three months than I ever wanted and was ready to stay in my room. I just wanted to be left alone. No one pressed me and I was grateful.

Surprisingly, it was Christopher who had the most challenging time.

Christopher:

I found myself overwhelmed with relief at having Cita back. Tristan and I had invited a nice bunch of men and women who were friends from all different facets of our life, and yet I found myself stuck in my own judgments. I wanted so badly for the alters to be accepted and felt very protective of them. I was hyper aware if someone was talking to an alter, but conversing as if they were talking to Cita. I would find myself wondering why they weren't asking about Tristan's art or what Chrissy liked to do. I wanted our guests to delve in and get to know how wonderful the alters were.

I had gained so much knowledge about myself by interacting with the alters these past three months. I had been called on my own behavior of ignoring them or not paying attention to whom I was talking. I realize now that I was projecting a lot of my own issues and insecurities on the guests.

For me, the Life Party turned out to be a beautiful day of reconnection. It was an introduction of our special internal family and of the unique way we all live, to our friends. That same night, Christopher asked SHE to keep the Gang blocked, and he made love to me. Afterward, as we were wrapped in each other's arms, he wept tears of relief and joy at my return. "Please don't ever do that again" were his last words as he drifted to sleep.

Part of the mural painted by Christopher on the ceiling for the Life Party.

37

❦

Pattee

ALTHOUGH WE HAVE TRIED TO keep our writing in chronological order, two important events occurred while Lou and I were captive internally. The first one was a visit from my stepmom Pattee and the second was a positive change in Q's ability to communicate, which we'll share more later.

The June before Lou's arrival, Pattee had planned on coming out from Montana for a two-week visit in August. On this trip, Pattee was to meet the Others for the first time. But Lou's arrival complicated matters in more ways than one. I let her know about Lou's presence, what was occurring, and that I'd understand if she wanted to postpone or reschedule her visit to a later date.

Below Pattee shares in detail what it was like having me as a stepdaughter and then learning about the alters. She refers to me as "Chris."

Pattee:

I can't say I was totally shocked because I always knew there was "something," but I just didn't know what. I knew nothing about MPD other than when I read the book and then saw the movie *Sybil*. They were real eye-openers for me as far as mental illness went. But that was years and years ago, and I hadn't thought of it since then. Chris felt she needed to tell me because everything was coming out now, and she couldn't keep the multiple personalities inside anymore. I think she wanted me to know that I could cancel the visit if I felt uncomfortable about it. Like that was going to happen. I didn't like the diagnosis, but I was happy there was one.

This visit was very difficult for me. Meeting a whole set of people living inside one body was, to say the least, stressful. Also, during the time I was meeting the Others, Lou came out and wasn't very nice and there were lots of sessions with her counselor. Coming to grips with this was difficult for me, but nothing like what it was—and still is—for Chris. I think in a way, she was happy that I knew about it but also scared I would turn away from her. For me, just knowing there finally was an explanation was helpful, but trying to learn to be with these other personalities while looking at Chris is very hard.

It took some doing on everyone's part, but I think we survived it fairly well. At least that's how I felt. Who knows, I could be living in a dream world. It certainly gave me more insight into why Chris acts the way she does. I needed to read books to get even a very small understanding of what she is going through. Is it hard for me? Yes, but nothing like how Chris will be dealing with it all.

As for me, I was so grateful and relieved when Pattee chose to still come out for her visit. Her loving, understanding presence was a gift to us all.

Pattee:

In retrospect, I think back to Chris's troubled teenage years and wonder which personality was there. I think about the times when Chris lied to us and that maybe it wasn't the Chris that she tried so hard to be. I know that through all that, she is still a kind and caring person. Is acting out and hurting oneself a way of reaching out? Too bad none of us knew what she was reaching out for. Could we have helped? Could we have even understood? I'm not sure that was possible back then for any of us.

While I was in Seattle this time, I met Rim, who would take over the driving or during sporting events (we watched the Olympics together); SHE, who would come out during times of extreme stress and with a clear head tell it like it was; Tristan, who loves doing jigsaw puzzles, likes to draw, and loves dragons (and is also a great help to Chrissy when she struggles to learn something); Q, who only came out periodically and was difficult to understand but is a great wit and loves Mariners baseball (we made beaded projects and she loves butterflies and the color green—she does make you laugh); and Chrissy (I call her "Bunny"), who likes to make things, loves Webkinz, and has learned how to use the computer to input all her Webkinz in their cute rooms.

Then there was Lou. I only met her during the sessions with Chris's counselor. It was during those times that I was a little afraid for Chris's safety. To be perfectly honest, I was afraid of Lou and I didn't like to look at Chris and see her.

During this visit, Chris allowed me to read what she wrote about Hope, who had been with her as long as she could remember. Was Hope the sweet one we saw so often? I have to admit I cried buckets while I was reading that. It makes me sad even now because it was very obvious from her words that Chris is still grieving over losing her (and I think the Others are too). I don't know why one personality gets to stay while the others go. Certainly it must have to be a part of the process. But I have no psychological knowledge and won't even go there.

Pattee's visit was far too short for me, but I'm sure she felt a sense of relief to get home and process all that she had witnessed and experienced.

Pattee:

After I left, the new personality continued to get stronger and Chris shut down. It was now up to the Others to take over and make sure they were safe. We didn't communicate very much for quite a while because Chris went inside and just left it to the Others. During those months I worried about the situation, but I knew it was only Chris and the Others who could do the work. I could love only from a distance, and to be perfectly honest I was glad I wasn't there to witness what was going on with Lou. I have to admit I did breathe a big sigh of relief when Lou left. I was very uncomfortable with her around and didn't like her at all.

I have always hoped that Chris could lead what most of us call a "normal" life. Maybe there isn't such a thing. Sometimes Chris seems like I remember her, but I don't know what she was years ago. What we probably saw was the portrait she painted for us to see and the rest was hidden inside. It breaks my heart to think this may be the way it will be for the rest of her life, and that other than to a few of us, she will remain hidden away. But that is not for me to know or to say, and I hope I can continue to give her the support she needs during her struggle to understand herself.

Chris is very important to me. Even though she isn't my biological daughter, I have always felt a strong connection to her. I believe that we come and go in other people's lives. We come for a reason and leave for a reason. Whatever that reason is, we are there at that particular time not by accident. I know I will be with Chris until I leave this world because she means so much to me. However far apart we live, I will be connected to her. Chris is a special person in my life and I believe I have grown because of her. I may never completely understand, but I can love.

38

⊸⊶⊰◈⊱⊷⊶

I Hear You!

THE SECOND EVENT THAT OCCURRED during the Lou phase revolved around Q. As we've stated before, Q did not reside in our internal home but in some separate niche in my brain. In addition, none of us could hear her, and she could not hear us, with the exception of Christopher and Mariana. If she wanted to communicate with us, she either left us a note when she had been out externally, or she shared with Christopher and he passed on the message.

Then shortly after Hope faded, Tristan and Q began to hear each other. We don't know why it occurred only for Tristan. But he is quite sensitive to the internal emotional currents that my body experiences, and he was mentally open at the right moment and connection was made. Again, it's only a guess.

Regardless, it was such a gift for Q to finally have someone to talk to besides the limited exposure she had with Christopher and Mariana.

Tristan:
Q couldn't contain her excitement, and for the first week she talked and talked and talked. She had so many questions and wanted more and more details on how the world worked and the memories that I shared of Cita's life. I was exhausted but so pleased to get to know Q better.

These slight changes in Q's world spurred Chrissy on to try and find Q and get her to live with them in Hope's old room. Chrissy ran up and down her internal hallway yelling Q's name, hoping she would hear her. She had Tristan bang on the outer walls and ceiling, but sadly no additional connection was made. With the arrival of Lou, we all went into survival mode, and no other energy was spent on finding Q. But Q was content to converse only with Tristan.

When late fall arrived, I had been internal with Lou for approximately forty days. Rim, who had sacrificed watching major league baseball to Q, was eager to watch our Seattle Seahawks NFL team compete. Just before the opening kickoff, Q shifted out and began acting as if she was going to watch the football game as a joke on Rim. It was moments later that Christopher heard Q squeal, "I hear you, Rim!"

Q:

I know I make sound of surprise. Just as I shifted out to pretend watching football, I actually hear Rim say, "Nice try Q, ha ha, now get your ass back inside." I so shocked and start laughing. I ask Rim if she hear me and she answer, "Yes!" Seconds pass and soon I hear Chrissy and Tristan laughing and with joy I hear Cita say, "I hear you too Q!" Soon many of us crying, Christopher too. I still not able see the internal Gang, but hearing them so very beautiful. It happiest day of life. Most special, hearing Cita. She and I talk long time learning more and more of each other. I get goosebumps when write these words.

Tristan:

Now Q was no longer the Quiet One.

Jennifer:

Once we got past the communication barrier, I discovered the sweetest, most caring, talented, and beautiful alter of them all!

I can't express the profound love that filled me when I could finally hear Q talk. Although I had regarded her initial arrival with a less-than-enthusiastic welcome, Christopher, Mariana, and other friends were sharing so many wonderful stories of the special individual Q was turning out to be. Now for the first time, I was able to hear for myself what a gifted and beautiful young woman Q was.

-◦◦◦-

39

One Foot in Front of the Other

THE YEAR 2008 WAS CERTAINLY filled with turmoil, pain, confusion, and joy. With Lou's integration seemingly permanent, it was time for us all to regain stability. To do this, I needed to continue pushing myself to take the necessary steps to live my own life.

With crisis mode over, our sessions with Mariana decreased from daily to twice a week, with an occasional third session added when needed. Shifting internally to hide from life was something I had been working on not doing since those first months of speaking out about the MPD in Mariana's office. With the unique situation I experienced with Lou, the months spent living internally made it that much harder to resurface and reclaim my life.

Even walking outside to our mailbox was often more than enough for me to cope with emotionally. To try and encapsulate the terror I was experiencing is really difficult. As a rational adult, I was fully aware that the danger level of walking outside was extremely low. However, it felt as if I'd been stripped bare—so exposed and vulnerable. If I opened the front door and heard a car about to drive down our street, I'd immediately shut the door and wait until it had passed. I was experiencing symptoms similar to people with agoraphobia live through: a fear of open spaces or crowded areas. However, I made myself do that task daily. It was a safe way to push myself and not hide. In addition to their assigned chores, the Gang was still asked to help with errands and daily tasks from time to time. Balancing their free time externally was a common topic in our counseling sessions as we continued to modify ways to comfortably live together.

Both Tristan and Q expressed desires to go to college, to travel, and to see the world, while Chrissy longed to have more friends and of course go to Disneyland. I wasn't able to provide those opportunities for them yet. In fact, where I once could shift internally and let someone else take over completely was no longer an option as our individual boundaries continued to evolve. Prior to speaking my truth about MPD, each of us—SHE, Hope, Rim, and the Others—all had strictly segregated emotions. If SHE was angry, WE might have been impacted by her acting out her rage, but those actual feelings of rage were experienced only by her. Now, if SHE expressed anger, her lingering emotional residue hung over me like a second skin. It might last for only a few seconds or minutes, but it was evident that our emotional boundaries were flexing.

Another example of the melding of our emotions might be a spike in my anxiety as we headed out to a local walking path for a short family stroll. Q and Tristan would also start feeling knots of anxiety, and this tension often overshadowed their enjoyment. It was easy to tell that it was my own neurosis filtering through them, and in time they would gently tell me to "breathe." We'd laugh about it and soon I could calm myself or be more conscious of blocking my emotions from them, something that I hadn't had to do in the past.

‑◦◦‑

40

Chrissy and Q Come into Their Own

MEANWHILE, CHRISSY WAS DEVELOPING INTO quite a young lady. She was allowed an hour a day on the computer, where the website she frequented the most was Webkinz. Their programs were educationally designed and they improved her vocabulary, spelling, and mathematical skills each day. This additional exposure to the outside world matured her in a way that she had not done living internally only.

Chrissy's birthday in April of 2009 was a monumental occasion, because Chrissy actually got to change the number of her age, from five to six. This should seem normal, but not in our situation. I mentioned earlier in the book that age and time are different when you exist internally. For example, I could be internally visiting with Tristan and Rim for what might feel like an hour, but when I shift back out, two hours might have passed. We aren't certain why this is, just that it occurs. When Rim shifts out to do an activity on the computer or chat with a friend, she's in my forty-five-year-old body, but internally her physical being is still twenty-eight years old.

Chrissy was now no longer behaving as a five-year-old would. She had matured, and so on her birthday she officially turned six. That was quite a feat for her since she'd been five for the past forty years!

Chrissy:
I never had a real birthday where I got to change a number of how old I was before. I even had a cake that Cita made for me with my name on it and it had six candles on it. The cake was

frosted in pink and the candles were all pink to. There were balloons and presents. I felt really special.

⁓⊛⊛⁓

In addition to Chrissy's growth, a new anomaly appeared that caused us all to step back and hold our collective breath. Earlier, Christopher had spoken about Chrissy talking in her sleep. By now, her night talking had increased to a constant chatter. It was as though she were carrying on an actual conversation with someone other than us. And when you have MPD, you tend to question when an alter has what appears to be an imaginary friend. When we addressed this with Mariana, she advised us to wait, watch, and that we didn't encourage this other being by asking Chrissy questions, like whether he or she had a name. Chrissy did not talk about this person when she was awake, and Mariana said for us to just let it be.

Needless to say, I was quite content having Chrissy talk with this person only during her sleep. I just wasn't ready to deal with a new alter—none of us were. So we took Mariana's advice and waited to see what the future had in store for us.

⁓⊛⊛⁓

I wasn't surprised when Tristan, Q, and Chrissy began to ask more questions about my relationship with my mother. They had always respected my right to not have contact with her, but since I had been talking with Mariana about what reuniting with my mom would be like, they must have felt I would be more comfortable with their inquiries.

Q:

I felt sadness for the loss of such a powerful dynamic. Cita was my mother figure and that relationship bring such joy in my world. I believed that together, Christopher, Us, Mariana, and Cita could provide enough support for her to begin to mend that tie between them.

Chrissy:

I wanted to have another Grandma. I love Mimi [stepmom Pattee] and feel sad that she lives so far away. I have memories of Cita when she was young like me. Hope let me shift out and play sometimes. I know I even talked to Sharon (Cita's mom) a few times to. I wanted to have her meet me and wanted her to love me.

With that in mind, they knew I would keep it under advisement, and I continued to do my work in therapy.

Q was also coming into her own. She was always so happy and seemed to genuinely love life. She made us all smile with her gregarious laugh and was developing quite a sense of humor. In addition, her beading hobby was growing.

Q:

I wanted to create jewelry that fit Cita, who was larger woman. Using memory wire and variety of glass, ceramic, wood, and metal beads, I able design beautiful and fun bracelets that fit women all sizes. I first make quite a few for Cita, one for Christopher, then for sister Jennifer, Pattee, and friend Sandy. From that had people calling and asking me make more. I make more and more. Jennifer ask me send to her and she sell in Arizona to her friends and coworkers. People who get them as gifts would call and ask for additional bracelets. It so exciting.

With Q's bracelets on demand, we researched the possibility of creating a web page and to sell her beaded items online. We went to a local used bookstore and purchased *Building a Web Site for Dummies*. After hours and hours of trying to create a web page for Q, WE all had to humbly admit that this book for dummies was far more advanced than WE were.

Tristan:
WE were dumber than the dummies the book was created for!

Fortunately a friend of Christopher's referred us to a wonderful man who did web design. After meeting him and weeks of emails back and forth, Q ended up with a beautiful website called Beads by Q. She learned how to add and remove her own pictures, load pricing and descriptions, and monitor the site's PayPal checkout system.

Q:
I so proud to see my items in color on my site and to get my first order. I can't describe how much joy I filled with. I wanted a commercial on TV saying check out my website but had to settle for word of mouth, mailings, and emails.

Q's business was active enough for her to average a hundred dollars in sales a month, sometimes less, but with holidays it increased. It was enough to keep her busy and happy, but not so much that any of us felt overwhelmed or cheated from our own time out.

Life now fell into a comfortable routine. We had our continued bouts of growing pains, but overall our days were becoming more stable, and a functioning family was blossoming.

41

Forgiveness

I THINK THE WORD FOR 2009 would be forgiveness. Throughout much of it, Tristan and Rim spent long hard hours working on their relationship. I was slowly healing from the trauma SHE had inflicted upon my life, and although I wouldn't claim to love her, I was beginning to warm up to her subtle charms. With all the work I had been doing on myself, I was finally realizing that I was someone worth loving. Now that I was feeling stronger, I could finally take the first steps to reunite with my mom.

And aside from my work, Rim and Tristan were sorting out their relationship once and for all.

Tristan:
We already shared the abuse that Rim inflicted upon me. Once I brought it to light in therapy, Rim was asked to no longer be physical with me, and with that she stopped almost all interaction with me. That isn't easy to achieve when you live together inside a person's mind, since there really aren't a lot of places to get away from each other. It was extremely uncomfortable and painful. It might not have been a healthy relationship, but it was the closest I'd experienced to having a girlfriend. To go from constant contact to the cold shoulder was difficult for me.

Through the years I had grown to love Rim and I felt as though my heart was breaking. In our sessions I asked to have everyone blocked so I could talk to Mariana in privacy. SHE is able to do that for us and through many tears, I realized that I needed to ask Rim to make time to talk to me. I needed to tell her how I felt.

The tension between the two of them was often uncomfortable for us all, but the work they were doing was necessary.

Rim:

I could feel Tristan's pain rolling off him in waves: sadness, anger, and confusion. I knew how he was feeling because I was experiencing the same; I just hid my emotions better than he could. What he took as cold and disinterested was just my way of shoving all the love and shame I felt toward him deep down inside. I'm not good with words. Expressing myself is not my forte, but I too had private time with Mariana trying to figure out how to pull my head out of my ass. I wasn't able to find a way to ask for his forgiveness, and I was so afraid to admit that I loved him too.

It was obvious that both of their emotions were coming to a head. They would either have a knockdown, drag-out fight, which wasn't likely as Tristan isn't much of a fighter, or they would kiss and make up. Of course, we were all hoping for the latter.

Tristan:

I remember getting more courage to confront Rim as the days went on. "Confront" seems negative, but with each passing day I was feeling more pissed that she wasn't willing to let me in.

I remember the actual moment vividly, as it was our birthday—April 24, 2009. I was on the couch in our internal living room and she was across from me sitting in a chair. I think we'd been in the same room together for over ten minutes, and that was a record for us over the past year. So, I sucked it up and strolled the ten feet over to where she sat. I nudged her leg, "Hey Rim, Happy Birthday." She was perfectly still for what felt like hours, and then she lifted her green eyes to me and with her crooked smile she whispered, "If you love me, kiss me now."

So I did.

That certainly didn't solve all our problems, but the road to healing was going to be much easier knowing we were working on it together. It was one of my happiest days ever.

Rim:

Ditto.

⟞⟨⟩⟜

SHE and I weren't quite so direct or lovey in our relationship growth. It was more of an easement for me or a quiet acceptance. After all, SHE had been a warrior for us all through my time with Lou; I hadn't wanted to admit it, but I had needed her strength and protection. I think we all did. I don't have a clear recollection of everything that occurred while I lived internally, and as I read the journal SHE had kept, I found myself in awe of her thoughtfulness. I began to appreciate how funny SHE was and to accept that SHE had changed.

Although I didn't want to kiss her, nor even hug her, for the first time in my life I truly came to see her as a person, not as a monster. I was surprised to find that I cared about her and at that time, it was more than enough.

SHE:

I am trying to think of something witty or sarcastic to add, but I actually find myself a tad speechless. Thank you for your words, Cita.

‑◦‑◦‑◦‑

After five years of separation, my mom and I took our first steps toward reconciliation in the summer of 2009. It was my mom who actually contacted Christopher and me first to let us know that she had finally decided to put our small vacation home on the market. It wasn't a surprise to us, knowing the cost of taxes and upkeep involved. My brother was in Arizona, and neither of us could assist her financially.

Mom's contact with me was threefold. The first was to let us know about the house going up for sale. The second was that we were more than welcome to come and stay at the cabin any time prior to the house actually selling. A lot of work was being done to it, but if she knew in advance, she'd make sure that we had the cabin to ourselves. And third, she wanted to see if Christopher had the time and desire to contract out for some of the projects that needed to be done.

I had many conversations with Christopher, the Gang, and Mariana as to what to do. I didn't want to plunge forth without reassuring us all that I was able to take care of myself in a healthy manner with my mom. I now felt much more confident in my abilities, as I knew I was no longer the victimized daughter of years past but an adult woman who was more than capable of being responsible.

But Mom still did not know about my MPD. SHE, Rim, and Hope had been the only ones to interact with her growing up, but under the guise of me as Christine or Christy, the familiar names she called me. I knew that I could not begin anew with my mom without her knowing the truth. How to balance getting reacquainted with her while sharing my truths was a quandary I needed to tackle.

It was equally important to me—and us—that Christopher was also comfortable with our reuniting. He remembered the days of me crawling deeper inside myself and seeing the lights go out in my eyes after a visit with Mom and her husband. He recalled how it sometimes took hours to bring me back to the surface. And he too had found himself intimidated by her assertive and often aggressive behavior, and he wasn't certain if he was at a place to take care of himself as well.

Less than a month after that first phone conversation with my mom, I returned her call. The conversation isn't clear in my mind, but I do remember sharing with her that I didn't know how to bridge the gap the years had made.

"Where do we go from here?" I gently asked.

"I don't know Christy, but forward is a good step," she replied.

A week later, we arranged to meet Mom and her husband up at the Camano vacation home. Christopher had agreed to do some repairs and it felt comforting for us to be together for this initial meeting. Of course, my intention was not to delve right into, "Hi Mom, lovely to see you and by the way, I have multiple personalities." The idea was for the three of us to share some time together. Then at some point I'd ask her if we could make a date for us two to talk.

But it didn't quite go as planned.

It was a gorgeous Pacific Northwest day when we headed out on the fifty-minute drive north to the cabin. The sky was blue with just a smattering of white billowing clouds. A slight warm breeze was blowing, which felt good against the cool nerves running through my body. All the confidence I had initially felt upon seeing my mom was slowly dwindling to a trickle. Internally I heard the Others rooting me on, along with Mariana's frequent phrase through the years, "Breathe Cita, just breathe." I reminded myself time and time again not to have any expectations, but I was badly hoping for the reunion to be a good one.

Tristan:

As we pulled down the driveway, WE all took a deep breath and exhaled, including Christopher. The nerves from Cita and

Rim and the excitement from Chrissy, Q, and I were keeping me pretty amped. My goal was to keep Chrissy entertained, as WE had agreed to have SHE block us for this initial contact. Chrissy was pretty bummed, but she understood why. WE all did.

The block was to help me keep my focus and not have one of the alters shift out unexpectedly. WE may have been living out in the open at our home, but it wasn't unheard of for the alters to be blocked for short lengths of time. However, If SHE blocked for more than a couple hours, I would start to get a headache. For the time being, we were playing it moment to moment.

The sea air helped calm me. I love Camano and being near the sea has always been restorative for me. I was sad to see this home sell but felt it was the right decision for everyone. When we saw Mom, she was warm and pleasant, but rather reserved. She was quick to fill any silence or awkwardness with chatter about the work that was going on at the place. We said our hellos to her husband, waved to the neighbors, and just enjoyed the scenic beauty around us.

Christopher started right in working, jotting down notes for additional supplies and tools needed for another trip out. For me, the time passed as if I were in a blur. While it felt wonderful to be in my mom's space, I was getting panicky about telling her of the MPD. I felt such an urgency to tell her NOW! I didn't know how she would react to the truth, and I felt my insecurities quickly surfacing. I looked to Christopher for strength, and we took a short walk together, during which time he held me and reminded me that I was loved. He whispered my old mantra, "I'm okay and it's okay for me to be me."

Dinner was ready upon our return. Although I couldn't tell you what we ate, I know that the boys congregated to the living room to watch TV. Mom and I cleared the table and in the privacy of the moment, I informed her that I'd like to set up a future date to share some things with her. We sat at the dining room table, with its huge windows looking out on the Puget Sound. Then she replied, "We have time now."

Truth be told, I wanted to vomit. I was so scared, but also relieved. I no longer needed to hold it all inside. Once and for all, I would let my mom in on our world.

"I have multiple personality disorder, Mom, and have for as far back as I can remember. These past years have been spent working on my own relationships with these alters in counseling."

And with that, I slowly spilled the details of the alters, giving her their basic stats and personality traits.

As Mom listened, she identified the personality traits of SHE, Rim, and Hope from memories of my youth.

Mom:

To acquaint me with the Clan, they invited me to play their favorite board game, *Sorry*. My daughter Christine/Cita was the official deck shuffler, and the rest of us all played in teams. Christopher was blue, Chrissy red, Tristan and Rim yellow, and SHE and Q green. Having all these voices coming from Christine was strange to say the least. It was a good way to learn to distinguish each alter. I had fun, but I was exhausted afterwards.

The game ended just as our neighbor stopped by to show me their new puppy. I went out to greet them both and the next thing I knew, my daughter was sobbing on her husband's shoulder. She was crying in a little girl voice (Chrissy's) that she wanted to pet the puppy too. She cried when Cita said she'd be too embarrassed if Chrissy came out.

Of course this broke my heart. I took a deep breath and forced myself to explain to my neighbor our dilemma. She was more than willing to bring the puppy over again for Chrissy to see too.

My memory of that afternoon is a hazy blur of nerves and amazement. But I was so relieved to have opened my life to my mother and truly happy to have her back in my life.

Over the following months we slowly began to see each other more often. With each visit the Gang worked on their own individual relationships with her. Q and Mom had an instant connection over her beading, Mom's love of jewelry, and going to local gem and bead shows.

Mom (Sharon):

Q is a wonderful part of Christine's inner family. Everyone loves her. Q's unique speech pattern led people to question what country she was from. This was odd for me at first, because when I'm introduced as "Mom," we don't sound alike. On those occasions I now reply, "This is my daughter and she has multiple personalities. This talented person is Q, one of her alters." Most take it very well.

Q:

I found meet Sharon exciting and intriguing. Visually such resemblance and could see where Cita get her beauty. More time spent I see how difficult Sharon be for Cita, but my time with Sharon enjoyable. I not hesitate say, "No I not like this." Or "No Sharon, that not what want do." Simple statement that Cita had found hard say. Then Sharon take me to bead show in Seattle and we best friends forever!

It was not always comfortable for me to watch the alters' relationships evolve with my mom. My mom can be easily distracted when you're having a conversation with her. We tease her by saying "Squirrel!" like in the Disney movie *Up*, in which the dogs lose their train of thought every time they see a squirrel, which happens frequently.

When Chrissy talked with Mom (whom she calls "Grandma"), Chrissy would get so frustrated at her for not listening. "Grandma, I'm trying to talk to you." Mom would return her attention to Chrissy and apologize. Each time Chrissy spoke candidly with my mom, I would squirm internally. I had never been entirely honest with anyone, especially my mother.

> **Mom:**
> Little Chrissy, to me, is that part of Christine that wanted to stay that cute, precious child that everyone adored. When I first met her, I loved her so much! But then I always did.

> **Chrissy:**
> I was so excited to meet Grandma Sharon. Grandma would ask me questions about things she remembered when Cita was a little girl like me. Sometimes I remembered and other times I remembered things that Cita and Rim didn't even remember. I loved having a grandma. The parts I didnt love were how Grandma and Grandpa Don [my stepfather] would fight a lot and also Don didnt like it when I was out.

My mom's husband did and still does have difficulty with the concept of my having multiple personalities. Early on, Mom shared that he felt by acknowledging the Others he was conceding that it was okay for me to behave this way. (As if I could choose not to have the alters.) It was just ignorance, but it continues to be a bone of contention years later.

⚜

Tristan's quick wit and sarcasm fit easily into our family, and soon he and Mom were sharing an easygoing banter.

Tristan:

I thought Sharon was a hoot. Her mind was so busy all the time. I think busier than Cita's if you can believe that. She could take in a whole room's conversation in a moment. That didn't make talking with her one-on-one easy, but if you said, "Hey Grandma, FOCUS," she would. She is a lot better now than during that first year of meeting her.

I liked how she immediately tried to ensure that WE all felt loved and separate from Cita. Sometimes after I meet people for the first time, they unconsciously refer to me as "she this or she that." I've learned to separate the times when I stay silent or correct them, "He. I'm a he!" With Sharon, I only had to do it once or twice. I appreciated her thoughtfulness.

SHE:

I don't remember our official moment of meeting that day. I know Sharon thought she recognized my gestures and gruff nature, but I'm fairly certain she was confusing me with Rim. When Cita was young, I just don't recall shifting out and actively participating in her life when others were around. If I was out, I was only causing physical harm to Cita's body. I didn't start playing well with others until after Cita first started talking about us with Mariana.

As her familiarity with the alters grew, Mom started sharing her own memories. She often confused memories of Rim with memories of SHE. WE continue to remind her that it's Rim she is thinking of, but on occasion she'll still confuse them both.

Mom:

When Christine was sixteen, her mannerisms when she drove were often strange to me. I would see her with her right arm on the back of the passenger seat and one hand on the wheel. She looked like her dad. When I first met SHE, I thought for sure that it must have been her driving, but the Gang is fairly certain it was Rim.

However, I believe I was aware of Rim in Christine's teenage years. Once in a while Christine had such a harsh uncaring response toward people, saying, "If they don't like it, that's just too bad!" I'd find myself wondering, "Who is this person?" Moments later, my girl would be back.

Christopher's initial hesitation in reuniting with Mom quickly dissipated once he saw how happy the Gang was to have her in their lives and he witnessed my ability to be in her space and hold my own.

Christopher:
I experienced several uncomfortable dreams during the hiatus between Cita and her mother. All of my dreams are littered with me avoiding confrontation with Sharon's more aggressive nature. Now that Cita and her mother have reunited, I feel that Sharon's disposition is calmer, and I'm more at ease. This is a complete turnaround, and I'm happy about it.

42

◦◦◦

Progress, Setbacks, and Cyndi

CAROL SAUER, THE OWNER OF Salon Retro, a hair salon in Everett, Washington, knew of the Others, although her interactions had been mainly between me and Q. In 2009, Carol invited Q to participate in a holiday open house in her salon, where Q could set up a small display and sell her bracelets.

I was less enthusiastic about the show. Although I was starting to come out about the MPD, I still felt pretty exposed and vulnerable in social settings. I panicked at the thought of someone I knew recognizing my face, but having it be Q out publicly. WE didn't exactly walk around with a sign on our head that declared, "I have multiple personalities." How would I handle that situation?

> **Q:**
> I not nervous only excited. I proud that Carol include me in her event. I not worried if someone thought I Cita. I tell them, "No I am Q, but know Christine. When I see her again I give message." What else to do? I not want miss out on opportunity from fear being seen. That said not want push Cita too hard either.

In session with Mariana, WE all discussed how we felt about Q selling her wares, including Christopher. We received the typical responses from Rim and SHE: "Leave us out of it and we'll be fine." Christopher and Mariana focused on my ability to handle this in a healthy manner and not regress in a depressive, downward panic. Knowing that I'd have support available and that this would be a safe place for me and have Q out selling her items, I agreed.

Q worked diligently to make many beautiful bracelets for this show—hours and hours, with much sacrifice from us all. Chrissy, however, really did enjoy the beading time.

Chrissy:

Q hired me to help. I got to put the extra beads away when she was done with a bracelet and sometimes she even let me put beads on the wire. I always made sure her workplace was clean and ready even when she was really really messy. Sometimes she would give me five dollars for helping, or she would get me neat stickers or colored pens. That was super cool but I would have helped anyway because I love Q and it was fun. My brother Tristan did not like it as much as I did though.

Tristan:

Let's see: Eat, sleep, and bead. In fact I think Q got a wooden sign for a Christmas gift that said exactly that. I remember that days before the event, I had an awful dream. In my dream I woke up sneezing and when I looked into my hands, I was sneezing beads out my nose. Still in the dream, I run to the bathroom and when I take a leak, I'm peeing out beads too! When I woke up, I told Q, "ENOUGH. No more BEADING. I need a timeout."

Christopher built a display to hold all the beautiful bracelets Q was making. Unfortunately, after all that hard work, WE came down with a chest cold and on the day of her show, WE were admitted to the hospital with pneumonia. Did I sabotage us with my deep-seated fear and have it manifest by getting sick? Who can say? What I did know was the true sadness and disappointment Q was experiencing.

Q:

I sad, not devastated. This my first time in hospital and never been sick before. I felt OK if stay internal, but when shift out and talk to Christopher it was hard breathe in Cita body. Yes, disappointed about show, but more worry about our health.

Christopher:

I was in a state of disbelief. Part of me just wanted to know that she would get better with a quick dose of antibiotics. I was not prepared for the seriousness of Cita's illness. For the first time, thoughts of Cita dying and possibly the Gang too crossed my consciousness; I lose one, I lose them all. That really hurt to think about.

Needing to take care of business, I contacted Carol at the salon and informed her of our situation. With complete compassion, Carol offered to help sell Q's bracelets for her at the show, even in our absence.

Q:

When Christopher shared with me, I not able stop crying. The kindness Carol and friends show to me fill me with much love.

The crew at the salon kept us informed of Q's sales throughout the evening, which ended up in excess of three hundred dollars!

WE stayed in the hospital for five days. Being there was emotionally hardest on Chrissy. To explain why, I needed to go back to the months after the alters began coming out as their own persons. During this time Chrissy began having nightmares. In the beginning, she couldn't remember what they were about, but she would cry into Christopher's arms until she fell back asleep. After a few weeks of these awful dreams, Chrissy began to remember the details of her recurring visions.

Chrissy:

I just remember that I was in a hallway that had lots and lots of windows and at one end I could see Cita and Christopher through the sliding doors at the end of the hallway. I wanted them to come and be with me but the doors would not open for them and I could not get to them and at another end of the hallway I could see Mariana. And she held her arms out to me and I ran down the hall into her arms. But when I turned my head I saw two men in white coats and she was taking me away with them. I did not like having those dreams.

Once Chrissy was able to tell us about her dreams, Mariana helped her process them. She told Chrissy that the next time she had that dream, she was to tell those men that Mariana would never let them take her and that she was safe with Mariana. Chrissy was eager to do just that. The next time she had her nightmare, Chrissy yelled at the men to go away and repeated what Mariana had advised her to say. Once Chrissy felt empowered, these dreams came less often and soon she didn't have them anymore.

These dreams also played a factor in the despair that Chrissy experienced while WE were sick in the hospital. Christopher stayed for as long as he could, but he had to work. Mom and our friend Sandy visited often, and this helped Chrissy feel more secure. However, just a week after WE were released from the hospital, Chrissy's "imaginary friend" whom she talked to at night began to make rapid appearances externally. During these quick moments, I felt that familiar sensation of "losing time" once again. They were so fleeting and disorienting that often I didn't even know they had happened.

SHE:

We've said before that there are times when the person shifted externally can block those of us internally to not hear or see the outside world. During such a block, the visual access WE have to the external world is closed. If I try to look out, it's just black. Shortly after WE came home from the hospital, I noticed a significant number of brief black moments. I checked with Cita to see if she had been closing her eyes or possibly dozing off, but that was not the case. I also checked with Q and Chrissy, who have not mastered blocking, to see if they were trying and that was the reason for these minuscule blips, but again the answer was no. When you are an alter inside a woman who has MPD, it doesn't take long to surmise that another alter is trying to surface.

Whether we wanted it to happen or not, the alter Cyndi appeared at 2 AM on January 1, 2010. Let me just say, "Happy Flippin' New Year's." Just like with Q when she first arrived, I was unable to hear Cyndi, and only Chrissy could see her.

Christopher:

On that New Year's evening we had gone to bed after 1 AM. Chrissy shifted out in her sleep, rolling Cita onto her stomach and chatting away with her internal friend Cyndi. For some reason I got the idea to ask Chrissy if Cyndi could shift out externally. Seconds later, Cita's head rose off the pillow higher and higher, and her arms extended to lift up her whole upper body. In a voice I hadn't heard before, the words were uttered, "Out? Out?"

This new alter looked with great curiosity out our bedroom window to our backyard. I couldn't believe it at first and was simply stunned. Seconds later Chrissy shifted out and lay back down on the pillow. I asked her, "Was that Cyndi?" But Chrissy really wasn't aware of what had just occurred. Moments later, Cita's head rose again, asking "Out? Out?" Then

Cyndi looked at me and laughed, giggling with utter excitement. I don't remember her saying a damn thing I could understand, but her enthusiasm at being shifted out and looking around was powerful.

Tristan:

I awoke with a start. I heard this small child and my first thoughts were that the infant Molly had come back. Then I heard Chrissy crying in her room. I immediately went to her to see if she was okay. She clung to me and cried, "Christopher's going to love her more!" "Who?" I asked. "Cyndi!" Chrissy replied. Then I realized that Chrissy's nighttime friend had made an official visit.

SHE:

I was like, "Shit!" Not a baby. Shoot me now.

Jennifer:

I concur; babies make me anxious and nervous. Not sure why Cyndi even likes me, but she does. I know she can smell the fear on me!

Mom/Sharon:

Cyndi could not walk, barely spoke, and on occasions wet her pants—i.e., Christine's pants. This was not good. My daughter is a grown woman who could at any provocation turn into an infant sucking her thumb. That was a hard adjustment, but the more time I spent with Cyndi, the more I was amazed at all her little nonsense songs, her funny little sounds, and how she breathes while sleeping, so clearly a young child. It's been extraordinary watching her.

The Gang, Christopher, family, and friends would try to let me know the minute I shifted back out from a visit by Cyndi. Christopher would even videotape her and I would see myself singing and acting like a baby. I was mortified. I had visions of being out in public as this self-conscious, overweight, middle-aged woman sucking her thumb and peeing my pants. (Yes, Cyndi wasn't potty-trained and we guess she was about two years old.)

But I admit that I did experience a jolt of smug righteousness when I realized that I couldn't hear Cyndi, but SHE could. I felt like SHE finally got her comeuppance for her past cruelty.

SHE:
Yes, isn't that special. In the middle of the night when Cyndi cries out, "Pee Pee Poppy," who takes her to the restroom? Me. If Cyndi is having a tantrum because she isn't getting her way, who can hear her screaming? Me. Nanny SHE is not in my résumé!

Q, however, was so excited by our new addition. Her dream of being a mom came true—albeit in a nonconventional way.

Q:
When Cyndi cry I let her know I hear and love her. If she shifting out to be external and not ask first, I verbally scold her and enforce rules. She learn from all of us, but look to me in maternal way. I laugh each time she say, "No no Koo." (She call me Koo instead of Q.)

Tristan:
I took Cyndi's arrival with a grain of salt. What could we do? Not a thing, so we dealt with her and it was much quieter at night, now that Chrissy wasn't talking to Cyndi all night long.

WE all worked hard at adapting to our new alter, but it was especially difficult for Chrissy, who certainly did not want to share Christopher with the new baby in the mix.

Chrissy:

I wanted to be a good big sister, but Christopher was my Poppy first and I didnt want him to like her more than me. I wanted Christopher all to myself and I felt mad and wanted to be mean to her.

Chrissy drew this shortly after Cyndi transitioned from someone Chrissy talked to at night while sleeping to a member of the Gang. Mariana is riding the horse. Chrissy is riding the bear, which represents Christopher. Written horizontally on the right side are the words, "I don't want to share." She was having difficulty sharing Mariana and Christopher with Cyndi.

Cyndi, on the other hand, loved her big sister. If Chrissy hurt her feelings, she'd cry out, "Yndi a no no," meaning Cyndi did something wrong. She would calm down only when Chrissy reassured her that she loved her. Cyndi often copied Chrissy, and that too caused a rift. If Chrissy wanted a pink balloon, then Cyndi wanted pink too. If Chrissy wanted to color, Cyndi wanted to also. Cyndi didn't want her own crayons; she wanted to use Chrissy's. When we asked Chrissy to share, then Cyndi would accidentally break one of Chrissy's good crayons and another war would take place. Other people have shared experiences of their own children and reassured us that this was all very normal. I was grateful that I missed out on at least half of the whining, since I couldn't hear Cyndi, but the Others and Christopher were now drawing deep from their well of patience.

I was selfishly content to not listen to the constant chatter of a two-year-old, but on the flip side, I missed out on Cyndi's joy and charm. I heard from the Others about her cute antics, new words she was learning, and her happiness at getting a new toy or using her finger paints. With Christopher taking quick videos of Cyndi, soon I was able to look past the image of myself acting like a baby and appreciate our newest member.

Q:
We learned quickly that Cyndi not like see her reflection. She would get mad at Cita. It was Cita's face she see. "No ita, Yndi out!" Each time she see Cita in mirror, she think Cita shifting out and Cyndi wanted to be the one out.

SHE:
Cyndi loves to take a bath, but in the beginning she would see Cita's breasts and become agitated. She'd slap at Cita's boob saying, "No ita! Yndi out."

It has taken over a year for her to not slap at my chest. Although she might not completely understand that she is a child inside my body, she's slowly adjusting to the concept.

Q:

It break my heart to hear Cyndi calling for her Poppy [Christopher] to carry her. She looking up into his face, her arms outstretched wanting to be held.

Christopher:

When Cyndi is sad or crying, she'll reach out to gather her comfort toys. She then tries to get her favorite stuffed animal to shift internally with her by repeatedly pressing it against her forehead. Cyndi will also ask me to come inside with her. At her request I lay my hand on her forehead and make a swooshing sound, like I am casting a spell. Cyndi laughs and is very comforted by my attempt. It's almost as if I really had gone inside with her. To this day, when she is hurting, I can place my hand on her head, "cast a spell," and then she is okay. It works every time.

Cyndi still tends to be active during the night. Less than ten minutes after my head hits the pillow, Cyndi will shift out and talk to me. Sometimes she's being goofy, just singing and squawking. Part of the reason she does it is to get a rise out of SHE. They go back and forth, with SHE telling her to settle down and let Poppy sleep and Cyndi saying, "No no he [SHE], yndi out."

Cyndi has experienced many growing pains when it comes to adjusting to being a small child in a large woman's body. I laugh when Christopher wakes me during the night and I find him squished beneath me.

Christopher:

Sometimes Cyndi shifts out half-asleep. She pushes herself up onto Cita's hands and knees, then just leans over and body-slams me. It's like waking up in the middle of a pro wrestling body slam.

Q:

We trying teach her be careful. In Cyndi's words she say, "Air-ful." It hard not laugh, but now when Cyndi shift out she say "Airful Poppy, Airful" right before she fall over onto Christopher. Obviously work in progress.

⋯⟨⊛⊛⟩⋯

Chrissy has now grown to be a wonderful big sister. It isn't perfect—like the time she told Cyndi she was a baby for crying. This caused Cyndi to bawl harder and yell, "Yndi no baby!" When Q caught on to what was happening, she gently mentioned to Chrissy that she might have hurt Cyndi's feelings. Sweet little Chrissy replied, "I know. I meant to!"

Fortunately those incidents are few and far between. Chrissy may feel anger toward Cyndi, but more often than not she is patient and supportive. She draws pictures for Cyndi to color, and she has let Cyndi pick out certain colors of her good pens that Cyndi can use as her own. At Christmas time, Chrissy sees the holiday lights and has Cyndi shift out to see them too.

Q:

We all make sure each girl feel love and have equal time to be out playing external.

I'm learning a lot about Cyndi through the Others and find her quite adorable. Whereas Chrissy is all girly-girl in her style (she loves the color pink, sparkling ponies, and fashion), Cyndi loves trains and monsters. If a scary show flashes on the screen when Christopher is changing the station, Cyndi will laugh. She finds zombies and beasts hysterical. Sirens, which I don't enjoy and Chrissy is bothered by, too, intrigue Cyndi and she starts to sing the theme song from the TV show *Cops*, "Bad boy bad boy what do ..." Well, that's Cyndi's version.

Cyndi was a definite challenge for all of us to adjust to, but together we have adapted to our new family member, whom we have come to love and adore.

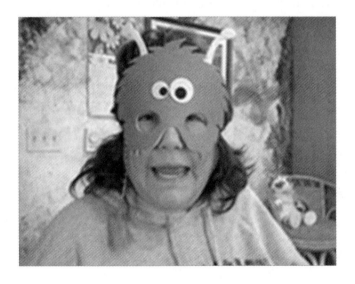

Cyndi excited to be a monster.

43

◄◦◙◦►

2011–2012

FOR THE NEXT TWO YEARS, OUR lives settled into a contented rhythm. WE continued therapy twice a week with Mariana. One session was for the Gang to use as they needed and the other hour was for me to focus on my own issues, such as weight, health, lack of self-esteem, and still wanting to hide from the world. Just little issues like that…

With his wife and Gang thankfully no longer in a constant state of crisis, Christopher found that his own neglected personal issues were starting to surface. Having participated in my sessions with Mariana for over thirteen years, he trusted her and immediately accepted her offer that he start coming in once a week for his own work.

One interesting item that Christopher tackled in counseling was his awareness of how often he had used his "poor sick wife" as an excuse to not get together with his brothers or friends. He never said that exactly, but it was easy to use my mental illness as the reason he wasn't facing his own relationship matters.

Christopher:
One day while I was on the phone with one of my five older brothers, Cita heard me say that I wouldn't be attending a family gathering that he was having the following weekend because I needed to spend the extra time with my wife and the Gang. That statement wasn't necessarily uncommon, but Cita's reaction when I hung up was.

A sign of my own growth was the fact that I no longer wanted to be the reason that Christopher didn't see his family. When he hung up with his brother, I gently informed Christopher that he was more than welcome to go to his family get-together and that we'd be just fine.

Christopher:
I was quick to defend my action, stating that he had invited both of us and that I was tired of showing up to functions without my wife. I wasn't comfortable coming up with another excuse as to why she wouldn't attend.

There was truth in his statement, but it was no longer accurate. I shared with Christopher that I felt ready to visit with his family. I couldn't promise that I would be able to participate for more than an hour or two, but that I'd like to try.

Christopher:
I remember responding that I was frustrated with the lack of acceptance and understanding that my family had in regard to the alters and that I didn't want to go to a function where they couldn't be embraced too.

Only a few occasions had occurred when the Others were introduced to some of Christopher's immediate family. Although a few members had met and even included the Gang during our visits, I told Christopher we'd need to take small steps and could slowly expand our social circle in time.

Christopher:
At that moment I realized how far my wife had come in her journey. I was filled with love and admiration. Then I laughed. After all we had just shared, I finally realized that it came down

to the fact that I just didn't want to go to my brother's that following weekend. Cita had made her point. It was time for me to work on my own personal relationships.

━◦❈·❈◦━

Another area of concern for all of us was Christopher's remodeling business. The current economy was in serious trouble and we had to determine if we could manage financially with the limited jobs he was able to find. It took him close to a year to gather the courage to step away from the work he'd done all his life. With the support of his family and Mariana, he eventually got hired with a school district as a custodian and in the process received good medical and dental benefits and even a retirement plan. WE were so proud of him.

Christopher:

I was eager for the opportunity and I was happy to be hanging up my carpenter bags for the winter and working inside. An added bonus was working the swing shift. I loved being home in the morning with the Gang and not having to rush out the door until after 1:00 PM.

━◦❈·❈◦━

Q also took a step forward in her beading business. Our friend Carol, who had invited Q to participate in her hair salon's holiday open house the previous year, moved her shop to a bigger location. The new salon's large reception area enabled Carol to sell retail items such as hair care products, purses, scarves, fun magnets, and jewelry. Carol asked Q if she would like to sell her beaded items there too.

Q:

I so happy and feel very humble that Carol open her business to me. Carol never charge me for my space, just let me be there from goodness in heart.

Q's wares sold consistently and stayed in the salon for about six months. The salon's customer base, however, is lighter on new customers and heavier with returning clients, so Carol encouraged Q to branch out. After researching craft shows, Q quickly registered herself in a holiday bazaar in the nearby quaint town of Snohomish, Washington.

Once again, Christopher helped Q with a much larger showcase that enabled her to display over seventy bracelets and thirty other beaded items. This bazaar spanned three full days, which made it much harder for all of us to manage it, but Christopher and my mom were by our side the entire time. I was grateful we never saw anyone who recognized me as Christine versus Q. The wonderful woman running the show was informed of our MPD in case there was an emergency, but other than that it was strictly Q's appearance.

Q:

It was much fun! Maybe twenty different vendor selling product. Across from me was another beader named Linda. She and friend had business "Beady Eyed Gals" and made beautiful earrings and necklaces.

WE spent so much time across from Linda that she began to notice that Q was a little more unique than the other people selling their wares. Christopher and my mom soon told her about the MPD. Linda was interested in learning more about us and really took Q under her wing.

Q:

I laughing just thinking about incident at show. Christopher
need leave for work. Without thought Christopher lean over
to kiss wife goodbye. I not plan for kiss. I never been kiss and
turn face away. He surprise, I surprise, and Linda not sure
what happening. We laugh and laugh now.

Q made eight hundred dollars at that show, and Linda invited her to
visit a specialty store in the same town called Grow Washington. This
store had been established by Carolyn Eslick, the mayor of the city of
Sultan. Grow Washington is an incubator store that allows small local
businesses to have a storefront through which to sell their retail items.

Q met with Carolyn, filled out the necessary paperwork, and was
given an area in the front of the store to sell her pieces. Again WE also
let Carolyn know of our MPD in case there was an emergency.

Q:

Part of contract to be at Grow is pay rent and volunteer one
day month run store. Whole days hard for Cita and Gang, WE
able to come in two half-days. First six month at store, Linda,
Christopher, or Cita's mom stayed at store with us. I comfortable by self, but Cita nervous and scared. With someone else
there it help calm Cita and easier for me do job.

Q was becoming more and more active. She was so confident being external. Nothing seemed to faze her. The more she did though, the more she
wanted to do. Often Q would sneak in additional days to cover the store in
Snohomish, and I'd be frustrated, telling her that she had to check with all
of us before she committed more time to Grow Washington. In response,
Q would defend her decision by stating that WE were all there when she
agreed to work and none of us had said anything...as if WE pay attention
to everything that goes on externally when WE are internal. Brat!

Chrissy:

Cyndi and I would moan when WE had to work at Grow Washington. It was sooooo boring having to stay inside all the time. The only thing that made it ok was a cupcake store really close to Grow. It had the cutest name of simply sweet. I was happy for something yummy in our tummy.

Q:

I share funny story, Grow Washington one block from train. Cyndi love trains. Even though SHE block little ones when working, when train toot horn Cyndi blasts right through SHE's block and cry out, "Choo Choo Poppy! Choo Choo." That always make interesting moment if customer or other vendor at store too.

Within that first year, I began to feel more secure with our time at Grow Washington and even visited briefly with Carolyn and Linda. WE tried to keep the focus on Q and her beading and not about my having multiple personalities. After that first year, more of the vendors learned about our MPD and WE spoke more openly any time someone had questions for us.

Q also took business courses offered through Grow Washington to give her the tools to assist in making Beads by Q successful.

Q:

It exciting have my things in store. I work two half-days in month, but items displayed seven days week. I never make enough for Cita retire, but cover my rent, pay for licensing, and most important more beads!

Want add one more story that crack me up. One day I at a craft store getting supplies for my business. Cyndi need go poop. Cyndi hate going big potty and cries and cries. I walk us to restroom and shift Cyndi out. While Cyndi crying, "No Poo Poo Koo," someone else enters bathroom. Nothing can do, so just let Cyndi stay out and fuss. I can't potty for her. After few minute I hear woman asking if Cyndi OK. Cyndi keep crying. Woman ask if Cyndi want her to get her Mommy. I think fast and shift back out saying, "No I right here. She just not like go poop." The woman laugh and tell me her grandson same. Now Cyndi done, but sit and wait for woman leave. Was not sure what she might think if only me walk out of stall and no physical child.

Q even began to contribute to our household budget on months when she did particularly well at Grow. It wasn't often, but it was very helpful and exciting.

⊷⧈⊶

Through the years Mom and the Gang have become closer and closer. One Christmas Mom gave Cyndi a yellow smiley-face tap light that we hung on the wall right by the bed. Cyndi loves that light, and from then on, she has referred to my mom as "Grandma Smiley," although Cyndi pronounces it "Randma Miley." However, that is a nickname only Cyndi uses, as Tristan had a sparkly T-shirt made calling my mom "Grandma Gray," referring to her gorgeous head of gray hair. Mom laughed and now wears it proudly.

By this time Mom had bonded with all of us, although Rim was still quite distant. Mom and SHE are hilarious together. SHE is always pushing the limit and Mom takes it in stride.

Mom:
I admire SHE's strength and her strong force in Christine. SHE takes on a lot of the hard jobs: doctors, dentist, driving,

and even puking if necessary. Stopping smoking was terribly hard for her. What a crabby—can I say "Bitch?" We have fun swapping sarcasms. SHE loves to try and get a rise out of me by flirting with me. It's Christine that gets rattled protesting, "That's inappropriate SHE—it's my mom!" We just laugh, knowing it's all in fun.

Those first years after Mom and I reunited, we avoided any discussion that dealt with our split. We continued to share memories that surfaced regarding "who was who" when I was little. And we discussed our current and future plans. However, anytime Mom mentioned our time apart, I immediately felt very defensive and was not willing to go there with her. It wasn't until I asked her to write some of her thoughts for this book that we were able to talk more openly about those lost five years.

> **Mom:**
> I believe that the main reason for the break between Christine and me was that I would have fought for her to try and contain the alters. My belief is that she might not have fractured so thoroughly if I had been able to get her help earlier. I think she didn't want my interference as she moved toward accepting her mental condition. In order for her to do this, she withdrew from her friends and her family.

There is some truth to my Mom's words, but they also reveal a lack of complete understanding. I've shared with her that my mind was fractured so very long ago—for as long as I can remember, in fact. What was occurring at the time of the split between her and me was my inability to contain the alters any longer. Mom's demand to keep me whole would have completely failed, and I still believe that I would have not survived had I not followed the path that Mariana advised.

Mom and I continue to walk a thin line around our difference of opinions, but what's special is that we do. I don't fall apart by telling her no, and she steps back and considers different opinions other than her own. It's a new way of being together.

⋯⟨✦⟩⋯

Mom and I weren't the only ones working on a new way of living. There was a beautiful dance starting between myself and the alters. WE were learning new ways to move and groove that helped us adapt into society. Our lives were constantly growing, and new and wonderful experiences occurred daily. WE all enjoyed outings with my mom or friend Sandy. WE also enjoyed visits from Jennifer, Pattee, and my brother Chuck. Through the years they had done all the traveling and I'm forever grateful for those visits. However, the Gang was getting more and more anxious to go on a family vacation.

Christopher and I had discussed going to Disneyland, but in reality, it wasn't in our budget. But when my mom sold the house on Camano Island, she gifted money to both my brother and me. Christopher and I knew that all the money should go to getting us out of debt and the balance straight to our retirement. But we finally asked each other that if we didn't do it now, when would we?

There are no guarantees in anyone's life, but the Gang had the added burden of not knowing if and when they might integrate fully. It wasn't something we liked to think about, but the possibilities were real.

So we went ahead and arranged our first family vacation destination: Disneyland.

44

Dreams Can Come True

IF WE HAD BEEN ABLE to keep Disneyland a secret from Chrissy and Cyndi until the night before our departure, it would have been a lot easier on all of us. However, as you might have guessed by now, keeping secrets from one another is quite difficult in our internal family, so WE didn't even bother. Looking back, I can only smile at so many magical moments and special memories, including the months of interrupted sleep when Cyndi would wake up declaring, "Mickey Mouse and Donald Duck Poppy."

Christopher in turn would try to explain to her that it was a long wait, but it was Chrissy who finally spoke to Cyndi in words that she could understand. Cyndi can count to three quite well. Anytime she's counting something that's more than three, she'll say, "1-2-3, 1-2-3." So Chrissy finally said to Cyndi, "Its 1-2-3, 1-2-3, 1-2-3, 1-2-3 until we go to Disneyland." Cyndi didn't like this answer, but she seemed to finally grasp that we weren't leaving for Disneyland right then. As the months turned to days and then hours, the thrill of what lay ahead filled us all with both happiness and stress.

> *Chrissy:*
> I was so excited and I felt like my insides were so full of happy that I was going to explode. It was so hard to wait and wait and wait and wait and wait.

The trip was to be special in other ways too. It was the first time for Q and Tristan to be on a plane, and as a whole it was our first "MPD family" vacation.

Unfortunately, two days before our departure, I tore a tendon in my ankle. I was completely overwhelmed by the injury, since I was already working through my own issues of self-consciousness just from my weight and how out of shape I was. Now I was incapacitated even more.

But everyone else took it in stride. Since Cyndi wasn't mobile anyway, we had already arranged to have a wheelchair at our hotel. Christopher said that he actually looked forward to the freedom the wheelchair would provide and had no hesitation at pushing us around. Really, the only obstacle in my way was me.

—◦◦◦—

When the day of our departure finally arrived, it was surreal. Everyone was beyond excited.

> ***Christopher:***
> Our morning went smoothly. We got to the airport on time, the excitement was mounting, and the youngest alters were behaving and cooperating the whole time. My biggest concern was getting situated on the plane.

We hadn't actually planned out ahead of time how we would handle being at the airport. As we began to go through security, it did seem that it would be less confusing for the TSA employees to have to encounter only one personality in me. (Imagine that!) Chrissy was busting at the seams and was more than happy to be the alter shifted out, so we let her take control. It was a relief to me, because then I could stay internal and keep working on my breathing and self-calming techniques. All of us were right there if Chrissy needed us, and the Others knew there would be more than enough time on our vacation for us all to be out and about.

Once we were seated, I was filled with relief at how efficiently the first stages of travel had proceeded. That is, until I realized that Christopher was telling the woman sitting next to him that his wife had multiple personalities. At that point, I felt some of the wind release from my high-flying sails. Already I was being identified as a freak, and I wanted to cry.

Christopher:
I sensed a mood change in Cita and quickly identified her discomfort in me sharing with the lady next to me. I hadn't intended to just blurt out our business, but with Cyndi and Chrissy leaning over me and the woman sitting at the window to see the view, I felt it was just best to explain our situation. As I related this to Cita, I could tell she understood, and she started to relax once again.

Rim, SHE, and I had all flown before, but it was all new for the Others. So many simple wonders, like the little fan and light buttons on the ceiling above our seats. Chrissy laughed at the tiny bathroom. When the plane began its departure down the runway, I wondered if Chrissy or Cyndi would be bothered, but no, they were just thrilled.

Q:
I never imagine how beautiful to see plane leaving cloudy Seattle and bursting into morning sun. You look down and see ocean of fluffy clouds beneath us. It breathtaking.

Tristan:
I thought it was amazing too, but I was more in awe of the technology and brainpower used to create this flying machine. If I looked through the windows across our aisle, I could see the massive wing and these flaps lifting up and down. The flaps

seemed so slight, and yet I pondered what would happen if even one of them didn't work.

SHE:

Once we were in the sky, I really didn't give a moment's thought to the "wow of flying." I was wasted from weeks of sleep deprivation. As soon as I got reassurance from Cita that all was okay in our world, I crashed. Guess that's not the best word to use while in flight. Instead I'll say I did a face plant and slept the entire flight.

I wasn't quite able to sleep, but for the most part, I found comfort internally while the rest of the Gang shifted in and out.

Our row partner, Mary, turned out to be quite a resource for Disneyland information. Mary was actually a ticket taker for Disneyland California Adventure Park, and she eagerly talked to Christopher and the Others about the process of entering the parks. She recommended that Chrissy get involved in pin trading, a popular way of purchasing and trading Disney pins. She also assured Christopher of how helpful the staff is and advised him to look for handicap-access lines on the rides. Thanks to Mary, by the time we landed, we all felt much more confident in our abilities to venture forth in the vast land of Disney.

During our descent, I sensed SHE's return from her nap, and I have to admit that I felt more secure in her presence. When we disembarked from the plane, I hobbled out onto a mobile ramp that zigzagged down to the tarmac. I was nervous with Chrissy maneuvering us down this steep slope for fear that she might trip and fall, so I asked SHE to intervene. SHE headed down the ramp quite quickly and confidently. As we made passed the flight attendants I heard them wish me a speedy recovery.

At the bottom, WE were greeted by an attendant with a wheelchair, who happily pushed us toward the airport building. However, instead of

Christopher walking with us, he had fallen a bit behind. I wasn't certain why, and I couldn't get his attention. Once we arrived at the baggage claim, the attendant tucked us out of the way and Christopher went to get our luggage. As we made our way to our shuttle pickup point, I asked Christopher if everything was okay. His mood had abruptly changed since the flight, and now he seemed agitated and distant.

Christopher admitted to having felt embarrassed, because he thought the flight attendants had noticed how fast WE had walked down the ramp from the plane, even commenting, "Wow, that was a speedy recovery." He added, "Cita, you can't *pretend* that you're more injured at certain times than you really are or people will assume you're faking the injury to get special privileges."

I was stunned by his words, and instantly tears welled up in my eyes. Instead of being able to discuss this with him rationally, I felt deeply hurt and ashamed. But at that moment we needed to get to our shuttle. I was unable to keep my emotions in check and shifted internally. On the shuttle, Tristan and Chrissy talked with Christopher until we reached our hotel.

Once we arrived in our room, the Gang was more than aware that Christopher and I needed some time to ourselves. SHE was quick to block, providing us with additional privacy. It only took a moment of sharing for the two of us to realize it had all just been a misunderstanding.

Christopher:
I obviously was having my own reactions and feeling a bit self-conscious. When young Chrissy is moving about, she is more animated and not as careful. I should have realized that someone else was walking down the ramp, but instead I panicked at being judged. I saw my wife, who had boarded the plane rather gingerly, racing down the ramp. Then when I thought the attendants were noticing the difference, I felt embarrassed.

I was still hurt that Christopher was so quick to be impacted by what others thought. I was certain that this wouldn't be the first time we'd experience scrutiny from other people, and if he couldn't handle it right from the start, I didn't believe I'd be able to stay strong on this trip. As for what the attendants did or didn't say, we just agreed that it didn't matter. After lovingly reassuring each other and a quick nap, we felt much better and happier.

⋅≼⋅§⋅≽⋅

Within an hour of our arrival at the hotel, my brother Chuck came in from Arizona. He had made a quick road trip to be with us and would have to head back on Monday morning. But it was an added bonus for us all, for me especially.

We let him get settled, then we headed out to stroll Downtown Disney, which was filled with shops, restaurants, street musicians, and fountains. We were told that although we wouldn't see any Disney characters there, we'd still have a fun time.

Christopher:

I could feel myself getting excited as we neared the main commons where the park gates were located: Turn right for Disney, left for California Adventure. We stopped and took in our surroundings, then saw glimpses of both parks that would be explored another day. Then all my emotions just hit me—so much anticipation wondering if Chrissy and Cyndi would ever get to be here, and now we were! Sheer relief, joy, excitement, and love flowed from my eyes. We spun in circles and laughed out loud.

Chrissy:

Looking at Disneyland I could see a building I thought was a castle but it was just a pretty building and because it was Halloween time there were giant pumpkins all across the gates to Disney. Cyndi loved them because they were carved to look like Mickey, Minnie, and even Donald Duck. When we were looking at the Adventure Park you could see a scarey earthquake building and Its a Bug's Life area. You could hear people screaming and laughing.

Once we entered downtown, we got our first hands-on experience in the world of Disney pin trading. There were so many kiosks dedicated to the pin business. As it turned out, it was a key part of the social experience that Chrissy had.

Chrissy:

I got a strap that I put over my head. Oh Tristan just told me it is called a lanyard and they make them in all different kinds of colors and I got the one with the Disney friends on it in Halloween pictures. When you get a pin you wear it on your lanyard and there is room for you to collect all kinds of pins. Then you buy some that are not your favorite and then you find workers and they will let you pick pins from their collection and you trade them one of yours. It was so cool.

Christopher:

I was really thrilled with the pin trading. It gave Chrissy a purpose and she was really outgoing. People were receptive and eager to trade with her. It made our Disney experience much more interactive and memorable.

We had been fortunate to have a very nice woman who worked at one of the kiosks take Chrissy under her wing and get her all set up with the tools of the trade. I will always be grateful for this kindness she showed.

After a nice dinner I felt the exhaustion of the day's travels and we headed back to our room to let my body and me take a nap.

Christopher:

My wife and the Others had been sleeping for close to two hours when Chrissy awoke to sounds of explosions coming from outside. I was in my socks, but we raced out to the balcony just in time to see a fantastic firework show coming from inside the park. It ended with a finale that only Disney could provide. Disney certainly spares no expense and it was incredible to get to share that experience with the alters.

The next day, morning came early to everyone but Chrissy. Both Chuck (who was sleeping on the foldout couch) and Christopher woke up to Chrissy's morning cries of "Is it time to go to Disney yet?"

Chrissy:

I got to decorate us [get us dressed and adorned with jewelry] and put on a beautiful bracelet that Q had made for me that had Mickey and Minnie beads and matching earrings too!

With the Gang and I nestled in our wheelchair, Christopher pushing us along, and Chuck by our side, we were off for our first day in Disneyland. As we passed through the gates, I was so surprised at how outgoing Chrissy was. She said hello to all the staff and received a pin that shared with the world that it was her first visit! She wore it proudly.

Just inside the main gates, we spotted the characters of Alice in Wonderland, the White Rabbit, and the Mad Hatter performing a musical jubilee. Cyndi squealed and bobbed our head up and down, chanting, "Dancing Poppy, Dancing!" Chrissy shifted back out to try to watch the performance. I'm certain that for anyone near us, we were a sight to behold and I had to really focus on the joy of our experiences and not be self-conscious. What helped me through my insecure moments was the sincere pride Christopher radiated while experiencing Disneyland with the alters. My brother appeared content too. Not thinking twice about the shifting back and forth, I felt safe and loved—not some freak of nature.

Chuck:
I was happy to be there to share this first-time experience with everyone. I was sad that they had to deal with the hurt ankle, but it didn't seem to take away from the experience for the youngsters.

Soon Christopher was steering us toward Main Street, where all the merchants were lined up on the sidewalk with big Mickey Mouse white gloves on their hands, waving and greeting us.

Chrissy:
Everyone was smiling and being so nice. I was given another pin that said honorary citizen of Disneyland and I hung it from my new lanyard.

Christopher:
I felt like we were on our very own float in a parade and everyone was paying attention to us—that's how special I felt walking down Main Street. I can't yet imagine how that feeling could be duplicated.

As we entered the roundabout at the end of Main Street, Chrissy caught her first glimpse of Sleeping Beauty's castle. In a reverent voice she whispered, "It's the princess castle! It's more beautiful than I ever thought it would be." Her bliss filled my eyes with tears.

We'd gone only a few more steps when Cyndi shrieked, "Mickey Mouse! Mickey Mouse, Poppy!" And there he was, jumping off a trolley, singing and dancing.

Q:

Cyndi kept laughing and crying out Mickey's name. When show over she was still calling after him, "Bye Mickey, Bye!" She was clapping and so happy. It pure joy to heart.

We traveled less than a block when Chrissy spotted Cruella Deville from the movie *101 Dalmatians*. For the month of October, Disneyland was featuring their Villain characters, so Cruella was the first of many who crossed our path.

Nearly an hour from the time we had entered the park entrance gates to our arrival at "It's a Small World," we were escorted down a separate ramp from the main waiting line. After parking the wheelchair, WE hobbled up to a special entrance and with minimal assistance were able to get on the ride right away.

Chrissy:

It was so beautiful. There were so many cute puppets and beautiful songs. The ride was so full of happiness and I did not want it to end. I knew we were in a magical place.

Chuck:

What I really enjoyed was watching the kids' expressions as Chrissy and Cyndi saw everything for the first time. Seeing it through their eyes allowed me to feel as though it was a new experience for me all over again.

We had been at the park for less than two hours when I began to notice that Chrissy was getting congested. She is normally my illness barometer; if she isn't feeling well, I can be certain that I will be feeling the same effects within twenty-four hours. I wasn't sure if it was sinuses or a head cold. I had sinus medicine with us, so WE took a dose and hoped that was all we'd need.

We had three-day passes to the parks, but only one more full day with my brother. After Star Wars, we agreed to head over to the new California Adventure theme park, which would be a first for us all.

Chrissy and Christopher with Cruella Deville at Disneyland.

California Adventure was simply spectacular. It featured Grizzly Mountain, which was built in the shape of a bear head. From its snarling mouth poured white water rapids that meander down the side of a mountain. A beautiful pier was nearby, and later as the day drew to darkness, stunning fountain shows would shoot out colored water choreographed to music and lights.

Christopher:
It was sunny with limited crowds and the Gang was just having a ball. The alters, Cita, and I were really in sync. There was so much cooperation, good communication, and an abundance of patience. I really felt as though we could work through any challenges we might come across.

And truly, the hitches were turning out to be "normal" versus MPD-specific. Such as Cyndi wanting every toy she saw with Mickey, Minnie, or Donald Duck on it. Chrissy was so sad when we missed the special appearance of Ariel from *The Little Mermaid,* and Cyndi threw a fit from sheer sensory overload and exhaustion. With each incident we became better prepared to handle something similar in the future, but really our family wasn't the only one dealing with these issues.

> **Q:**
> Our first ride in the new park was called "Grizzly River Run." I had much fun. Most time try let Chrissy and Cyndi out for rides, but Chrissy and Cita got scared and Cyndi asleep. Tristan not big fan of wet, so they let me be out. We got special entry again and had huge round raft to ourselves. Chuck, Christopher, and I got in and sat in already wet seats so we know it be a splash ride. We spun and flew around and around down beautiful river setting. I had most fun on that ride. I couldn't stop laughing.

Soaking wet and happy, we headed off to another ride. As we sauntered about, Q shared with me that she didn't feel afraid on rides. I asked her how she was able to do that and she replied that it was Disneyland, after all. They wouldn't have unsafe rides. Her words really helped me. I wasn't completely fear-free after that, but I certainly felt calmer. It turned out that the river ride was one of two that we went on more than once. Q's laughter is so contagious. I was moved to tears several times just experiencing the thrill and exhilaration the alters felt throughout our Disney adventure. Chrissy was ecstatic over the Little Mermaid Ride, while Donald Duck and Minnie Mouse brought Cyndi sheer ecstasy.

As the day neared an end, we had to accept that it was not allergies Chrissy was experiencing. Whatever WE had was blooming into a full-blown nasty cold. Even though we made the best of it, we were all pretty drained after that, so we grabbed something to eat and slowly made our way out of the park.

-◄◈◈►-

Monday came too quickly, and none of us were ready to say goodbye to Chuck. After a nice breakfast and another trip through Downtown Disney, we bade a tearful goodbye to my brother.

Chuck:
Shortly after I returned home, Cita asked if I wanted to share anything further that might benefit people reading their story, and I do.

On my drive back, I thought a lot about my sister and the Others too. I believe each alter is a different aspect of my sister's personality. I love my sister and therefore I love them all. I also think we all have different characteristics of our own personality. I know I have the scared little boy, the curious little kid, the horny teenager, and many other aspects to my own personality. The difference for most of us is that they haven't manifested as separate personalities.

Tristan:
Did he just call me a horny teenager?

SHE:
If the shoe fits…

WE spent the remainder of Monday recouping in the hotel room in hopes that some rest would work magic on our cold. On Tuesday, fully medicated with over-the-counter cold-and-cough drugs, WE managed another full day of pin trading, magical rides, and autographs of Disney stars.

By Wednesday our health had spiraled into major chest and sinus congestion. Propped up on pillows, WE stayed in bed the entire day. In fact the only time WE left was for a wonderful trip to the emergency room that night.

SHE:

I woke Christopher up around midnight letting him know WE needed to see a doctor. WE were coughing and spewing and I feared if WE waited until WE got home, that pneumonia would set in. He called the front desk but was told there weren't any walk-in clinics. They advised that going to the ER was our best option.

Tristan:

Just a quick note: That was one long and creepy night. Many readers might say I have no place to cast judgment on the sanity of a few of the patients in that waiting room, but compared to some, WE appeared quite normal!

Sadly, that was true. In fact, the attending nurses actually moved us and a family to another room that was much quieter and less scary.

Tristan:

Less scary until WE were placed in a curtained-off room right across from a man handcuffed to his bed and two police officers by his side. WE of course had SHE block the little ones, who for the most part remained sleeping.

It was yet another memory in the making of our Disney vacation. After finally getting seen by a doctor, we left with three prescriptions that needed to be filled and rode a taxi back to the hotel.

On Thursday, Christopher spent the day on city transit filling our prescriptions and again WE spent the day sick in our room. WE had a slight reprieve by Friday morning, enough that we opted to make our rounds through the parks for our last day at Disney. It was disappointing to feel so lousy, but we were all anxious to get out of the hotel and make the best of it.

Christopher tried to lighten the mood by pushing us all over both parks. Then we made the mistake of going on the California Screamin', which was a looping rollercoaster. What were we thinking? I was petrified and made it clear that I would not be out and participating. Chrissy was with me, but Tristan and Q were game, so we went for it. It was hell!

Q:
Tristan got squeamish right away. I tried to keep out but after loop I feel like throw up. SHE came to rescue.

SHE:
It takes a lot to make me wimp out on something, but when I shifted out for Q it was all I could do not to spew all over us. I closed my eyes and focused on our breathing. Once the ride was over, I got us back in the chair and told Christopher, "Don't touch us. Move us gently out of the way and get us some 7-Up." Fifteen minutes passed and I still wanted to hurl. It sucked big time.

I'm pretty sure our packed sinuses didn't help make that ride a success for us. It was hours before the nausea left us completely.

Christopher:
When Cita told me that ride ruined the whole morning for her, I was really kicking myself. I knew she didn't like going on rollercoasters. I wanted to go on the ride and felt strongly about having Q or Tristan get to experience it too. I just didn't think past my own desires. I can't even explain how bad I felt.

I could have said "No way," and there was no reason why Christopher couldn't have gone on a ride without us. But knowing that I was the only reason why Q and Tristan wouldn't get to experience the rollercoaster, I caved in, against my better judgment. Oh well... live and learn.

Once WE recovered, Christopher took us on the Downtown Disney monorail. That was a calming ride that had Cyndi yelling, "Choo choo Poppy Choo Choo." Even though the day had been overshadowed by our illness and the added nausea, we still left the park that evening filled with Disney bliss.

Christopher:

Our time together and the wonderful experiences we shared at Disney were so special. The happiness I felt was still present a week later. It will always be a treasured memory of my time together with my very special family.

Cyndi back at the hotel, with her Disney prizes.

45

-◄◈·◈►-

Our Final Thoughts

OUR VACATION TO DISNEYLAND WAS a huge milestone for me, for all of us. My goal of integrating into society to live cohesively as a woman with alternate personalities came true there. Disneyland was a triumph and a wonderful way to end this story. So in this final chapter, I will have each of us share one last quip, quote, story and words of wisdom.

Mom:

As a mother, my goal would still be to have my daughter whole. I realize that is not my choice and in part it doesn't seem to be an option for her either. With that in mind, I have accepted and grown to love all of her alters. It may not be what I'd wished for her, but I'm proud of the work they are doing to become a "whole" functioning person with multiple personalities.

Pattee:

When I first met the alters, it was during "Lou Time" and it was a very scary time for Cita and the Gang. I was a bit terrified for them. Just having learned about the MPD diagnosis and then meeting Lou made it difficult to comprehend what was going on. I was never sorry that I came during such a difficult time. I am glad I didn't get scared off because I do believe that getting to know the Gang during this process and learning more about mental health issues has helped me a great deal in dealing with the death of my sister, who committed suicide; I learned afterward that she had been diagnosed as bipolar. Rim has told us she is not good with expressing herself and I must say that neither am I. However, if I had one wish for the alters, it would be that you can live happy and content with your limitations of being separate but still one. My wish for Christine would be that you can stand tall and be proud of your beautiful self. It is an honor to know such a beautiful person(s). Christine, Rim, SHE, Tristan, Chrissy, Q, and Cyndi: You are wonderful in your own right and bring me joy and laughter. Thank you for being a part of my life and helping me to understand how truly extraordinary you all are.

Tristan:

Do I ever feel like I got a bum rap being an alter and having to live as a male inside a woman's body? Finding myself at times in pink flannel pajamas with red reindeer on them? Or how about seeing myself in the mirror when I'm shifted out and viewing a woman with huge knockers and a vagina?

Sure, I'd like it to be different. I'd like it better if I was my own physical person who exists outside of Cita, coming over to visit Ma and Pa on the weekends and holidays. I'd love to have my own job, be going to college, and have a driver's license with my picture on it.

The point is that I am very much aware that will never, ever happen. But I'm not going to waste too many pity parties on the impossible. Instead, I'm grateful for the family I've been given. It isn't paradise, but we've made the best out of a crazy situation. Christopher is the balm and I love him dearly. He is my father figure, even if he didn't bear me from his loins. The Gang, Cita, and Christopher are my family and I'll do anything to keep us safe and happy.

No one has any guarantees in life. As WE all continue with our therapy is there a higher risk that one or more of us may integrate? I think yes, but it's not gonna stop us from trying to become the best that WE can be. I'm happy for my life, my internal family, and for my external family and friends.

SHE:

Sharing Cita's body is all I know. I'm fine with it. I'm not good with people, so the shorter moments of external living are better for me. That doesn't mean I don't have wishes. Do I wish our internal walls were built with better soundproofing to block out young Cyndi's tantrums and cries? Hell yes.

What I long for is an additional female alter whom I could customize to my flavor, who of course is attracted to females too and in particular to me. I'd be quite content to have some internal arm candy and romance; lack of companionship and sex is a definite bummer.

I also know that I don't help Cita in regard to our obesity. I figure I've given up sex and cigarettes—so leave my fuckin' food alone. With the help of Mariana, I realize that our dying from a stroke or heart attack doesn't suit any of us and I'm trying to make better choices in my eating habits.

Rim:

My original statement was only, "Power to the people. Now leave me alone." After additional consideration and talking with Mariana, I want to elaborate some more. I gave my permission to have my shit displayed across the pages of this book for the good of our cause. That doesn't mean that I don't feel violated, exposed, and vulnerable knowing that other people will be reading about my life. I don't believe that this book will stop child abuse in the future, but I do hope that it might help free others who have been tortured from abuse they have experienced.

Q:

I only know life as alter, but does not stop me from wish had boyfriend. I never experience sex. I never get married or have baby. The last make me very sad. It seems lot I don't have, but not true. I rich in love, rich with family and friends. I love life and not regret the one I given.

Chrissy:

Sometimes when I dream, I see Tristan and me running in a field and Christopher and Cita are holding hands nearby. Cyndi is sitting next to them and Hope is a bird with lots of bright colors flying over our heads. I love that dream. When I wake I am sad cause I know that I am still inside but then I smile because I love everyone and I know they love me too.

Being around other kids is hard and they laugh at me and I get mad. I want to be in a pink dress with pink shoes playing on the playground to but they just think I am a weirdo and I feel sad. Christopher loves me and sees me for me and I am glad for that. My grandmas and aunts do too.

I have friends now through Grow Washington where Q sells her beaded things and Sandy has loved me for a long time. I miss people who dont want to see us anymore and Cita says its not because of me but its still hard. I feel sad right now but mostly I am happy and love my family even if some people think we are weird.

Cyndi:

Mickey Mouse! Donald Duck!

Christopher:

The first day I was introduced to the alters it was amazing, but not shocking. It was exciting and incredible, but never was it bizarre. I experienced anxiety from SHE and am grateful now for SHE, though SHE still loves to make me squirm. Lou was downright scary, but together and with Mariana's support we were able to make it through unharmed.

I've struggled with my sadness. This family has grown so much, yet the alters are trapped and their fate is sealed. This may well end suddenly. When they do go, everyone will be gone. No grandkids on the horizon for this clan.

I now look back on the journey my life has taken me on as an incredible mixture of tragedy, perseverance, love, transformation, and resilience. As I sit here writing, I'm amazed at how content I feel with my life. I'm at peace. I am loved and I am able to love.

I have not overcome all of my own personal issues. Take the MPD out of my equation and I still have low self-esteem, wrestle with social phobias, and am overweight. Until I take the appropriate steps to say directly to someone who is treating me in an unhealthy manner, "This is not acceptable behavior and you may not treat me this way," or "That is not okay with me, you need to stop," I will continue to battle with my own emotional health. I'm not talking about getting physically or sexually abused any longer, but emotional abuse is equally debilitating.

Continuing to spend time with family members who are not accepting of the alters, not letting my mother know immediately if she's overstepped a boundary, and spending money beyond our means—all of these points keep me out of integrity with my relationships and with myself. This is my continued work and one of the main reasons I continue to see Mariana for therapy.

For the longest time—years and years—I worried that Mariana would decide that I was too much to handle and no longer want to counsel me. In time I began to ask her what would happen if she retired. She always laughed, and it became a sweet, reassuring gesture as each time she'd tell me that she was here for me.

It's been over eighteen years that we've been working together and neither one of us are spring chickens any longer. I no longer ask her what will happen when she retires—I don't want to know. I'm content that for now she's here and available to me and to us when I need her, as she always has been. That's enough to keep me stable.

I'm not the same person I was when I first walked into her office. I am more than capable of keeping myself and the alters safe and healthy. And that's just what I plan on doing.

The end, for now...

The Gang's all here, by Christopher 2013. From left to right: Rim, Tristan, and Q holding Cyndi; below is Chrissy and Dixie. I and Christopher with SHE above us.

Profiles: Our Traits

Rim suggested it might be useful and fun for readers to know some basic statistics and character traits about each of us, similar to the back of a baseball card.

Name	Christine Louise Pattillo
Alternate personality	No, I am the woman with alternate personalities
Nickname	Cita, Christy, Chris
Age	46
Height	5'11"
Weight	NOYB (none of your business!)
Hair color	Brown
Eye color	Hazel
Freckles	Not many
Body art	Yes, a tattoo of a tiger on my back right shoulder thanks to alter Rim
Favorite color	Purple
Favorite animal	Dolphins, dogs, quail, beavers
Favorite candy	Fresh 3 Musketeers candy bars
Favorite meal	Mom's BBQ ribs
Favorite dessert	Uncle Seth's pink-frosted cookies
Favorite season	Winter
Favorite time of day	An hour after waking up
Favorite song	"I Am, I Said" by Neil Diamond
Favorite movie	*Legal Eagles, Pretty Woman,* and *Apollo 13*
Favorite book/author	*Gone with the Wind*, Nora Roberts, J. D. Robb

Name	Christine Louise Pattillo
Favorite car	Jeep, Land Rover
Fears/phobias	Falling, people being mad at me, Christopher leaving me, loud sudden noises
Hobbies	Reading, writing, knitting, cross-stitch, jigsaw puzzles
Irritating things	Talk radio, debates, people who like to hear themselves talk, people rude to the alters
Ocean, mountains, river, or lake?	Ocean any day of the week!
Favorite flower	Yellow tulips
Favorite smell	Leather
Three adjectives to describe myself	Funny, creative, and intuitive
If I could change one thing about myself?	My weight
My perfect career choice?	Author

Name	SHE
Alternate personality	Yes
Nickname	Sheera
Age	30-something
Height	5'6"
Weight	None of your frickin' business
Hair color	Light brown
Eye color	Hazel
Freckles	Some
Body art	No

Name	SHE
Favorite color	Orange
Favorite animal	Wolf
Favorite candy	5th Ave and Reese's Peanut Butter Cups
Favorite meal	All of them; burgers and fries
Favorite dessert	Hostess Powdered Mini Donettes
Favorite season	Fall
Favorite time of day	After everyone's asleep
Favorite song	"China" by Tori Amos
Favorite movie	*Hangover*
Favorite book/author	Connor Hawthorne Mystery series/Lauren Maddison
Favorite car	Hummer
Fears/phobias	Cita dying and taking us with her
Hobbies	Reading, eating
Irritating things	People who are mean, stupid, and selfish
Ocean, mountains, river, or lake?	Mountains
Favorite flower	Any coming from a beautiful woman
Favorite smell	Pine trees
Three adjectives to describe myself	Abrasive, honest, and impatient
If I could change one thing about myself?	My past behaviors
My perfect career choice?	Something not involving people

Name	Rim
Alternate personality	Yes
Nickname	None
Age	28
Height	5'10"
Weight	150 pounds
Hair color	Brown
Eye color	Vivid green
Freckles	I get some across my nose from the sun
Body art	Tiger tattoo
Favorite color	Gray
Favorite animal	One that isn't near me
Favorite candy	Nestlé Crunch
Favorite meal	Pizza
Favorite dessert	Chocolate sundae
Favorite season	Spring
Favorite time of day	Afternoon
Favorite song	"Time after Time" by Cyndi Lauper
Favorite movie	Mystic Pizza
Favorite book/author	Deb MacComber, some Nora Roberts
Favorite car	1964 and 1966 Mustang, 2011 Camaro
Fears/phobias	Having to talk about emotions, and being in the hot seat in counseling
Hobbies	Reading and watching sports; used to be partying and playing sports
Irritating things	Uncontrolled children, crying babies, and stupid people

Name	Rim
Ocean, mountains, river, or lake?	Ocean
Favorite flower	Yellow roses
Favorite smell	Roses
Three adjectives to describe myself	Quiet, detailed, and serious
If I could change one thing about myself?	I'd like to be less nervous
My perfect career choice?	Race car driver
Addition information	Big on the 1980s; love the music, clothes, and of course mall bangs

Name	Tristan
Alternate personality	Yes, the only male
Nickname	T-Man, Trist, Scout, and Nilla
Age	19ish
Height	5'10"
Weight	Not sure; I say svelte, others say skinny
Hair color	Blonde
Eye color	Blue
Freckles	No
Body art	No
Favorite color	Brown
Favorite animal	Dog
Favorite candy	Snickers and Reese's
Favorite meal	All of them; love tacos
Favorite dessert	Apple pie à la mode

Name	Tristan
Favorite season	Summer
Favorite time of day	Evening
Favorite song	Not sure
Favorite movie	*Star Trek* (2009, with Chris Pine)
Favorite book/author	No favorite, just love reading and learning
Favorite car	2011 Camaro
Fears/phobias	Merging on the freeway
Hobbies	Reading, drawing, jigsaw puzzles, and writing children stories
Irritating things	Rain, not being recognized as a guy, people not accepting us, and wearing pink
Ocean, mountains, river, or lake?	I like them all, but I'd say ocean; I like it best in some place warm
Favorite flower	Anything that blooms
Favorite smell	Fooooooood!
Three adjectives to describe myself	Sarcastic, quick-witted, and intellectual
If I could change one thing about myself?	I'd like to exist physically outside of Cita's body.
My perfect career choice?	Storm chaser baby; I'd also love to go to college for any type of career!
Addition information	Cita and all the other alters are right-handed; I'm left-handed

Name	Quiet One
Alternate personality	Yes
Nickname	Q or QY because ask so many questions
Age	Unknown; 22 to 30
Height	5'8"
Weight	No idea
Hair color	Dark brown
Eye color	Light green
Freckles	Yes, across cheek and nose
Body art	No
Favorite color	Green
Favorite animal	Butterfly
Favorite candy	None
Favorite meal	Baked potato and no-meat meals
Favorite dessert	Fruit salad
Favorite season	Summer
Favorite time of day	All times
Favorite song	Not good with song names. I will think more
Favorite movie	*Sound of Music*
Favorite book/author	*National Geographic*
Favorite car	I like idea of hybrid, but want safety of bigger car
Fears/phobias	Someone I care about get hurt
Hobbies	BEADING
Irritating things	Dishonesty; someone not being nice to Others and cruelty

Name	Quiet One
Ocean, mountains, river, or lake?	All, but cried first time saw ocean
Favorite flower	Orchids
Favorite smell	I like the smell of fresh air
Three adjectives to describe myself	Opinionated, curious, happy
If I could change one thing about myself?	I would like to have my physical body exist externally from Cita
My perfect career choice?	Beading and going to college
Addition information	One of two alters that came to exist when Cita adult. I don't live in internal home with Others. I have speech impediment that make me sound different. None of Others can see me, only hear me.

Name	Hope
Alternate personality	Yes
Nickname	None
Age	27ish
Height	5'11"
Weight	175 pounds
Hair color	Blonde
Eye color	Brown
Freckles	Very few
Body art	None
Favorite color	Light blue
Favorite animal	Doves

Name	Hope
Favorite candy	None
Favorite meal	Stir-fry
Favorite dessert	Granola, strawberries, yogurt, and a little Cool Whip
Favorite season	Spring
Favorite time of day	Afternoon
Favorite song	"Candle in the Wind" by Elton John
Favorite movie	*Fried Green Tomatoes*
Favorite book/author	*Little Women*/Louisa May Alcott
Favorite car	None
Fears/phobias	Cita giving up on life
Hobbies	Reading and cross-stitching
Irritating things	Rude people, wasteful people, and litter bugs
Ocean, mountains, river, or lake?	Mountain meadows
Favorite flower	All of them
Favorite smell	Just after the first rain
Three adjectives to describe myself	Patient, kind, and loving
If I could change one thing about myself?	Integrating
My perfect career choice?	Horticulture
Addition information	Christine and the Gang completed Hope's stats, as she is no longer with us

Name	Chrissy
Alternate personality	Yes
Nickname	Bunny, Squirt, and Bun-Meister
Age	6ish
Height	4'
Weight	58 pounds
Hair color	Brown and I like to wear them in two ponytails
Eye color	Hazel
Freckles	Just a few
Body art	No
Favorite color	Pink
Favorite animal	Ponies, goats, penguins, dogs, and Webkinz
Favorite candy	M&M's
Favorite meal	Donuts
Favorite dessert	Cupcakes
Favorite season	Summer and Christmas
Favorite time of day	Mornings with Christopher before anyone else is awake
Favorite song	Rudolph
Favorite movie	*Bolt and Tarzan*
Favorite book/author	*Dr. Seuss*
Favorite car	I like Smart cars because they make me giggle
Fears/phobias	Being joked about, loud things, mean people, and Christopher leaving us
Hobbies	Coloring, drawing, swimming, and helping Q bead

Name	Chrissy
Irritating things	Being laughed at and being ignored
Ocean, mountains, river, or lake?	Ocean and lake
Favorite flower	Sunflowers
Favorite smell	Tyler's donut store
Three adjectives to describe myself	Sunny disposition [Chrissy pronounces it "deposition"], happy, and loving
If I could change one thing about myself?	That I could exist with my body outside of Cita
My perfect career choice?	Work with animals at the zoo or in the water

Name	Cyndi
Alternate personality	Yes
Nickname	Gangster-Monster-Pudd'n Pie (she says them all together at the same time)
Age	2ish
Height	Little
Weight	Unknown
Hair color	Dark blonde
Eye color	Hazel/brown
Freckles	Some on her cheeks and shoulders
Body art	No
Favorite color	Pink because Chrissy likes Pink
Favorite animal	Mickey and Minnie Mouse, Donald Duck, alpacas, Mater from the movie Cars, and monsters
Favorite candy	Ring Suckers

Name	Cyndi
Favorite meal	She doesn't like eating much, but she loves strawberries
Favorite dessert	Strawberries
Favorite season	Anytime when she gets to open presents
Favorite time of day	When Christopher is home to play
Favorite song	Itsy-Bitsy Spider and the Happy Birthday song
Favorite movie	*Mickey Mouse Club Cartoon*
Favorite book/author	*Mr. Brown*
Favorite car	Mater from the Disney movie Cars
Fears/phobias	Loud noises and strangers
Hobbies	Finger painting and she loves to sing
Irritating things	She doesn't like to be splashed or have her fingers wet or sticky
Ocean, mountains, river, or lake?	As long as we're together she likes them all
Favorite flower	The pretty kind
Favorite smell	Unknown
3 adjectives to describe myself	Impatient, silly, and loud
If I could change one thing about myself?	Not living with the rest of the alters
My perfect career choice?	Unknown
Addition information	Cyndi fractured fully when Christine was an adult; no one but Chrissy can see her. Everyone but Christine can hear her

Name	Christopher
Alternate personality	No, I'm Cita's husband
Nickname	Chief, OP (stands for "O Great Provider") and Mr. Man
Age	51
Height	5'11" with short hair, 6'1" when hair is longer, because of my curls
Weight	235 pounds
Hair color	Grey, but was red when I was younger
Eye color	Blue
Freckles	Yes, lots
Body art	No
Favorite color	Blue
Favorite animal	Goats, dogs
Favorite candy	Frozen Snickers
Favorite meal	Thai food
Favorite dessert	Mint Dilly Bar
Favorite season	Fall
Favorite time of day	Morning
Favorite song	"Come Down in Time" by Elton John
Favorite movie	*True Grit* (John Wayne) and *The Godfather*
Favorite book/author	*For Your Own Good*/Alice Miller
Favorite car	Pickup truck
Fears/phobias	Bees trapped in my curly hair (don't laugh—it's happened!)
Hobbies	Sports, piano playing, drawing, gardening, and cooking

Name	Christopher
Irritating things	Drivers who wait until the last second and cut in front, and the shame I feel when I do the same
Ocean, mountains, river, or lake?	Rivers
Favorite flower	Nasturtiums
Favorite smell	Freshly baked pastries
Three adjectives to describe myself	Artsy-fartsy, contrarian, work in progress
If I could change one thing about myself?	30 pounds lighter
My perfect career choice?	Cartoonist
Addition information	One day I'm ambitious and the next day I'm not

Name	Dixie
Alternate personality	No, I'm their black lab dog
Nickname	Boo, Thumbalina
Age	11
Height	Average
Weight	68 pounds
Hair color	Black
Eye color	Brown
Freckles	On my underbelly
Body art	No
Favorite color	Tennis ball color
Favorite animal	Christopher
Favorite candy	Happy Hips (treats)

Name	Dixie
Favorite meal	Breakfast and dinner
Favorite dessert	Cheetos Puffs
Favorite season	All seasons
Favorite time of day	Breakfast and dinnertime
Favorite song	"Who Let the Dogs Out"
Favorite movie	*Marmaduke*
Favorite book/author	*The Dog Whisperer*/Cesar Millan
Favorite car	Any that let me ride in them
Fears/phobias	Nails being cut and being left behind
Hobbies	Chasing balls and chewing on wood
Irritating things	Flies, bath time, and football season
Ocean, mountains, river, or lake?	I love it all, but beaches are cool
Favorite flower	Clover; I love to chase me a bee.
Favorite smell	Urine. I love checking my pee-mail. (My brother used this phrase when Dixie was sniffing a tree trunk.)
Three adjectives to describe myself	Happy, relaxed, and cute
If I could change one thing about myself?	Stronger joints
My perfect career choice?	Major League Baseball center fielder

Suggested Resources

Multiple Personality- and DID-Specific

Books

Baer, Richard K. *Switching Time: A Doctor's Harrowing Story of Treating a Woman with 17 Personalities.* New York: Three Rivers Press, 2007.

Casey, Joan Frances. *The Flock: The Autobiography of a Multiple Personality.* New York: Ballantine Books, 1992.

Chase, Truddi. *When Rabbit Howls.* New York: Jove, 1990.

Giller, W. *Multiple Personality Disorder from the Inside Out.* Baltimore, MD: Sidran Press, 1991.

Oxnam, Robert B. *A Fractured Mind: My Life with Multiple Personality Disorder.* New York: Hyperion, 2006.

Trujillo, Olga. *The Sum of My Parts: A Survivor's Story of Dissociative Identity Disorder.* Oakland, CA: New Harbinger Publications, 2011.

Movies and Television

The Three Faces of Eve. Twentieth Century Fox Film Corporation, 1957. (The film stars Joanne Woodward in an Academy-Award-winning performance. As you watch it, remember the year it was made.)

United States of Tara. Showtime, 2009.
(When WE first heard of this series, WE were not eager to watch it because WE thought it would be mocking of our condition. Encouraged by friends, Christopher, the Gang, and I did watch one episode and soon we watched all three seasons. Although it does not perfectly represent our own experience, it is accurate, emotionally stirring, and funny. We think it's worth seeing.)

Schizophrenia-Specific

Saks, Elyn R., *The Center Cannot Hold: My Journey Through Madness.* NY: Hyperion, 2007. (Although WE do not suffer from schizophrenia, as I read her book, I related to Saks's emotional journey and felt as if she was writing about my own feelings and pain.)

Miscellaneous

Bradshaw, John. *Healing the Shame That Binds You.* Deerfield Beach, FL: Health Communications, 1988.

Frey, James. *A Million Little Pieces.* New York: Anchor Books, 2005.

Halpern, Howard M. *Cutting Loose: An Adult's Guide to Coming to Terms with Your Parents.* New York: Fireside, 1990

Katherine, Anne. *Boundaries: Where You End And I Begin: How To Recognize And Set Healthy Boundaries.* New York: Fireside, 1991.

Lerner, Harriet. *The Dance of Anger: A Woman's Guide to Changing the Patterns of Intimate Relationships.* New York: Perennial Currents, 2005.

Love, Patricia. *The Emotional Incest Syndrome: What to Do When a Parent's Love Rules Your Life.* New York: Bantam, 1990.

Miller, Alice. *The Drama of the Gifted Child: The Search for the True Self.* New York: Basic Books, 1997.

Miller, Dusty. *Women Who Hurt Themselves: A Book of Hope and Understanding.* New York: Basic Books, 2005.

Westberg, Hannah. *Hannah: My True Story of Drugs, Cutting, and Mental Illness (Louder Than Words).* Deerfield Beach, FL: Health Communications, 2010.

Whitfield, Charles L. *Healing the Child Within: Discovery and Recovery for Adult Children of Dysfunctional Families.* Deerfield Beach, FL: Health Communications, 1987.

Helpful Tips

WE would like to share our thoughts regarding how someone might help another person who has MPD. Before WE respond, I first need to stipulate the following:

Know if there is any alter who is a physical threat to themselves or to you.

If the answer is yes, then you need to find out what you need to do to keep them and yourself safe. The most direct route would be to ask the person themselves. Keep in mind that each individual experiencing the MPD, whether it is the host or alter, is undergoing his or her own unique situation. For instance, my alter Lou would have lied to you about her identity. And if you didn't know Us well, you might not have caught on that it was Lou, who had no misgivings about putting us in direct danger if you listened to her.

Another option is to ask caregivers, spouses, family, or medical staff if you are in danger or if there are any special needs you should be aware of. I once read about a man with MPD who had an alter who would experience violent rage whenever a certain song played on the radio. This would be important to know before turning on music around him. My alter Lou also couldn't stand to be touched and would react violently. Again, it's this type of information that might ease your way when you interact with someone who has multiple personalities.

Here are some other tips for getting to know alters:

- Ask the names of each of the alters. Write them down if necessary. If there are too many to remember, then ask that they each introduce themselves when they are out talking. My family will say, "Hi, this is Tristan" or "Hi, I'm Chrissy" when they are with people who are new to our situation. Usually people start to recognize them individually, but that may be harder in someone else's situation.

- Remember that what works for us might be a total mishap with someone else. As Tristan has stated so many times, the only way you'll learn is to ask questions. Ask and ask some more. If you ask something that someone is uncomfortable answering, then they can just tell you that. And be understanding, respectful, and patient.

- Also, each alter has his or her own likes and dislikes. Find out what the alter you're talking to enjoys doing or the type of music they like to listen to. Ask them the same kind of questions you would ask anyone you're meeting for the first time. Remember, an alter can be male or female, regardless of the host's gender, and that's important to know so that you can say "he" versus "she."

- Play a board game and see if some of the other alters will play too. If they are young, draw with them or read them a story. Do age-specific projects.

- If the person and alters you are visiting are in "crisis mode," offer to bring a meal over. While they may not want company for long, their spouse or caregiver could likely really use some support too.

- Find out if they need errands done, such as picking something up at the store or medications. Also ask if they need rides to appointments.

- If you know that younger alters are coming over for a visit, bring some stickers for them or a jigsaw puzzle or a movie.

- Try to treat them with respect and honesty. It's okay to say, "I'm really uncomfortable and not sure how to proceed."

- Just don't treat them like a novelty or a freak of nature. It's different for sure, but the alters are all individually unique selves. As WE have stated in the book, it's like being in a room with a group of people, but with only one physical body.

- Once you take the time to learn more and understand one, two, or even all of the alters and their host too, you will find it easier to be around them. Often they are just as nervous about meeting you as you might be of them!

- One last note: It is not okay for alters to mistreat you or misbehave. Just because someone has MPD doesn't give them the excuse to be insensitive or rude. And it is okay to advise them that a particular behavior is unacceptable. They may decide that they don't agree, but keep your boundaries as they should keep theirs.

Crisis Information

If you are in crisis, please contact 9-1-1 or the Volunteers of America Care Crisis Response Services at 1-800-584-3578.

Also, most counties have care crisis lines that you can look up online or in your local phonebook.

Your safety is important; please take the time to call someone!

I hear the chimes sing to me
I feel the wind caress me
I watch the trees dance for me
Mother Earth has truly blessed me

Chris Pattillo 2010

About the Author

Having lived with multiple personality disorder all her life, Christine Pattillo began writing during the traumatic loss of one of her alternate personalities. Christine hopes that by sharing her story she might make a difference for others who also suffer with mental illnesses. She and her family live in the Pacific Northwest.